120 GREAT HISTORY PROJECTS

120 GREAT HISTORY PROJECTS

Bring the past into the present with
hours of creative activity

General Editor: Leon Gray

Consultants: Rachel Halstead and Struan Reid

southwater

Contents

Houses and Homes

Fashion and Accessories

Science and Technology

Customs, Arts and Entertainment

Early farmers in northern Europe, c. 5000BC

Houses and Homes

Homes provide shelter from the elements first and foremost, but they can be much more than simply a resting place. They can give clues as to what materials were locally available at the time of their construction, and reflect the owner's status and taste. This section investigates a whole host of homes from a variety of different cultures. It takes a look inside to examine some typical features, and recreates some popular dishes of the past.

Different Homes

P eople have always needed to shelter from the weather, and somewhere warm and comfortable to sleep at night. The design of most homes throughout the world depends on the climate. People living in hot countries need their homes to be as cool and airy as possible, while people in cold countries need their homes to be snug and warm. The materials that people use to build their homes usually depend on what they can find around them. Stone, mud, straw and wood are all natural materials that have been used to build homes for thousands of years. By contrast, many modern homes are built from artificial materials such as concrete, steel and glass.

▲ Cool currents

The ancient Greeks built their houses from sundried mud bricks laid on stone foundations. The roofs were covered with pottery tiles. Rooms were arranged around an open courtyard so that cool air could build up and circulate through the rooms during the heat of the day.

King of the castle ▶

During the Middle Ages, between 1000 and 1500, castles were built all over Europe, in Scandinavia, Britain, France and Germany, and south to the Mediterranean Sea. They were also built in the Middle East during the Crusades. Castles were built by important people such as kings or queens. They were not only splendid homes that the owners could show off to their friends, but military bases from which the surrounding lands were defended.

◀ Outdoor rooms

The Incas lived in the Andes Mountains in what is now Peru. They built their homes from large blocks of granite, which they quarried from the nearby mountains. The blocks fitted together without mortar. The resulting thick walls provided insulation against the bitter winter cold. A courtyard acted as a large outside room and was used just as much as the inside of the house for everyday living.

Etruscan palace ▶

The Etruscans lived between the Arno and Tiber rivers in western Italy around 2,500 years ago. Wealthy Etruscan families built luxurious palaces decorated with beautiful figurines, bronze statues and engraved mirrors. The Etruscans grew rich by mining copper, tin and iron and trading with the neighbouring Greeks and Phoenicians.

◀ Wood and bark

The Iroquois people lived in a densely wooded region of North America. They built their long-houses using a wooden framework covered with sheets of thick bark. The barrel-shaped roofs allowed the rain to run off. These houses were huge because several families lived in each one.

Hunter's home

People have always needed protection from the weather. For most of human history, the Earth's climate has been much colder than it is today. Early humans lived in huts out in the open during summer but moved into caves when the harsh winter weather came. They built stone windbreaks across the entrances. Inside, there were inner huts made of branches and animal bones to provide further protection from the cold. Hunters following herds of game built temporary shelters of branches and leaves in the summer. Families lived in camps of huts made of branches and animal skins. Farther north, where there were no caves and few trees, people built huts from mammoths' leg bones and tusks. Wherever they settled, however, it was very important to be near a supply of fresh water.

▲ A place to shelter
At Terra Almata, southern France, hominids (early humans) lived in groups. They established camps made up of several simple shelters, to which they returned year after year. The huts were made of tree branches and weighted down with stones.

YOU WILL NEED
Self-hardening clay, cutting board, modelling tool, twigs, ruler, scissors, card, brown and green acrylic paint, water pot, paintbrushes, PVA glue and glue brush, fake grass or green fabric.

◄ Skin huts
Huts at Monte Verde, Chile, were made of wood covered with animal skins. They are the earliest evidence for human-made shelters in the Americas. The remains were preserved in peaty soil, along with other items, such as a wooden bowl and digging sticks.

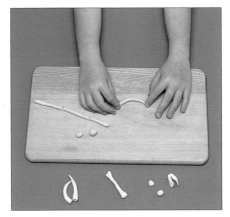

1 Roll out lengths of self-hardening clay, and shape them to look like long and short mammoth bones and tusks. Then make some small clay stones in different sizes.

2 Use the modelling tool to shape the ends of the bones. Then use it to make the stones look uneven. Lay the bones and stones on the cutting board to dry.

3 Lay the twigs next to a ruler. Then use a pair of scissors to cut the twigs so that they are about 15cm long. You will need about eight evenly sized twigs in all.

4 Roll out some more clay and spread it unevenly over a piece of card. Paint the clay a brown-green colour to look like soil and grass. Do not leave the base to dry.

5 Push the twigs into the clay base, and arch them over to form a cone-shaped frame. Glue a few stones on to the clay at the base of each of the twigs.

6 Cover the twigs with pieces of fake grass or green fabric. Leave a gap at one side for the entrance. Glue the pieces in place. Take care not to cover up the stones around the base.

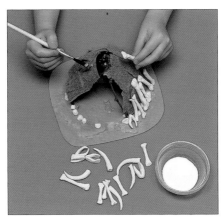

7 Neatly glue the long mammoth bones and tusks all over the outside of the hunter's shelter. Fill in any gaps with smaller bones. Leave the hunter's home to dry.

When wood was scarce, the heavy bones of an elephant-like animal called a mammoth were used to weigh down the grass and animal hides that covered the hunter's shelter.

Mud-brick house

The great cities of ancient Egypt were built along the banks of the River Nile. Small towns grew up haphazardly around them. Special workers' towns, such as Deir el-Medina, were also set up around major burial sites and temples to be close to the building work.

Mud brick was used for most buildings, from royal palaces to workers' dwellings. Only temples and pyramids were built to last – they were made from stone. Most homes had roofs supported with palm logs and floors of packed earth. In the evenings, people would sit on the flat roofs or walk in the cool, shady gardens.

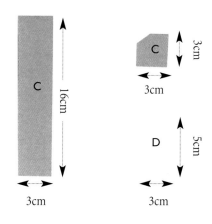

▲ Tomb workers

The village of Deir el-Medina housed the skilled workers who built the royal tombs in the Valley of the Kings. The men were required to work for eight days out of ten.

clay

▲ Mud brick

The Egyptians dried bricks in the sun using the thick clay soil left behind by the Nile floods. The clay was taken to a brick yard and mixed with water, pebbles and chopped straw.

Templates

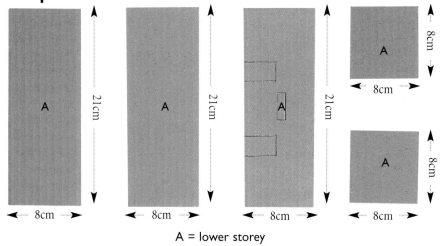

A = lower storey

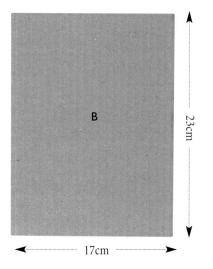

B = base

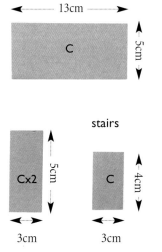

stairs

C = upper storey

D = sunshade roof

YOU WILL NEED

Thick card, 4 x 3cm thin card (for stairs), pencil, ruler, scissors, PVA glue and glue brush, masking tape, balsa wood, plaster of Paris, water pot and brush, acrylic paint (green, white, yellow and red), paintbrush, sandpaper, straw.

1 Use the templates to measure and cut out the pieces for the house. Glue together the base board, walls and ceiling of the lower storey. Reinforce the joints with masking tape.

2 Glue together the roof and walls of the top storey. Fold the thin card as shown for the stairs, and glue into place. Tape joints to reinforce. Glue the top storey to the lower storey.

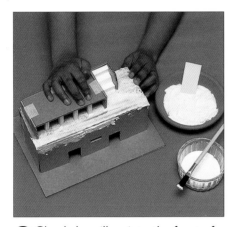

3 Glue balsa pillars into the front of the top storey. When the house is dry, cover it in a wet paste of plaster of Paris. Paint the pillars red or another colour of your choice.

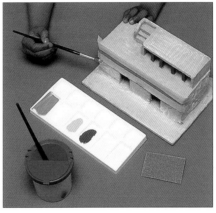

4 Paint your model the same colour as dried mud. Next paint a green strip along the wall. Use the masking tape to ensure the edges are straight. Sand any rough edges.

5 Now make a shelter for the rooftop. Use four balsa struts as supports. Glue the piece of card (D) and cover it with pieces of straw. Glue the shelter into place.

Mediterranean Sea

Giza
Saqqara — Dashur
Meidum

Western desert

Red Sea

River Nile

Eastern desert

▲ **Living by the river**
Egyptians built their homes along the banks of the River Nile. Many pyramids, such as those at Giza, are found here, too.

Egyptian houses had a large main room that opened directly into the street. In many homes, stairs led up to the roof. People slept there during hot weather.

Roman house

Only the wealthiest Romans could afford to live in a private house. The front door opened on to a short passage leading to the *atrium*, a central court or entrance hall. Front rooms on either side of the passage were usually bedrooms. Sometimes, though, they were used as workshops or shops and had shutters that opened out to the street.

The centre of the atrium was open to the sky. Below this opening was a small pool to collect rainwater. If you were a guest or had business, you would be shown into the office, or *tablinium*. The dining room, or *triclinium,* was often the grandest room of all. Extremely wealthy Romans also had a summer dining room, which looked out on to the garden.

▲ **House and garden**
The outside of a Roman town house was usually very plain, but inside it was decorated with colourful wall paintings and intricate mosaics.

Templates

Cut out the pieces of card following the measurements shown.

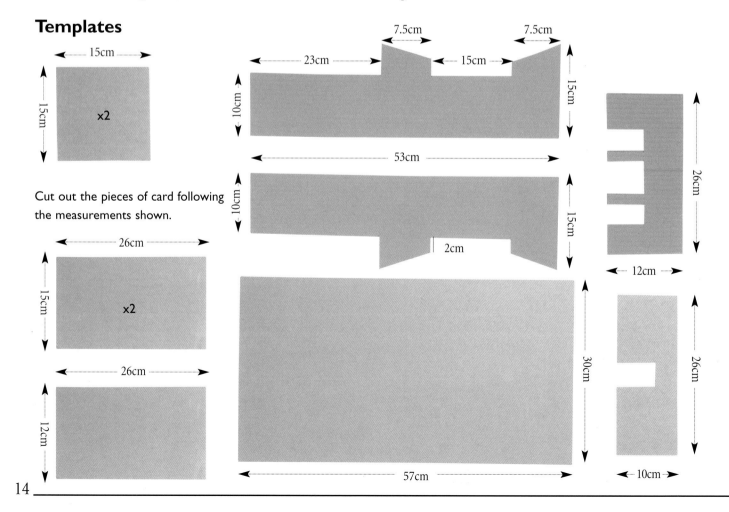

YOU WILL NEED

Pencil, ruler, thick card, scissors, PVA glue and glue brush, masking tape, corrugated card, acrylic paints, paintbrushes, water pot, thin card.

ivy

rose

▲ **Garden delights**

Trailing ivy and sweet-smelling roses often grew in the beautiful walled gardens of a Roman house.

1 When you have cut out all the templates, edge each piece with glue. Press the templates together and reinforce with masking tape as shown. These form the walls of your house.

2 Measure your model and cut out pieces of corrugated card for the roof sections. Stick them together with glue as shown above. Paint all of the roofs with red paint.

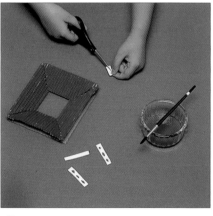

3 Rain water running down the roof above the atrium was directed into a pool by gutters and water spouts. Make gutters from strips of thin card and pierce holes for the spouts.

4 Paint the walls of the house, using masking tape to get a straight line. Glue on the roof sections. You could then cover the walls of the house with some authentic Roman graffiti.

Roman houses had high, windowless walls to keep out the sun, making it cool and shady inside. High ceilings and wide doors made the most of the light from the open atrium and garden. Houses were made from whatever building materials were available and included stone, mud bricks, cement and timber. Clay tiles usually covered the roof.

Celtic roundhouse

It was dark and smoky inside a Celtic roundhouse but quite cosy and comfortable. A thatched roof kept the house warm in the winter but cool in the summer. Houses were heated by a wood or peat fire burning in a pit in the centre of the room. The hearth was the heart of the home, and the fire was kept burning day and night, all year round. Smoke from the fire escaped through the thatch.

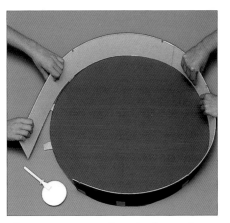

straw

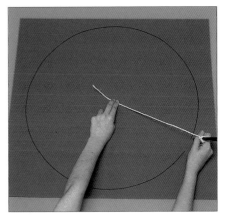

1 Use the piece of string, a ruler and a felt-tipped pen to draw a circle with a radius of 25cm on the brown card. Carefully cut out the circle using a pair of scissors.

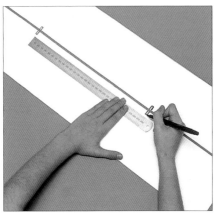

2 Draw a mark every 30cm along the edges of the two pieces of white card. Cut into each mark to make a notch. Glue the two pieces of card together at one end.

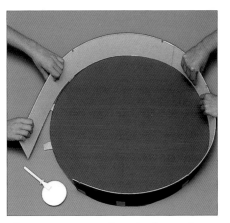

3 Fit the card wall to the base of your house, making sure that the notches are along the top. Glue the wall in place and secure it with masking tape.

4 Roll out the modelling material into sections 13cm wide. Sprinkle straw on to the modelling material and roll it into the surface. Make enough sections to cover the card wall.

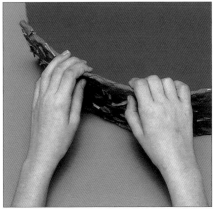

5 Firmly press each modelling material section on to the card wall until the whole wall is covered. Remember to leave a space where the notches are at the top of the wall.

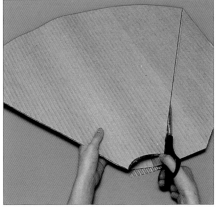

6 Cut a large circle with a diameter of 91cm from the corrugated card. Cut a small circle in the centre. Cut the large circle into sections 56cm wide along the edge.

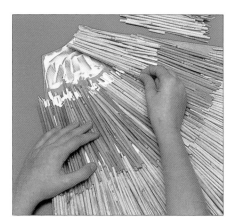

7 Glue pieces of straw on to each piece of card. These will form the roof sections. Start on the outside edge and work your way in towards the centre. Use three layers of straw.

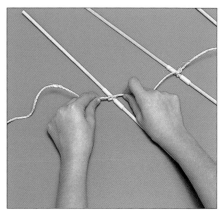

8 Wrap two pieces of masking tape 1cm apart around the middle of six lengths of dowelling. Tie string between the pieces of tape. Allow a 13-cm length of string between each stick.

9 Place one length of dowelling in the middle of the base. Secure it with modelling material. Place the tied sticks over the base as shown above. Lodge the sticks into the wall notches.

10 Fix the sticks in place in the wall notches using modelling material. Cover with an extra piece. Tie the top of the sticks to the upright stick using more string.

11 Tie together the ends of the string between the last two sticks that make up the roof section. Remember to keep the string taut to stop the roof from collapsing.

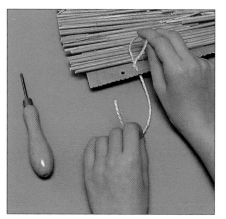

12 Use the bradawl to pierce two holes on both edges at the top and bottom of each straw roof section. Carefully thread a piece of string through each hole.

13 Use the ends of the string to tie the straw roof sections firmly on to the roof structure. Carry on adding the straw sections until the roof is completely covered.

Most houses had no windows. The only light came through the open door. Doorways were low and protected by a porch to keep out the wind and rain.

Native American tipi

Many Native American tribes, such as the Cheyenne of the Great Plains, were nomadic. Their life was dependent on the movement of buffalo. The animals supplied the tribe with food, clothing and shelter. Many tribes lived in tipis, which were easy to build and also easy to pack up when it was time to move on.

Your tipi is a simple version of a Plains tipi. These were large, heavy shelters made from stretched and tanned buffalo skin.

YOU WILL NEED

An old double sheet (measuring around 250 x 78cm) cut into a semicircle with a diameter of 152cm, scissors, pencil, tape measure, large and small paintbrushes, acrylic paints, water pot, string, 12 bamboo sticks, three small sticks, large stones.

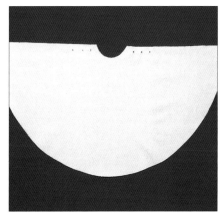

1 Cut out a smaller semicircle 46cm across and 20cm deep as shown. Make three evenly spaced holes either side of this semicircle. Start 6cm from the centre and 3cm from the flat edge.

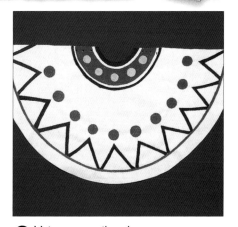

2 Using a pencil and tape measure, draw out a pattern of triangles, lines and circles on the sheet. Make the pattern bold and simple, similar to the one shown. Paint it and leave it to dry.

3 Tie three bamboo sticks together at one end and arrange them on the ground to form a tripod. Lean the remaining bamboo sticks against the tripod. Leave a gap for the entrance.

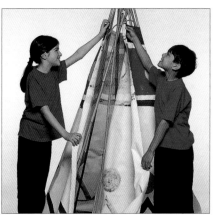

4 Now take the painted sheet (your tipi cover) and wrap it over the bamboo frame. Overlap the two sides at the top of the frame so that the holes you made earlier join up.

5 Insert a small stick through the two top holes to join them. Do this for each of the other holes. You can place stones around the bottom of the sheet to secure your tipi.

Arctic igloo

In the Inuit language, the word *iglu* was actually used to describe any type of house. A shelter such as the one you can build below was called an *igluigaq*. Most Inuit igloos were simple, dome-like structures, which were used as shelters during the winter hunting trips. A small entrance tunnel prevented cold winds from entering the igloo and trapped warm air inside. Outside, the temperature could be as low as –70°C. Inside, heat from the stove, candles and the warmth of the hunter's body kept the air at around 5°C.

YOU WILL NEED

Self-hardening clay, cutting board, rolling pin, ruler, modelling tool, scissors, thick card (20 x 20cm), pair of compasses, pencil, water pot, white paint, paintbrush.

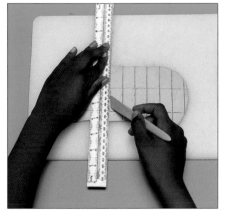

1 Roll out the self-hardening clay. It should be 8mm thick. Cut out 30 blocks of clay. Twenty-four of the blocks must be 4 x 2cm and the other six blocks must be 2 x 1cm.

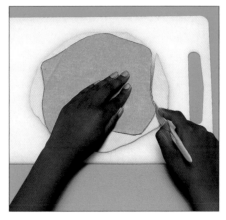

2 Cut out some card to make an irregular base shape. Roll out more clay (8mm thick). Put the template on the clay and cut around it to make the base of the igloo.

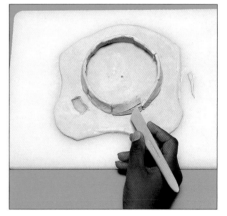

3 Mark a circle (diameter 12cm) on the base. Cut out a rectangle on the edge of the circle (2 x 4cm). Stick nine large blocks around the circle using water. Cut across two blocks as shown.

4 Using your modelling tool, carefully cut a small piece of clay from the corner of each of the remaining blocks of clay as shown above. Discard the pieces of cut clay.

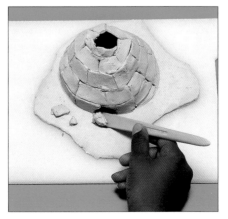

5 Build up the igloo dome, slanting each block in as you go. Use the six small blocks at the top and leave a gap. Form an entrance behind the rectangle cut into the base. Then paint it white.

Inuit hunters made temporary shelters by fitting ice blocks together to form a spiralling, dome-shaped igloo. Only firmly packed snow was used to make the ice blocks.

Medieval castle

In the Middle Ages, castles were built as fortified homes for wealthy lords. The castle needed to be big enough for the lord's family, servants and private army, and strong enough to withstand attack. The outer walls were very high to prevent attackers from climbing over them.

Building a castle ▶

Hundreds of workers were needed to build a castle. Raw materials, such as stone, timber and iron had to be transported to the site, often over great distances.

Templates

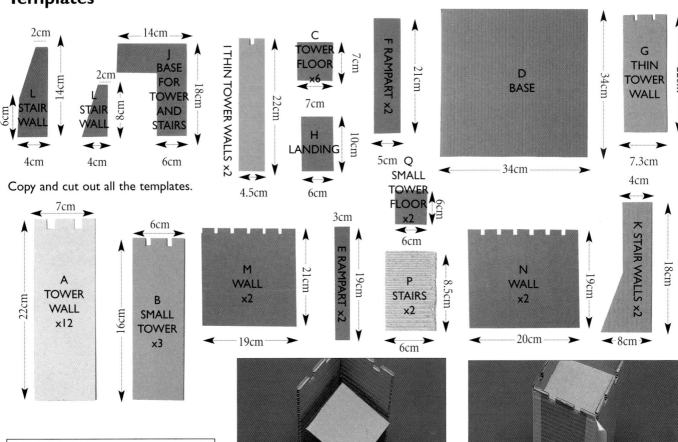

L STAIR WALL — 2cm, 14cm, 6cm, 4cm

L STAIR WALL — 2cm, 8cm, 4cm

J BASE FOR TOWER AND STAIRS — 14cm, 18cm, 6cm

I THIN TOWER WALLS x2 — 22cm, 4.5cm

C TOWER FLOOR x6 — 7cm, 7cm

H LANDING — 10cm, 6cm

F RAMPART x2 — 21cm, 5cm

D BASE — 34cm, 34cm

G THIN TOWER WALL — 22cm, 7.3cm

Q SMALL TOWER FLOOR x2 — 6cm, 6cm

K STAIR WALLS x2 — 4cm, 18cm, 8cm

Copy and cut out all the templates.

A TOWER WALL x12 — 7cm, 22cm

B SMALL TOWER x3 — 6cm, 16cm

M WALL x2 — 21cm, 19cm

E RAMPART x2 — 3cm, 19cm

P STAIRS x2 — 8.5cm, 6cm

N WALL x2 — 19cm, 20cm

YOU WILL NEED

Ruler, pencil, scissors, four sheets of A1 size (50 x 76cm) thick card, 19 x 7cm sheet of thin card, 50 x 15cm sheet of corrugated card, PVA glue and glue brush, masking tape, pair of compasses, acrylic paints, paintbrush, water pot.

1 Cut the stairs from the corrugated card, thin tower wall (G) from thin card and the rest from thick card. Glue two A walls on to tower floor C. Glue upper floor C in place.

2 Glue the open edges of the floor, tower base and standing wall and stick the other two walls in place. Tape strips of masking tape over all the outside corners of the tower walls.

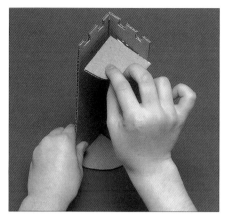

3 Draw a 9.5cm-diameter circle on thick card. Mark it into quarters. Cut out two quarters for the thin tower floors. Glue the two right-angled walls I and the floors into position.

4 Glue the edges of the thin tower walls I. Curve thin card wall section G and stick it onto the right-angled walls. Strengthen the joins with masking tape. Glue tower on base D.

5 Glue the other towers at each corner of the castle base. Glue the bottom and side edges of the walls M and N and stick them between the towers. Glue ramparts E and F to the walls as shown.

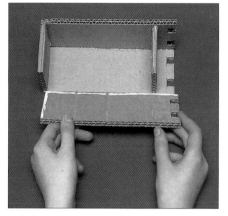

6 Make the small tower B in just the same way as you have made all the other towers. Put two of the walls in place, then the floors and finally the third wall.

7 Glue the small tower at the end of the longer arm of the castle's stair base section J. Glue the two long stair walls K and each stair wall L into place as shown above.

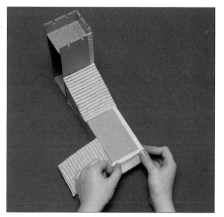

8 Glue landing H on to the straight edges of the stair walls. Stick stairs P on to the sloped edges. Secure with tape. Then stick the whole structure to one side wall of the castle.

9 Cut out some pieces of thick card and glue them to the walls of your castle and stair-tower. When you have finished, paint the castle to look like stone and paint in some windows.

The walls of a real stone castle were up to 5m thick and built of individual stones painstakingly cemented together.

Inside the Home

▲ Elaborate patterns

The Native American tribes of south-western North America were renowned for their beautiful pottery. Each tribe used geometric designs and bright colours to decorate household objects such as this striking tankard.

*U*nless they happened to be very rich, most people throughout history have lived in simple but extremely functional homes. Most families had few pieces of furniture or other household items. Their homes consisted of one large room, which was used for a number of different activities, such as cooking, eating and sleeping. By contrast, modern homes are arranged so that separate rooms are used for specific activities, and each room is furnished for that purpose.

▲ Spacious layout

The rooms of a Chinese house from the Han Dynasty (206BC–AD220) were built around a courtyard and small garden. Family rooms were separate from the main reception area, which was used for entertaining.

▲ Greek vase

This Greek vase is in the Geometric Style, dating from between 1000BC and 700BC. The detailed pattern took a long time to create so it was very expensive to buy. The vase would have been used only for special occasions.

Lasting tradition ▶

Many modern lifestyles have not changed much over the centuries. The Japanese have long favoured simple interior spaces divided by light partitions instead of solid walls. Traditional paper windows have been replaced by glass, which captures the effect of paper.

◀ All in one

Huts made from stone, turf and animal bones were built by the Thule people of the Arctic. The main feature of the inside of the hut was a fire. Animal skins were draped on the walls and floor to give insulation against the bitter cold.

House and garden ▶

Wealthy Japanese nobles lived in huge *shinden* (single-storey homes) with many different rooms. The various members of the noble family, and their servants, lived in different parts of the shinden. Streams flowed from the garden through the rooms of the house.

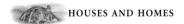

Egyptian tiles

The ancient Egyptians loved to decorate their surroundings. Wealthy citizens had the walls of their homes plastered and painted in bright colours. The rooms of their houses included bedrooms, living rooms, kitchens in thatched courtyards and workshops. Homes were furnished with beds, chairs, stools and benches. Many beautiful tiles have been found in the tombs of the pharaohs, and it is thought that they were used to decorate the furniture and floors of their magnificent palaces.

YOU WILL NEED

Two sheets of card, pencil, ruler, scissors, self-hardening clay, cutting board, rolling pin, modelling tool, sandpaper, acrylic paint (blue, gold, green and yellow ochre), paintbrush, water pot.

1 Copy the two tile shapes, about 5cm deep, on one sheet of card. Cut them out. Draw around them on the other sheet to make the whole pattern. Trim the edge as in step 2.

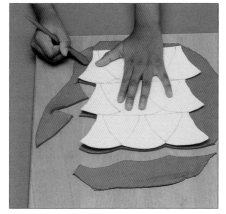

2 Roll out the clay on to a cutting board with a rolling pin. Place the overall outline over the clay and carefully trim the edges using the modelling tool. Discard the extra clay.

3 Mark the individual tile patterns on to the clay. Cut through the lines but do not separate them fully. Score patterns of leaves and flowers on to the surface of the clay. Separate each tile.

4 When one side of each tile has dried, turn the tile over and leave the other side to dry. When the tiles are fully dry, use a piece of sandpaper to smooth off the edges.

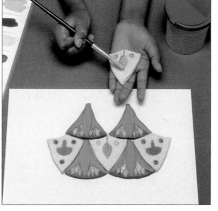

5 The tiles are now ready to paint. Use bright colours to paint over the patterns you made earlier. When you have finished, leave the tiles to dry in a warm place.

The tiles you have made are similar to ones found at a royal palace in Thebes, the capital city of ancient Egypt. The design looks rather like a lotus, the sacred flower of ancient Egypt.

Greek dolphin fresco

Frescoes – paintings on plaster – were a popular way of decorating the walls of palaces on the Greek island of Crete. To make the frescoes last as long as possible, they were painted directly on to wet plaster. Most Greek frescoes show scenes from palace life and the natural world. The paintings are a vital source of information for modern historians. A large fresco decorated the walls of the queen's apartments in a magnificent palace at Knossos. The fresco shows lively dolphins and fish swimming underwater.

YOU WILL NEED

Pencil, sheet of white paper (21 x 19cm), rolling pin, self-hardening clay, cutting board, rolling pin, modelling tool, ruler, pin, sandpaper, acrylic paints, paintbrush, water pot.

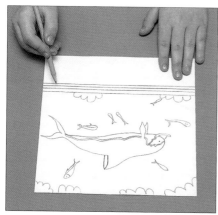

1 Draw a picture of a dolphin on to the sheet of white paper. Add some smaller fish and some seaweed for decoration. Refer to the final picture as a guide for your drawing.

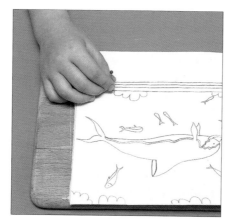

2 Roll out some clay. Tidy up the edges using the modelling tool and ruler. Place your picture over the clay and use a pin to prick holes through the outline on to the clay below.

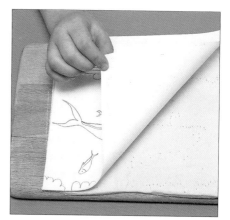

3 Peel the paper off to reveal your picture marked out in dots. Leave the base to dry completely. Then sand it down with fine sandpaper for a smooth finish.

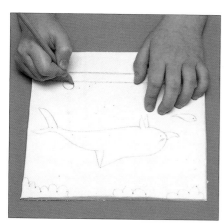

4 Use your pencil to join up the dots on the surface of the clay. Do not press too hard on the clay. When you have finished, you will have a replica of your original drawing.

5 You can then begin to paint the picture. When you have finished, paint in two stripes at the bottom of the picture. These indicate where the fresco would have ended on the wall.

Today, the frescoes at Knossos are copies based on fragments of the original pictures. They are a valuable source of information about Minoan customs.

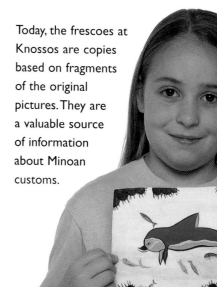

Roman mosaic

The Romans loved to decorate their homes, and the floors of some wealthy houses were covered with mosaic pictures. These pictures might show hunting scenes, the harvest or Roman gods. They were made by using *tesserae* – cubes of stone, pottery or glass – which were pressed into soft cement. Making a mosaic was rather like doing a jigsaw puzzle.

tesserae

Tiny tiles ▲

The floor of a room in an average Roman town house may have been made up of over 100,000 tesserae.

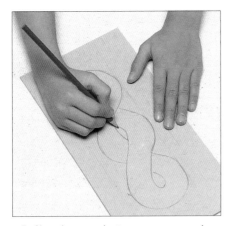

1 Sketch your design on to a rough sheet of paper. A simple design is always easier to work with. Cut the sheet of card to measure 25 x 10cm. Copy your design on to it.

2 Roll out the clay on the cutting board. Use a ruler to measure out small squares (your tiles) on the clay. Cut out the tiles using the modelling tool and then leave them to dry.

3 Paint the dry tiles different colours as shown above. When the paint is dry, you can give the tiles a coat of varnish for extra strength and shine. Leave the tiles to dry completely.

4 Spread plaster paste on to the sheet of card, a small part at a time. While the paste is still wet, press in your tiles, following your design. Use the rough sketch as an extra guide.

5 When the mosaic is dry, use a muslin rag to polish the surface of the tiles. Any other soft, dry rag will do. When you have finished, you can display your mosaic in your house.

Mosaics were displayed in dining rooms and courtyards where visitors would see them.

Roman kitchen

The kitchens of wealthy Romans were equipped with all kinds of bronze pots, pans, strainers and ladles. Pottery storage jars held wine, olive oil and sauces. Herbs, vegetables and joints of meat hung from hooks in the roof. There were no tins, and no fridges or freezers to keep the food fresh. Instead, food had to be preserved in oil or by drying, smoking, salting or pickling. Food was boiled, fried, grilled and stewed. Larger kitchens might include stone ovens for baking bread or spits for roasting meat.

YOU WILL NEED

Ruler, pencil, thick card, scissors, PVA glue and glue brush, masking tape, acrylic paints, paintbrush, water pot, red felt-tipped pen, plaster paste, sandpaper, balsa wood, self-hardening clay, cutting board, modelling tool.

1 Glue pieces of card to make the walls and floor. Secure with masking tape. Paint the floor grey and pencil in stone tiles. Paint the walls yellow and blue. Draw on stripes with the red pen.

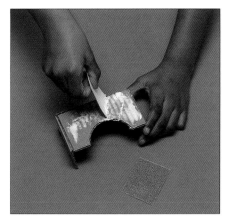

2 Use some card to make a stove and coat it with plaster paste. When it is dry, rub it smooth with sandpaper. Make a grate from two strips of card and four bits of balsa wood, glued together.

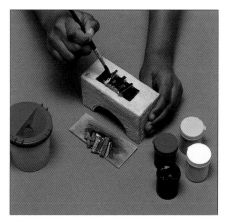

3 Use some acrylic paints to colour the stove as shown above. Use small pieces of balsa wood to make a pile of wood fuel to store underneath the stove.

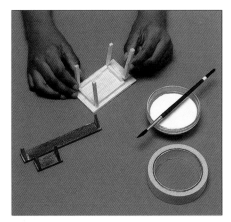

4 Make a table and shelves from pieces of balsa wood as shown above. Glue them together and secure the joins with masking tape. Leave them to dry before painting them brown.

5 Use a piece of clay to model pots, pans, bowls, storage jars, perhaps even a frying pan or an egg poacher. Leave the utensils to dry before painting them a suitable colour.

Foods in a Roman kitchen were stored in baskets, bowls or sacks. Wine, oil and sauces were stored in pottery jars called *amphorae*.

Chinese lantern

Chinese festivals are linked to agricultural seasons. The festivals include celebrations of sowing and harvest, dances, horse racing and the eating of specially prepared foods. The Chinese festival best known around the world today is the New Year or Spring Festival. Its date falls on the first full moon between 21 January and 19 February. At the end of the Chinese New Year, dumplings made of rice flour are prepared for the Lantern Festival. This festival began during the Tang Dynasty or 'Golden Age' (AD618–906) – a time when the arts prospered, new trade routes opened in foreign lands and boundaries expanded as a result of successful military campaigns.

▲ Bright lights

During the Lantern Festival, lanterns are hung outside the house to represent the first full moon of the Chinese New Year. Lanterns were once made from silk or glass and decorated with ornate images or calligraphy (handwriting).

Templates

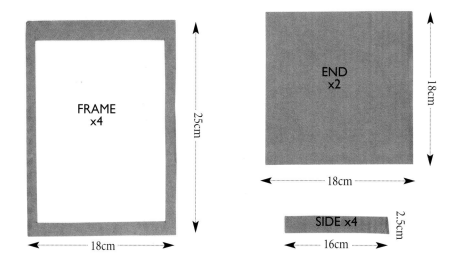

FRAME
x4

18cm

25cm

END
x2

18cm

18cm

SIDE x4

16cm

2.5cm

Using the measurements above, draw the ten templates on to thick card (the templates are not drawn to scale). Cut them out carefully using a pair of scissors.

▲ Fire power

You could decorate your lantern with a firework display. The Chinese invented gunpowder in the AD700s. It was first used to make fireworks in the 900s.

YOU WILL NEED

Thick card, pencil, ruler, scissors, pair of compasses, PVA glue and glue brush, red tissue paper, blue acrylic paint, paintbrush, water pot, thin blue and yellow card, wire, masking tape, bamboo stick, small torch, fringing fabric.

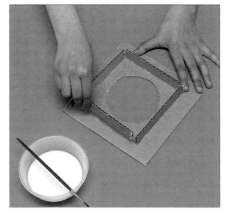

1 Using a pair of compasses, draw an 8cm-diameter circle in the middle of one of the end pieces. Cut out the circle using the scissors. Glue on the four sides.

2 Glue together the four frame pieces. Then glue both end pieces on to the frame. When it is dry, cover the frame with red tissue paper. Glue one side at a time.

3 Paint the top of the lantern blue. Cut the borders out of blue card. Glue to the top and bottom of the frame. Stick a thin strip of yellow card to the bottom to make a border.

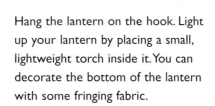

Hang the lantern on the hook. Light up your lantern by placing a small, lightweight torch inside it. You can decorate the bottom of the lantern with some fringing fabric.

4 Make two small holes opposite each other at the top of the lantern as shown above. Pass the ends of a loop of wire through the holes. Tape the ends to secure the wire.

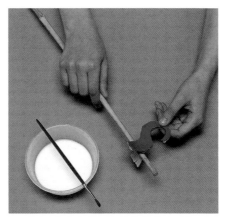

5 Make a hook from thick card. Split the ends opposite the hook as shown above. Wrap the ends around the bamboo stick and glue them together, securing with masking tape.

Japanese paper screen

Builders faced many challenges when they designed homes in ancient Japan. Not only did buildings have to provide shelter against extremes of climate, they also had to withstand earthquakes. Lightweight, single-storey houses were made of straw, paper and wood. These would bend and sway in an earthquake. If they did collapse, or were swept away by floods, they would be less likely than a stone building to injure the people inside.

Japanese buildings were designed as a series of box-like rooms. A one-room hut was sufficient for a farming family. Dividing screens and partitions could be moved around to suit people's needs. Many houses had verandas (open platforms) beneath overhanging eaves. People could sit here taking in the fresh air, keeping lookout or enjoying the view.

paper

wood

▲ Screened off

Wood and paper were used to make screens for both the outer and inner walls of many Japanese homes. The screens were pushed back to provide peaceful garden views and welcome cool breezes during the hot summer.

▲ Fine work

Folding screens became decorative items as well as providing privacy and protection from draughts. This panel was made during the Edo period (1603–1868), when crafts flourished.

Simple living ▶

Modern rural Japanese homes are built in the same way and using similar materials to those of ancient Japan. Screens and sliding walls can be moved to block draughts and for privacy. Straw and rush mats, called *tatami,* cover the floor.

YOU WILL NEED

Gold paper (48 x 44cm), pencil, ruler, scissors, thick card (48 x 22cm), craft knife, cutting board, PVA glue and glue brush, fabric paints, paintbrush, water pot, fabric tape.

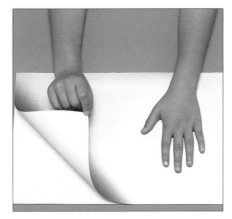

1 Cut two pieces of gold paper to measure 48 x 22cm. Use a craft knife to cut out a piece of card the same size. Stick the gold paper to each side of the card.

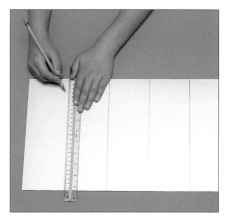

2 When the glue has dried, use a ruler and pencil to mark out six panels of equal size on one side of the gold-covered card. Each panel should measure 22 x 8cm.

3 Now turn the card over. Paint a traditional picture of Japanese irises in shades of blue and green fabric paint as shown above. Leave the paint to dry.

4 Turn the screen over so the plain, unpainted side is facing you. Using scissors or a craft knife, carefully cut out each panel along the lines that you marked earlier.

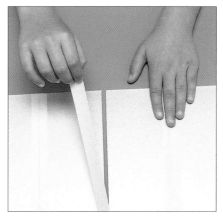

5 Now use fabric tape to join each of your panels together, leaving a small gap between each panel. The tape will act as a hinge for each section of your Japanese screen.

Irises are a popular image in Japanese homes. The pretty blue flowers are a symbol of absent friends.

Native American tankard

The Native Americans were skilled craftspeople. Most tribes wove baskets and blankets from plant fibres. Some baskets were coiled so tightly that they could hold water. The tribes of the Southwest were renowned for their pottery. The Apache tribe made black and white bowls that became known as burial pots. This was because they were broken when their owner died and buried with the body. Archaeologists have also found beautiful pots dating back to around 1000BC.

YOU WILL NEED

Self-hardening clay, cutting board, rolling board, water pot, pencil, selection of acrylic or poster paints, selection of paintbrushes, non-toxic varnish.

1 Roll out a slab of clay into a flat circle about 10cm across. Roll two sausage shapes. Dampen the perimeter of the circle and then stick one end of the sausage to it as shown above.

2 Coil the sausage around. When the first sausage runs out, use the other clay sausage. Use your damp fingers to smooth the coils into a tankard shape and smooth the outside.

3 Roll out another small sausage shape of clay to make the handle of the tankard. Dampen the ends and press it on to the clay pot to make a handle shape. Leave it to dry.

4 Using a sharp pencil, mark out a striking design on your tankard. You can follow the traditional Indian design shown here, or you could make up one of your own.

5 Using poster paints or acrylic paints, colour in the pattern. Use a fine brush for tiny checked patterns and thin lines. When it is dry, coat the mug with one or two layers of varnish.

Each tribe had its unique designs and used certain colours. The geometric patterns on the tankard above were common to tribes of the Southwest.

Viking drinking horn

The Viking sagas (long stories) tell of many drunken celebrations. They helped relieve the strain of the long dark winters. Warriors would have toasted each other with beer or mead (an alcoholic drink made by fermenting honey). They drank from drinking horns made from the horns of cattle. Unless a drinking horn was being passed around a number of people, it could not be put down and the contents had to be consumed in one go. Drink was ladled out from giant barrels and tubs.

YOU WILL NEED

Thick paper, pencil, ruler, scissors, mug, masking tape, brown paper, self-hardening clay, newspaper, water pot, acrylic paints, paintbrush, silver paper, PVA glue and glue brush.

1 Cut the thick paper into 28cm-long strips all with different widths. Roll the widest strip into a ring using the rim of a mug as a guide. Secure the paper ring with masking tape.

2 Roll up the next widest strip, and secure it with masking tape. Place the small ring inside the large ring and fix with tape. Make more rings, each one a bit smaller than the one before.

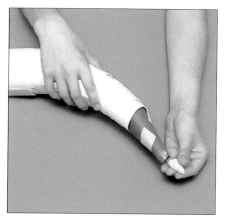

3 Place each small ring into the next largest, binding with tape to make a tapered horn. Roll brown paper into a cone to make a point and bind it in position. Round off the end with clay.

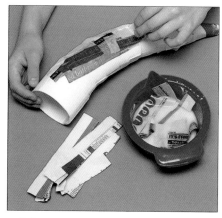

4 Cover the horn with papier mâché. Cut strips of newspaper, soak them in water and glue them to the horn. Leave to dry and then add more layers of papier mâché. Leave to dry again.

5 When dry, paint the horn white, giving it a black or brown tip. Cut the silver paper into a pattern and glue it to the rim of the horn. Viking horns were often decorated with silver.

Drinking horns were used on special occasions such as festivals and victory celebrations.

Arctic oil lamp

The Arctic is one of the wildest, harshest, environments on Earth. Arctic winters are long, dark and bitterly cold. A thick layer of snow and ice blankets the region for much of the year. A fire was the main feature of an Arctic home. In Inuit shelters, seal or whale blubber were burned in stone lamps to provide light and additional heat. With fires and lamps burning, the shelters could be surprisingly warm and bright.

▲ Underground houses

Ancient Arctic peoples built their houses under the ground to protect them from the freezing conditions above. Often, the walls and floor were lined with animal skins to provide extra insulation against the cold.

▲ Colony in the cold

When Viking warrior Erik the Red landed in Greenland in AD983, he and his men built houses of turf and stone. These shelters provided excellent insulation against the cold.

A harsh climate ▶

The Arctic lies at the far north of our planet within the Arctic Circle. Much of the Arctic is a vast, frozen ocean, surrounded by the northernmost parts of Asia, Europe, North America and Greenland. The Arctic is characterized by low temperatures, often as low as −70°C in the winter. For anyone living in the region, it is vital to keep as warm as possible. Homes may be buried underground, with an entrance through the roof.

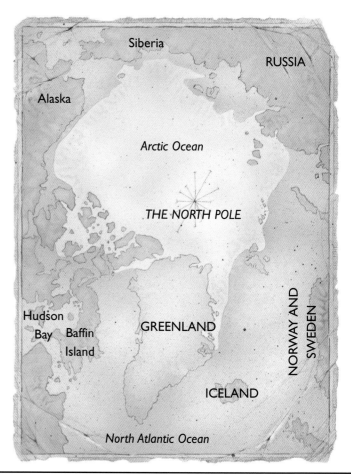

YOU WILL NEED

Self-hardening clay, rolling pin, cutting board, ruler, pair of compasses, sharp pencil, modelling tool, water pot, dark grey and light grey paint, small paintbrush.

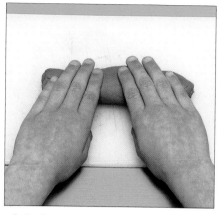

1 Roll out a piece of clay. Draw out a circle with a radius of 5cm, and cut the circle out using the modelling tool. Roll more clay out into a long sausage shape 30cm long and 2cm thick.

2 Wet the edge of the clay circle and stick the sausage shape around it. Use the rounded end of the modelling tool to blend the edges firmly into the base.

3 Use your modelling tool to cut a small triangular notch at the edge of the circle. This will make a small lip for the front of your oil lamp.

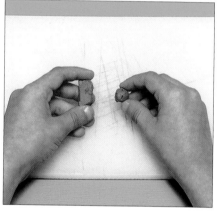

4 Shape a piece of clay into a small head. Use another piece to shape some shoulders. Stick the head to the shoulders by wetting the clay and holding the pieces firmly together.

5 Stick the small figure just off centre on the base of the oil lamp. Then use the modelling tool to make a small groove on the base. This is for holding the oil.

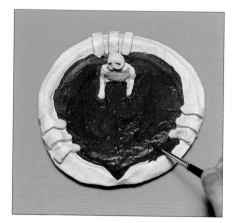

6 Decorate the edge of the lamp with extra pieces of clay. Once dry, paint the lamp using dark grey and light grey paint. *Safety note: do not attempt to burn anything in your lamp.*

Stone lamps burning seal or whale blubber (fat) cast a warm glow in homes throughout the Arctic region. A lighted wick of moss or animal fur was placed in a bowl filled with fat, and the lamp was left to burn slowly.

Food and Feasts

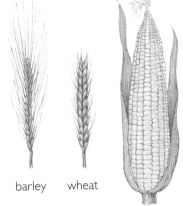

barley wheat

maize

squashes

▲ Fruits of the soil

The first plants to be cultivated already grew in the wild. For example, wheat and barley were grown from wild plants in the Middle East. Maize, squashes and beans were the first to be grown in Central America.

A great change in human history took place around 10,000BC. Instead of gathering the seeds of wild plants, people began to grow their own food. They selected and sowed seeds from the healthiest plants to produce crops to harvest for food. People also began to breed cattle, goats and sheep for meat and milk. Different traditions surrounding the preparation, cooking and eating of food developed. Food was a way of showing hospitality to family and strangers. Some foods were given a religious meaning and came to be used for special festivals.

◀ Back-breaking work

Early farmers gathered grain from edible wild grasses and then planted seeds from the plants for the following year's harvest. They had only simple tools and the crops were harvested using wooden sickles set with sharp flint blades.

▲ Jobs for the family

Farmers on this settlement in Germany are thatching the roof of a longhouse. The women are grinding grain between stones to make bread. They will add water to the flour and shape the dough into flat loaves, which will be baked in a clay oven.

▲ A farming village

The farmers of this village in southern England have built round, thatched houses next to their wheat fields. They also keep domesticated cattle for milk, meat and skins. Every morning the cattle were led from the village to pastures outside.

cattle

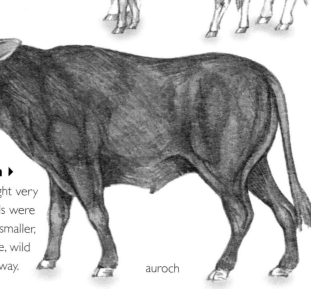

Domestication ▶

When people changed from hunting to farming, they caught very young animals to raise by hand. Larger, more aggressive animals were killed. Gradually, new domesticated strains evolved from the smaller, more docile animals. Domestic cattle were bred from large, wild animals called aurochs in this way.

auroch

Stone Age food

The hunter-gatherers of the Stone Age had a varied diet. Gradually, they learned that they could eat certain plants and got to know where and when they could find them. From spring to autumn, women and children foraged for berries, nuts, eggs, and the roots, shoots and leaves of vegetables. In summer, fruits and plant seeds were picked and stored to eat or sow later.

dandelion leaves

woodland fungus

◀ Foraging for food

The food that prehistoric people ate came mostly from plants. Woodlands in autumn were a rich source of food, with plenty of fruits, fungi and nuts.

YOU WILL NEED

A large saucepan, 500g blueberries, 500g blackberries, wooden spoon, 200g whole hazelnuts, honeycomb, tablespoon, ladle, serving bowl.

1 Choose fruit that is fresh and firm. Wash your hands before you start, and ask an adult to help you cook. Wash the blueberries and pour them into the large saucepan.

2 Next wash the blackberries and pour them into the pan with the blueberries. Use a wooden spoon to stir the fruits gently without crushing them.

3 Take the whole hazelnuts and pour them into the pan with the blueberries and blackberries. Carefully stir the contents until the fruits and nuts are thoroughly mixed.

4 Add six tablespoons of honey from the honeycomb. (You could use honey from a jar instead.) Then ask an adult to help you cook the mixture, gradually bringing it to the boil.

5 Simmer the fruit and nut mixture for about 20 minutes. Take the pan off the stove and leave it to cool. Use a ladle to transfer your dessert into a serving bowl.

In prehistoric times, people cooked fruit in this way to preserve it as jam. Clay pots were used for cooking and storing the jam.

Egyptian pastries

People in ancient Egypt were often given food as payment for their work. Foods such as bread, onions and salted fish were washed down with sweet, grainy beer. Flour was often gritty, and the teeth of many mummified bodies show signs of severe wear and tear. An Egyptian meal could be finished off with nuts, such as almonds, or sweet fruits, such as figs and dates.

onions

◄ Fruits and vegetables
Onions, leeks, cabbages, melons, grapes and many other fruits and vegetables were grown in ancient Egypt.

YOU WILL NEED
Mixing bowl, wooden spoon, 200g stoneground flour, ½ tsp salt, 1tsp baking powder, 75g chopped butter, 60g honey, 3 tbsp milk, floured surface, caraway seeds, baking tray.

1 Mix the flour, salt and baking powder in the bowl. Add the chopped butter. Using your fingers, rub the butter into the mixture until it resembles fine breadcrumbs.

2 Add 40g of honey and combine it with the mixture. Stir in the milk to form a stiff dough. Shape the dough into a ball and place it on a floured board or work surface.

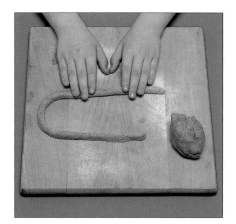

3 Divide the dough into three. Roll each piece into long strips as shown above. Take each strip and coil it into a spiral to make a cake. Make two other cakes in the same way.

4 Now sprinkle each spiral cake with caraway seeds and place them on to a greased baking tray. Finish off by glazing the cakes with the remainder of the honey.

5 Ask an adult to bake the cakes in an oven at 180°C/Gas Mark 4 for approximately 20 minutes. When they are ready, take the cakes out and leave them to cool.

Egyptian pastries were often shaped in spirals. Other popular shapes were rings like doughnuts. The Egyptians did not have sugar, so their cakes were sweetened with honey.

Greek pancakes

Meals in ancient Greece were based around fish, home-baked bread and vegetables such as onions, beans, lentils, leeks and radishes. Chickens and pigeons were kept for their eggs and meat, and a cow or a few goats or sheep for milk and cheese. Pancakes like the ones in this project made handy snacks.

dried apricots

olives

raisins

◀ **Drying fruits**

Raisins (dried grapes) and apricots, and olives, were plentiful in the Mediterranean and used for cooking.

YOU WILL NEED

8 tbsp clear honey, spoon, small bowl, 100g flour, sieve, mixing bowl, fork, 200ml water, frying pan, sesame seeds, 1 tbsp olive oil, spatula, serving plate.

1 First measure the honey into a small bowl. Then make the pancake mix. Sieve the flour into a mixing bowl. Then, using a fork, stir the water into the flour. Mix into a runny paste.

2 Spoon the honey into the pancake mixture a little at a time. Mix it with a fork, making sure that the mixture is nice and smooth, and that there are no lumps.

3 Ask an adult to help you with the next two steps. Heat the frying pan. Sprinkle in the sesame seeds and cook them until they are brown. Set the seeds aside to cool.

4 Heat a tablespoon of olive oil in a frying pan. Pour a quarter of the pancake mixture into the frying pan. Cook on both sides for about four minutes until golden brown.

5 Serve the pancake on a plate. Sprinkle on a handful of sesame seeds and pour extra honey over the top. Cook the rest of the pancake mixture in the same way.

Pancakes were popular among theatre-goers in ancient Greece. Stalls were set up around theatres to catch the crowds as they left.

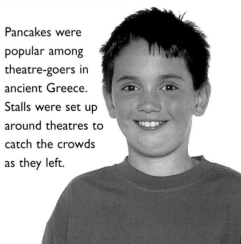

Roman honeyed dates

Many Roman town-dwellers lived in homes without kitchens. They ate takeaway meals brought from the many food stalls and bars in town. Breakfast may only have been a quick snack of bread, honey and olives. Lunch, too, was a light meal, perhaps of eggs, or cold meats and fruit. The main meal of the day was *cena* (dinner). This might start with shellfish or a salad, followed by a main meal of roast pork, veal, chicken or goose with vegetables. Cena finished with a sweet course of fruit or honey cakes.

1 Slit open the dates with the knife on the chopping board. Remove the stone inside. Be sure not to cut the dates completely in half and use the knife carefully.

2 Set aside the hazelnuts. Chop up the rest of the nuts. Use a pestle and mortar to grind them into smaller pieces. Stuff a small amount into the middle of each date.

3 Pour some salt on to the chopping board and lightly roll each of the stuffed dates in it. Make sure the dates are coated all over, but do not use too much salt.

4 Slowly melt the honey in a frying pan on a slow heat. Lightly fry the dates for about five minutes, turning them with a wooden spoon. Ask an adult to help you use the stove.

5 Arrange the stuffed dates in a shallow serving dish. Sprinkle over the whole hazelnuts, some of the chopped nuts and a few fresh mint leaves. The dates are now ready to eat!

The Romans loved sweet dishes made from nuts and dates imported from North Africa. They also used dates to make sauces for savoury fish dishes.

Indian chickpea curry

The diet of most people in ancient India depended on what plants were grown around them. In the areas of high rainfall, rice was the main food. In drier areas, people grew wheat and made it into bread.

Religion affected diet, too. Buddhists did not agree with killing animals, so they were vegetarians. Most Hindus became vegetarian, too. Hindus believed the cow was holy, so eating beef was forbidden. Muslims were forbidden to eat pork, although they did eat other meats. Chickpeas, peas, lentils and cheese provided healthy alternatives to meat.

The Indians used many spices in cooking to add flavour, to sharpen the appetite or aid digestion. Ginger, turmeric, cinnamon and cumin have been used from early times. Chillis were introduced from the Americas after the 1500s.

▲ Staple food

Rice cultivation has been the dominant agricultural activity in most parts of India since ancient times. The starchy, grain-like seeds form the main part of most Indian dishes. A rice plant's roots must be submerged in water, so a reliable irrigation system was essential if farmers were to obtain a good yield.

YOU WILL NEED

Knife, chopping board, small onion, 30ml vegetable oil, wok, wooden spoon, 4cm cube of fresh ginger root, two cloves of garlic, ¼ tsp turmeric, 450g tomatoes, 225g cooked chickpeas, salt and pepper, 2 tbsp chopped fresh coriander, 2 tsp garum masala, coriander leaves for garnish, a lime.

1 Ask an adult to help you cook. Finely chop the onion. Heat the oil in a wok or frying pan). Fry the onion in the oil for two to three minutes until it is soft.

2 Finely chop the ginger and add it to the wok. Chop the garlic cloves and add them to the wok, too, along with the turmeric. Cook gently for another minute.

3 Peel the tomatoes, cut them in half and remove all the seeds. Roughly chop the tomatoes up and add them to the onion, garlic and spice mixture in the wok.

4 Add the cooked chickpeas to the pan. Gently bring the mixture to the boil, then simmer gently for around 10-15 minutes until the sauce has reduced to a thick paste.

turmeric

cardamom pods

black mustard seeds

5 Taste the curry and add salt and pepper as seasoning if required. The curry should taste spicy but not so hot that it burns your mouth – or those of your guests!

6 Add the chopped fresh coriander to the curry, along with the garum masala. Garnish with a scattering of fresh coriander leaves and serve with a slice of lime.

▲ Essential spices

Turmeric is ground from the root of a plant to give food an earthy flavour and yellow colour. Black mustard seed has a smoky, bitter taste. Cardamom gives a musky, sugary flavour suitable for both sweet and savoury dishes.

mango leaves

limes

rice flour

Chickpeas are an extremely popular ingredient in Indian cooking. They have been grown as a crop in India for thousands of years.

▲ Good luck food

Various foods and plants were placed at the entrance of an Indian home for good luck. Rice-flour pictures were drawn on the step, and mango leaves and limes were hung above the door.

Chinese bean soup

Rice was the basis of most meals in ancient China, especially in the south where it was grown. It was often added to soup. People from the north made noodles and buns from wheat flour instead. They also made pancakes and dumplings, as well as lamb and duck dishes. For most people, however, meat was a luxury.

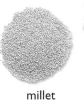

rice

millet

mung beans

sesame seeds

◄ Cooking in China

Mung beans, rice, millet and sesame seeds are all important additions to Chinese dishes and sauces.

YOU WILL NEED

Measuring jug, bowl, water, scales, 225g aduki beans, 3 tsp ground nuts, 4 tsp short-grain rice, tangerine, saucepan, wooden spoon, 175g sugar, liquidizer, sieve, serving bowls.

1 Measure out 1 litre of water in the jug. Weigh, wash and drain the beans, nuts and rice and put them in a bowl. Add water and leave overnight to soak. Do not drain off the water.

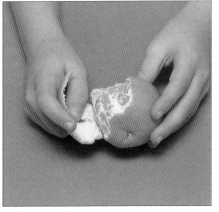

2 Wash and dry the tangerine. Then carefully use your fingers to ease off the peel in one long, continuous strip. Leave the peel overnight to become hard and dry.

3 Put beans, rice and liquid into a saucepan. Add the peel and 500ml water. Ask an adult to help you bring the mixture to the boil. Cover the pan and simmer for two hours.

4 Use the scales to weigh out the sugar. When the water has boiled off and is just covering the beans, add the sugar. Simmer until the sugar has completely dissolved.

5 Remove and discard the tangerine peel. Leave the soup to cool. Then liquidize the mixture. Strain any lumps with a sieve. Pour the soup into bowls and serve.

Most peasant farmers lived on a simple diet. Red bean soup with rice was a typical meal.

Japanese rice balls

Food in Japan has always been simple and healthy. The diet is based on rice, millet, wheat or barley, which is boiled, steamed or made into noodles. Many foods are flavoured with soy sauce, made from fermented soya beans. Another nutritious soya product, tofu (beancurd), is made from soya beans softened and pulped in water. The pulp is formed into blocks and left to set.

seaweed

mussels

◄ **Treasures from the sea**
Japan is an island, so seafood, such as mussels and seaweed, is an important part of the Japanese diet.

YOU WILL NEED

7 cups Japanese rice, saucepan, sieve, wooden spoon, mixing bowls, 1 tbsp salt, chopping board, 1 tbsp black sesame seeds, ½ sheet yaki nori seaweed, knife, cucumber, serving dish.

1 Ask an adult to help you boil the rice. When the rice is cooked, drain it in the sieve but do not rinse it. The rice should remain sticky. Place the rice in one mixing bowl and salt in another.

2 Wash your hands thoroughly. Then wet the palms of both hands with cold water. Next, put a finger into the bowl of salt and rub a little on to your palms.

3 Place about one eighth of the rice on one hand. Use both your hands to shape the rice into a triangular shape. You should press firmly but not too hard.

4 Make seven more rice balls in the same way. When you have made them all, sprinkle some of the sesame seeds over each one to add some flavour to the rice balls.

5 Cut a strip of yaki nori seaweed into four pieces and wrap some of your rice balls in it. Put the *onigiri* on a serving dish and garnish them with sliced cucumber.

Rice was introduced from China in AD100 and remains the staple food of Japan.

Celtic cakes

In Celtic times, you would have had to watch how many oatcakes you ate. The Celts did not approve of people getting too fat. Roman writers reported that Celtic warriors were told not to let out their belts, but to lose weight when clothes around their waists became too tight. The Celts produced most of their own food on their farms. All they needed to buy were products such as salt.

apples

◄ Home-grown fruits

In Celtic times in northern Europe, many fruits were available that are familiar to us today.

1 Under adult supervision, preheat an oven to 220°C/Gas Mark 7. Put the oatmeal into the bowl. Sieve the flour into the bowl and add the salt. Mix all the ingredients with a wooden spoon.

2 Add the baking soda. Mix it in well and then put the bowl to one side. Melt the butter in a small saucepan over a low heat. Add it to the oat and flour mixture.

3 Boil some water and put it in a heat-resistant glass. Gradually add the hot water to the oatmeal and flour mixture and stir well until you have a firm dough.

4 Turn the dough out on to a board sprinkled with a little oatmeal and flour. Roll the dough until it is about 1cm thick. Use a glass to cut the dough into about 24 circles.

5 Place the circles of dough on a greased baking tray. Bake in an oven for about 15 minutes. Allow the oatcakes to cool on a wire tray before serving them.

Enjoy your oatcakes plain or eat them with butter, honey or cheese.

Viking bread

A typical Viking family ate twice a day. The food was usually prepared on a central hearth, although some large farmhouses had separate kitchens. Oats, barley and rye were made into bread and porridge. The hand-ground flour was often coarse and gritty. Poor people added split peas and bark to make it go further, and their teeth became worn down. Dough was mixed in large wooden troughs and baked in ovens or on stone griddles. Goat, beef and horse meat were roasted or stewed in cauldrons over a fire.

YOU WILL NEED

2 cups white bread flour, 3 cups wholemeal flour, sieve, mixing bowl, 1 tsp baking powder, 1 tsp salt, 1 cup edible seeds, 2 cups warm water, wooden spoon or spatula, baking tray.

1 Sieve the flours into a bowl. Add the baking powder and salt. Stir half of the seeds into the bowl. Sunflower seeds give a crunchy texture, but you could use any other edible seeds.

2 Add two cups of warm water and stir the mixture with a wooden spoon or spatula. At this stage the mixture should become quite stiff and difficult to stir.

3 Use your hands to knead the mixture into a stiff dough. Before you start, dust your hands with some of the flour to stop the mixture sticking to them.

4 When the dough is well kneaded and no longer sticks to your hands, put it on a greased baking tray. Sprinkle the rest of your seeds over the top of the loaf.

5 Put the baking tray in a cold oven. Ask an adult to turn the oven to 190°C/Gas Mark 5. Cook the bread for one hour. Cooking the bread from cold will help the loaf to rise.

The Vikings put split peas in bread to add flavour and bulk, but sunflower seeds are just as tasty! Bread made from barley was most common, but wealthy Vikings ate loaves made from finer wheat flour.

Native American corn cakes

Tribes of North America have hunted, fished and gathered their own food from the earliest days. The Inuit fished from kayaks or through holes in the ice. Calusa tribes of the Southeast farmed the sea, sectioning off areas for shellfish. Tribes of the Northwest coast also harvested the sea. They therefore had little reason to develop farming, although they did cultivate tobacco.

For many peoples, however, farming was an important way of life. The Pueblos of the Southwest cultivated corn (maize) and made a thin bread, rather like your tortilla. Tribes on the fertile east coast, such as the Secotan, set fire to land to clear it for farming and then planted thriving vegetable gardens. As well as the staple maize, squash and beans, they grew berries, tomatoes, vanilla pods and asparagus. Archaeologists have found evidence of a tyoe of popcorn dating from 4000BC.

artichoke

plums

▲ Offerings to the dead

The Shawnee Feast of the Dead was held each year to honour the spirits of the dead tribal members. They would place luxurious fruits and food, such as artichokes and plums, on the graves and light candles all round.

seal

Inuit fisherman

Chipewyan canoe

Cree

beaver

Tsimshian

salmon

maize

Huron

Haida house

Sioux

Iroquois

Hopewell Mound

Paiute basket-maker

N

Secotan

Cheyenne warrior hunting bison

Navajo

Kiowa camp

Cherokee village of Echota

Apache   Comanche

Calusa

eagle

▲ Harvesting the land

The area and environment tribes lived in determined what they ate. Tribes of the Northwest who lived on the coast took their food from the sea. For many tribes on the fertile eastern coast, farming was an important way of life.

maize

squashes

mixed beans

▲ Vegetable crops

Maize, or corn, was the staple food for most Native American tribes. Two other important vegetable crops were squashes and beans.

YOU WILL NEED

200g corn tortilla flour or plain flour, measuring scales, sieve, mixing bowl, jug, cold water, metal spoon, chopping board, rolling pin, frying pan, a little vegetable oil for cooking, honey.

I Measure out 200g of the corn tortilla flour or plain flour using the measuring scales. Carefully sieve the flour into the mixing bowl. Fill the jug with cold water.

2 Slowly add the water to the flour in the mixing bowl. Add a little water at a time, stirring all the time as you pour, until the mixture forms into a stiff dough.

3 Using your hands, gently knead the mixture. Keep kneading the dough until it is not too sticky to touch. You may need to add a little more flour to get the consistency right.

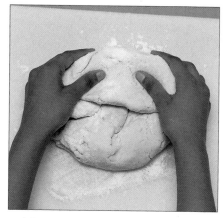

4 Sprinkle flour over the board. Take the dough from the bowl and knead it on the floured chopping board for about ten minutes. Leave the dough to stand for 30 minutes.

5 Pull off a small lump of dough. Roll it between your hands to form a flattened ball. Repeat this process until you have made all the dough into flattened balls.

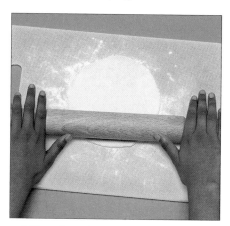

6 Keep kneading the dough balls until they form flat, round shapes. Finish them off by using the rolling pin to roll them into flat, thin cakes called tortillas.

7 Ask an adult to help you cook the tortillas. Heat a heavy frying pan or griddle. Gently cook the cakes in a little oil one by one until they are lightly browned on both sides.

Tortillas were usually eaten with savoury food, but they also taste delicious with honey.

Aztec tortillas

Mesoamerican people usually ate their main meal around noon and had a smaller snack in the evening. Ordinary people's food was plain – but very healthy – as long as there was enough of it. Everyday meals were based on maize (which was ground down for tortillas), beans, vegetables and fruit. Peppers, tomatoes, pumpkins and avocado pears were popular, and the Aztecs also ate boiled cactus leaves. Soup made from wild herbs or seeds boiled in water was also a favourite. Meat and fish were luxuries. Deer, rabbit, turkey and dog were cooked for feasts, as well as frogs, lizards and turtles. The Aztecs also ate fish eggs and algae from the lakes.

tomato

avocado pear

▲ New food

Today, many Central American meals still include tomatoes, peppers, chillis and avocado pears. These fruits and vegetables were first introduced to Europe and Asia in the years after the conquest of Mesoamerica.

mixed beans

prickly pear

▲ Vegetarian diet

Beans were an important part of the Mesoamerican diet. So was the fruit of the prickly pear cactus. The fine spines had to be carefully removed first!

◀ Floating gardens

Chinampas were very productive floating gardens. Layers of twigs and branches were sunk beneath the surface of a lake and weighted with stones. The government passed laws telling farmers when to sow seeds to ensure there would be a steady supply of vegetables for sale in the market.

YOU WILL NEED

Measuring scales, 225g plain flour or maize flour, 1 tsp salt, mixing bowl, 4g butter, water jug, 120ml cold water, teaspoon, rolling pin, chopping board, a little vegetable oil for frying, non-stick frying pan.

1 Weigh out all the ingredients. Mix the flour and salt together in a bowl. Rub the butter into the mixture until it looks like breadcrumbs. Then pour in the water a teaspoon at a time.

2 Use your hands to mix everything together until you have a loose mixture of dough. Do not worry if there is still some dry mixture around the sides of the bowl.

3 Knead the dough for at least ten minutes until it is smooth. If the dough on your hands gets too sticky, you could add a little plain flour to the bowl.

4 Tip the dough out of the bowl on to a floured chopping board. Divide it into egg-sized balls using your hands or a knife. You should have enough for about 12 balls.

5 Sprinkle the board and the rolling pin with a little plain flour to stop the dough from sticking. Then roll each ball of dough into a thin pancake shape called a tortilla.

6 Ask an adult to help you fry the tortillas using a non-stick frying pan. Fry each tortilla for one minute on each side. You can use a little oil in the pan if you want to.

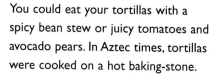

You could eat your tortillas with a spicy bean stew or juicy tomatoes and avocado pears. In Aztec times, tortillas were cooked on a hot baking-stone.

Inca bean stew

The wealthiest members of Inca society entertained their visitors with banquets of venison, duck, fresh fish and tropical fruits, such as bananas and guavas. Honey was used as a sweetener. Peasants ate squash and other vegetables in a stew or soup like the one in the project, and added fish if it was available. Families kept guinea pigs for meat, but most of their food was based on a vegetarian diet. The bulk of any meal was made up of starchy foods. These were prepared from grains such as maize or quinoa, or from root crops such as potatoes, cassava or a highland plant called *oca*. A strong beer called *chicha* was made from maize.

cassava

sweet potatoes

▲ **Common crops**
Many of the world's common crops were first grown and then cultivated in the Americas. These include cassava and sweet potatoes.

chilli peppers

peanuts

▲ **Tropical taste**
Chilli peppers and peanuts are just two of a number of tropical crops that grow in the Americas.

◄ **A fertile land**
Maize was common across Central and South America. Potatoes and quinoa were grown in the area occupied by present-day Chile, Peru and Ecuador. Squashes and beans were cultivated mainly in Central America.

CENTRAL AMERICA

VENEZUELA

Atlantic Ocean

COLOMBIA

ECUADOR

BRAZIL

PERU

SOUTH AMERICA

BOLIVIA

Pacific Ocean

PARAGUAY

URUGUAY

N

CHILE

ARGENTINA

YOU WILL NEED

250g dried haricot beans, bowl, cold water, sieve, large and medium saucepans, 4 tomatoes, knife, chopping board, 500g pumpkin, 2 tbsp paprika, mixed herbs, salt, black pepper, 100g sweetcorn.

1 Wash and then soak the beans in water for four hours. Drain and then put them into a large saucepan. Cover with water. Ask an adult to help you boil the beans. Simmer for two hours.

2 While the beans are cooking, chop up the tomatoes into fine pieces. Then peel the pumpkin and remove and discard the seeds. Cut the fleshy part of the pumpkin into 2cm cubes.

3 Ask an adult to help you heat 100ml of water in a medium saucepan. Stir in the paprika and bring to the boil. Add the tomatoes and a pinch of mixed herbs. Season with salt and pepper.

4 Simmer for 15 minutes until the mixture is thick and well blended. Drain the beans and add them to the tomato mixture. Add the pumpkin and then simmer for 15 minutes.

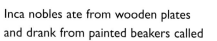

Inca nobles ate from wooden plates and drank from painted beakers called *keros*, but most peasants drank and ate from the dried, woody shells of gourds.

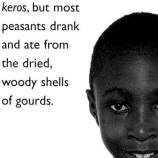

5 Add the sweetcorn and simmer the tomato mixture for an additional five minutes until the pumpkin has almost disintegrated and the stew is nice and thick.

6 Carefully taste the tomato and bean stew, and add more salt and pepper if you think it is necessary. Serve in bowls. Cornbread or tortillas would be an ideal accompaniment.

Medieval flan

It was quite usual to have a mixture of sweet and savoury dishes in one course at a medieval castle feast. The flan you can make here mixes savoury cheese with sugar and spice, all in one dish. Other sweet pies might have been made with cream, eggs, dates and prunes. In medieval times, food was often coloured with vegetable dyes such as saffron, sandalwood or sometimes even gold. The pinch of saffron in the cream cheese mixture of this dish gives the flan a rich yellow colour. Saffron is expensive because it comes only from the flowers of a type of Mediterranean crocus and is difficult to get hold of. For hundreds of years, it has been seen as a sign of wealth and status.

Remember to wash and clear up your mess when you have finished cooking. Before the days of cleaning products and dishwashers, dirty pots and pans were scoured clean using sand and soapy herbs.

▲ **Tasty titbits**

It was not considered to be good manners to feed the castle dogs and cats from the table, but leftover bones and scraps of food were usually tossed on the floor. People also spat on the floor (this was considered to be polite), which quickly became dirty and was not cleaned very often. Straw covered the floor and would be changed for new straw periodically.

YOU WILL NEED

Measuring scales, two mixing bowls, four small bowls, plate, egg cup, tea strainer, fork, whisk, spoon, chopping board, rolling pin, greased paper, 15cm-diameter flan tin, knife, two large eggs, pinch of saffron, hot water, 170g cream cheese, 1 tbsp caster sugar, 1 tsp powdered ginger, salt, 250g pack of readymade shortcrust pastry, flour.

1 Have all your bowls and utensils laid out and ready to use. Weigh out all the ingredients carefully using the scales. Place them in separate bowls on the work surface.

2 Break each egg in turn on to a plate. Place an egg cup over the yolk. Tip the plate over a bowl and discard the egg whites. Transfer the yolks into a bowl.

3 Put the saffron in a bowl. Heat some water and pour a little of it over the saffron. Leave until the water turns golden and then strain the liquid into another bowl.

4 Use a metal fork to mash up the cream cheese in a mixing bowl. Carry on blending until there are no lumps and the cream cheese is of a soft and creamy consistency.

5 Add the tablespoon of caster sugar to the egg yolks. Use a whisk to beat the egg and sugar together. Continue until the mixture has thickened a little.

6 Gradually add the cream cheese to the egg and sugar mixture. Use the whisk to gently beat in the cream cheese until it has completely blended with the egg and sugar.

7 Add the powdered ginger, salt and saffron water to the cream cheese and egg mixture. Stir all the ingredients thoroughly. Ask an adult to preheat the oven to 210°C/Gas Mark 6 or 7.

Sweet cheese flan was one of the earliest known sweet puddings. Another favourite was fried bread flavoured with sugar and sherry.

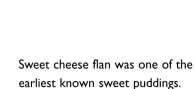

8 Roll the pastry on a lightly floured board. Smear greased paper over the flan tin and cover with the pastry. Press the pastry into the edges of the tin and trim the excess pastry.

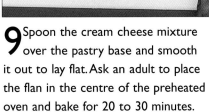

9 Spoon the cream cheese mixture over the pastry base and smooth it out to lay flat. Ask an adult to place the flan in the centre of the preheated oven and bake for 20 to 30 minutes.

Hallowe'en feast

Cook some scary food for a Hallowe'en party on 31 October. Then, the sun was said to be so low that the gates of the underworld were opened to let in the light. As the gates opened, demons and spectres escaped on to Earth.

Cat and bat cookies

1 Scale up the bat and cat templates. Draw them on to the thick card, and then cut them out. You could make other shapes such as jack-o'-lanterns, pumpkins, witches' hats and ghosts.

2 Put the butter into a mixing bowl. (Take it out of the fridge in advance to soften it.) Add the caster sugar and stir with a wooden spoon until mixture is fluffy and creamy.

3 Add one beaten egg, the plain flour and a few drops of black food colouring to the bowl. Stir the mixture until it forms a stiff dough. Make sure the food colouring blends in well.

4 Roll the dough out on to a chopping board until it is about 1cm thick. Place the cat and bat templates on to the dough and cut around them with a blunt knife.

5 Roll out the leftover dough and cut out more bat and cat shapes. Place them on to a non-stick baking tray. Ask an adult to bake the animal cookies for 20 minutes at 190°C/Gas Mark 5.

6 When they are done, remove the cookies from the oven and place them on a wire tray. When cool, use red and green icing to add features such as eyes and noses.

Scary potato face

1 Ask an adult to bake a large baking potato. When it has cooled, use a knife to cut off the top. Then spoon out the insides into a mixing bowl. Add green food colouring and mix well.

2 Add the butter and grated cheese and season the potato mixture with salt and pepper. Mix thoroughly with a fork. Spoon the potato mixture back into the potato skin and keep it warm.

3 Use a knife to slice the carrot, red pepper and onion ends into strips for hair, mouth and eyebrows as shown above. Slice the sausage to make eyes. Sprinkle with grated orange cheese.

Ghoulish drink

1 You need one plastic straw for each drink you make. Use a glue brush to dab glue near one end of the straw. Fix a toy spider firmly in place. Leave to dry completely.

2 Put the glass on to a small plate. Put three of four tablespoons of ice cream in the glass. Mint chocolate chip looks good, because it is a ghoulish green colour.

3 Pour a fizzy drink over the ice cream. A lime drink works well because it is a ghastly green colour like the ice cream. Pour in enough so that the ice cream really froths up.

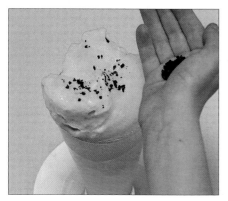

4 Sprinkle little flakes of chocolate over the top. You could add mini marshmallows or hundreds and thousands instead. Stick a decorative straw into each drink you make.

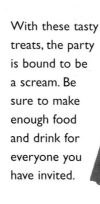

With these tasty treats, the party is bound to be a scream. Be sure to make enough food and drink for everyone you have invited.

Cowboy cookout

People were constantly on the move in the West. Native Americans followed herds of buffalo, settlers travelled in wagon trains and cowboys drove cattle. Everyone had to carry food with them and hunt animals for fresh meat.

Whatever food the cowboys carried with them was stored in their rolling kitchen, which was called the chuck wagon. One man had the job of cooking for all the others. This project shows you how to make the kind of meal a group of cowboys would have eaten on the trail.

▲ **Hung out to dry**
Native Americans hung strips of buffalo meat over poles in the open air. The Sun's heat dried and preserved the meat.

YOU WILL NEED

Two frying pans, cooking oil, garlic, wooden spoon, tin of tomatoes, mild chilli powder, teaspoon, sieve, tinned beans, stock cube, mixing bowl, 250g plain flour, 50g cornmeal, salt, knife, warm water, chopping board, rolling pin, spatula.

1 Ask an adult to help you with your cowboy cookout. Heat a little oil in a frying pan. Crush two cloves of garlic and fry gently until soft and a light golden brown colour.

2 Open the tin of tomatoes and add the contents of the tin to the garlic in the frying pan. Heat the tomatoes for a few moments until they are warmed through.

3 Stir one teaspoon of mild chilli powder into the tomato sauce. Taste it to see if it is spicy enough. If not, add a little more chilli powder, but make sure not to add too much.

4 Drain the liquid from the different tins of beans. Kidney beans, butter beans and pinto beans are a delicious combination. Stir the sauce and warm it through for a few minutes.

5 Crumble a stock cube into the tomato and chilli bean sauce and stir it in well. If the mixture becomes too dry, you may need to add a little hot water from a kettle.

6 Cook the bean sauce over a low heat for about ten minutes. Remove it from the stove, and leave it to one side. You can now make the tortillas for your cowboy feast.

7 Add the flour, cornmeal and a pinch of salt into the bowl and pour in a little warm water. Gradually add more and more water until the mixture forms into a stiff dough.

8 Sprinkle some flour over a chopping board and vigorously knead the dough until it feels stretchy and elastic. If the dough is too dry, try adding some more water to it.

9 Divide the dough mixture into six equal portions. Use your hands to shape each one into a ball. Then coat the outside of each ball lightly with a little flour.

10 Dust the chopping board with more flour. Using a rolling pin dusted with flour, roll out each ball into a flat circle. You should try to roll each one as thin as you possibly can.

You might like to invite a few friends over for this delicious cowboy feast. Serve your tortillas on tin plates, just like the ones used by real cowboys.

11 Heat some oil in the second frying pan. Place one dough circle, called a tortilla, into the pan. When the edges curl, use a spatula to flip it over to cook on the other side.

12 When each tortilla is cooked, put it on a plate. Reheat the tomato and chilli bean sauce. Spoon some over half the tortilla. Fold over the other half. Serve immediately.

Mesoamerican workers making accessories with feathers

Fashion and Accessories

Some clothes are made for work and comfort, while others are designed to show how important the wearer is. Jewellery and other accessories, such as headwear, are often a sign of the wearer's wealth. This section looks at the practical clothes worn by people through the ages. It also examines the distinctive styles, fashions and materials adopted by different cultures throughout the world.

Fashion and Clothing

U nlike animals and birds, humans do not have fur and feathers to keep them warm. One of the main reasons we wear clothes is to protect ourselves from the weather, from heat as well as the cold. However, clothes are much more than just a form of protection. They have long been used as statements about the people who wear them. Special clothes worn by different groups of people indicated their position in society, their religious beliefs or the sort of work they did. From the very earliest times, people also cared about how they looked. So they decorated their clothes with shells and beads, and coloured threads were woven together to produce brightly patterned materials.

▲ **The first clothing**
Animals were hunted by early people not only for their meat but also for their skins. These were scraped clean and shaped with sharp stone tools. Later methods of treating the skins made them soft and supple and therefore comfortable to wear.

◄ **Cool, crisp linen**
The clothes worn by the ancient Greeks were simple and elegant. The most common piece of clothing was a loose linen tunic. This was cool and comfortable to wear during the hot summer months.

◄ Wedding clothes

The Aztec people of Mexico wore clothes made of cotton. Here a man and woman are shown in their wedding outfits. Their cloaks have been tied together to show that the couple are now bound together in marriage.

◄ A warrior's clothes

The samurai were an elite warrior class of old Japan. The formal clothes of a samurai were called *kami-shimo*. They showed his high status. The outfit consisted of a winged jacket, known as a *kataginu*, with matching trousers, called *hakama*, worn over a long tunic called a *kimono*.

▼ Rich embroidery

This picture shows the Hindu god Brahma wearing red pantaloons and a gold hat. The woman to the left is wearing a traditional Indian form of dress called a sari. The clothes are very simple, but they are made from beautifully embroidered silk, which indicates the importance of the people wearing them.

Stone Age dyed cloth

The hunters of the last Ice Age were the first people to wear clothes to protect them from the cold. They sewed animal hides together with strips of leather. The first clothes included simple trousers, tunics and cloaks, decorated with beads of coloured stones, teeth and shells. Fur boots were stitched together with leather laces.

Furs were prepared by stretching out the hides and scraping them clean. The clothes were cut out and holes were made around the edges of the pieces with a sharp, pointed stone called an awl. This made it easier to pass a bone needle through the hide. Cleaned hides were also used to make tents, bags and bedding. After sheep were domesticated in the Near East, wool was used to weave cloth. Plant fibres, such as flax, cotton, bark and cactus, were used elsewhere. The cloth was coloured and decorated with plant dyes.

oak bark

dyer's broom

birch bark

▲ Nature's colours
Stone Age people used the flowers, stems, bark and leaves of many plants to make brightly coloured dyes.

▼ Mammoth shelter
During most of the last 100,000 years, the Earth's climate has been much colder than it is today. Stone Age people dressed warmly. Their clothes kept out the cold and the rain.

YOU WILL NEED

Natural dyes (such as walnuts, elderberries and safflower), tablespoon, saucepan, pestle and mortar, water, sieve, bowl, chamois leather, rubber gloves (optional), white card, white T-shirt, wooden spoon. (Many natural dyes can be found in good health food shops.)

1 Choose your first dye and put between 8 and 12 tablespoons of the dye into an old saucepan. You may need to crush or shred the dye with a pestle and mortar.

2 Cover the dye with water and ask an adult to bring it to the boil and then simmer for one hour. Leave it to cool. Pour the dye through a sieve into a bowl to remove the lumps.

3 Test the dye using a piece of chamois leather. Dip the chamois leather into the dye for a few minutes. You could wear rubber gloves to stop any dye getting on to your hands.

4 Lay the chamois leather patch on to a piece of white card and leave it to dry. Be careful not to drip the dye over clothes or upholstery while you work.

5 Make up the two other dyes and test them out in the same way. When all three pieces of chamois leather are dry, compare the patches and choose your favourite colour.

6 Dye a white T-shirt by preparing it in your chosen dye. Try to make sure that the T-shirt is dyed evenly all over. Make sure it is completely dry before you try it on.

The bark, leaves and husks of the walnut dyed fabric a deep brown colour. Elderberries gave cloth a rich purple-brown colour. The flowers of the safflower plant were picked when first open, then dried. Fabric dyed with safflower was light brown in colour.

Greek chiton

Clothes were styled simply in ancient Greece. Both men and women wore long tunics. These draped loosely for comfort and were held in place with pins or brooches. Heavy cloaks were worn for travelling or in bad weather. Clothes were made of home-spun wool and linen. Fabrics were coloured with dyes made from plants, insects and shellfish.

cotton

linen

◂ Style at a price

Only the wealthiest Greeks wore clothes made from cotton or linen. Poorer citizens wore clothes made from home-spun wool.

YOU WILL NEED

Tape measure, rectangle of cloth – the width should measure the same as the height of your shoulder, scissors, pins, chalk, needle, thread, 12 metal buttons (with loops), cord.

1 Measure your arm span from wrist to wrist and double the figure. Measure your length from shoulder to ankle. Cut your cloth to these figures. Fold the fabric in half widthways.

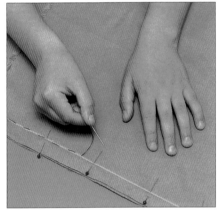

2 Pin the two sides together. Draw a chalk line across the fabric, 2cm in from the edge. Sew along the line, turn the material inside out and re-fold the fabric so the seam is at the back.

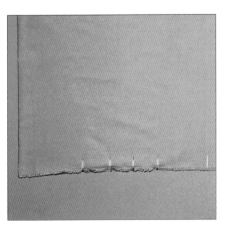

3 At one of the open ends of the fabric, mark a central gap for your head. Pin the fabric together there. From the head gap, mark a point every 5cm to the end of the fabric.

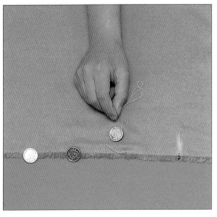

4 Pin together the front and back along these points. At each pin, sew on a button to hold the two sides of fabric together. To secure the button, sew through the loop several times.

Tie the cord around your waist. If it is too long, cut it to the right length, but leave enough cord to tie. Bunch the chiton material up, over the cord.

Roman toga

Most Roman clothes were made of wool that had been spun and woven by hand at home or in a workshop. The most common style of clothing was the tunic, which was practical for active people such as workers and slaves. Important men also wore a garment called a toga. This was a 6m length of cloth with a curved edge, wrapped around the body and draped over the shoulder.

◀ **A change in colour**

Roman women wore a long dress called a stola over an under-tunic. Only married women wore dresses dyed in bright colours. Girls dressed in white.

YOU WILL NEED

Double-sided sticky tape, purple ribbon, old white sheet, scissors, long T-shirt, cord.

1 Use double-sided sticky tape to stick the ribbon along the long edge of the sheet. Cut one corner off as shown. Put on a long white T-shirt tied at the waist with a cord.

2 Get a friend to hold the long edge of the fabric behind you. The cut corner should be on your left hand side. Drape about a quarter of the toga over your left arm and shoulder.

3 Bring the rest of the toga round to the front, passing it under your right arm. Hook the toga up by tucking a few folds of the material securely into the cord around your waist.

4 Now your friend can help you fold the rest of the toga neatly over your left arm, as shown above. If you prefer, you could drape it over your left shoulder.

Boys from wealthy families wore togas edged with a thin purple stripe until they reached the age of 16. Then they wore plain togas.

Indian sari

Clothing has always been very simple in India. Noble people, both men and women, usually wore a single piece of fabric that was draped around the hips, drawn up between the legs and then fastened securely again at the waist. Women wore bodices above the waist, but men were often bare-chested. Although their clothes were simple, people had elaborate hairstyles with flowers and other decorations. Men and women also wore a lot of jewellery, such as earrings, armbands, breastplates, nose rings and anklets. The Hindu male garment was called the dhoti, and the female garment gradually evolved into the sari – a single large cloth draped around the body, with a bodice worn underneath.

▲ A guide for the gods
A Brahmin (priest) looks after the temple and is a go-between for the worshipper and a god. He wears a sacred cotton cord across his chest to symbolize his position.

◄ Noble warriors
Society in ancient India was divided into three castes (classes). The noble warrior class (Kshatriya) was the next highest class after the Brahmin. Noble warriors wore expensive jewellery and used weapons such as bows and arrows, daggers, spears and swords.

▼ Holy water
Hindus have bathed in the sacred River Ganges for centuries. The religion states that bathing in its waters washes away sin. People wear their dhotis or saris when they bathe.

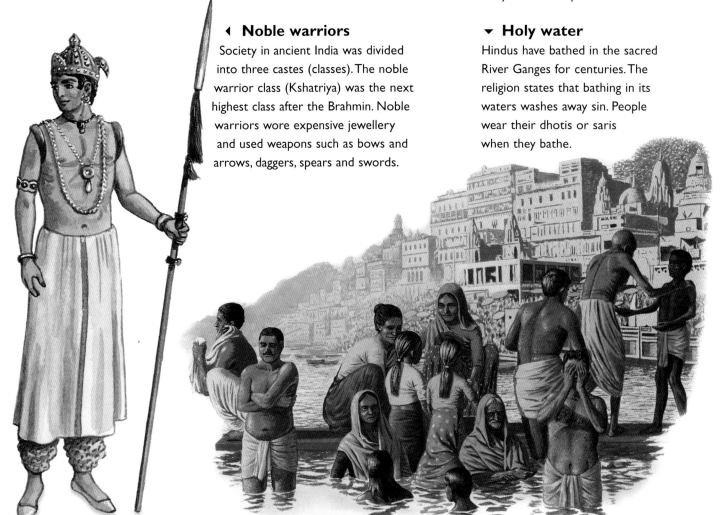

YOU WILL NEED

Silky or cotton fabric measuring 4 x 1m, one large safety pin. Dip a cork into gold paint and press it along one long edge of the fabric to add decoration to the sari. Leave to dry before trying it on.

1 Hold one corner of the fabric to your stomach with the decorated border on the outside. Wrap the long side of the fabric once tightly around your waist.

2 Make a number of pleats where the fabric comes back around to the front of your body. Make them as even as you can. The pleats act as the underskirt of your sari.

3 Tuck the pleated section of the sari into the waist of the underskirt. You could use a safety pin to hold the pleats in place, while you practise tying the sari.

4 Take the excess length of fabric in your left hand and pass it all the way around your back. Take extra care that the pleats do not come out.

A sari is a single large cloth that covers both the upper and the lower body. Saris were first worn in eastern India over 1,000 years ago.

5 Now take the rest of the sari fabric in your right hand and lift it up so that it is level with your shoulders. Do this in front of a mirror if possible, so that you can see what you are doing.

6 Swing the fabric over your left shoulder. The fabric should fall in gentle folds from your shoulder, across your body to the level of your waist. You may need to practise doing this.

Native American robe

The clothes of most Native Americans were made from the skins of bison (American buffalo). Hunters performed elaborate dances before a hunt, and then headed off in search of animal tracks. Early hunters stalked the animals on foot, often disguised as other animals. Later, horses made the job a lot easier. Once the bison was killed, women and elder children usually processed the carcass. The skin was taken off in one piece and used to make clothes and covers. Meat was prepared for a feast to celebrate the successful hunt.

YOU WILL NEED

Three pieces of an old bed sheet (one measuring 140 x 60cm and the other two measuring 40 x 34cm), pencil, tape measure, scissors, large needle, brown thread, felt (red, yellow, dark blue and light blue are the best colours to use), PVA glue and glue brush, black embroidery thread, red thread.

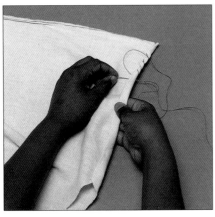

1 Fold the larger piece of fabric in half for the body. Draw and cut a curved neckline 22 x 6cm on the fold. Roll the fabric over at the shoulders and stitch it down with brown thread.

2 Open the body fabric out flat and line up the two smaller fabric rectangles for the arm pieces with the centre of the stitched ridge. Stitch the top edge of the pieces on to the body.

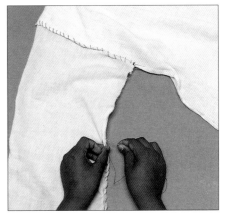

3 Fold the fabric in half again to see the shirt's shape. Now stitch up the undersides of the sleeves. (Native Americans did not usually sew the sides of skin robes together.)

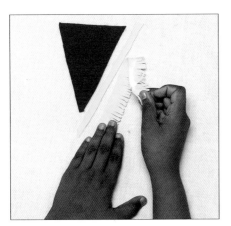

4 Your shirt is ready to decorate. Cut out strips and triangles of coloured felt and glue them on to the shirt. Make decorative fringes by cutting into one side of strips of felt.

5 Make fake hair strips by cutting 8cm lengths of black embroidery thread and tying them in bunches. Tie red thread tightly around the top, and then glue the fake hair on to your shirt.

Native Americans made their clothes from young bison, and the resulting animal hide was called buckskin.

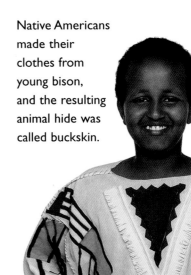

Inca tunic

The standard of Inca weaving was very high. The Inca people had to weave cloth for the state as a form of tax, and woven cloth was often used to pay officials. Inca men wore a loincloth around the waist, secured by a belt. Over this was a knee-length tunic, often made of alpaca – a fine, silky wool. Women wrapped themselves in a large, rectangular piece of alpaca.

◄ Fighting force

Inca warriors decorated their war dress with brightly coloured feathers.

YOU WILL NEED

40cm square of red felt, 160 x 65cm rectangle of blue felt, PVA glue and glue brush, tape measure, scissors, needle and thread, pencil, ruler, cream calico fabric, fabric paints, paintbrush, water pot.

1 Place the blue felt flat on the table with the long side facing towards you. Position the red felt in the centre of the blue felt to form a diamond. Glue the red felt in place here.

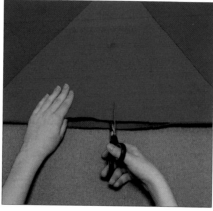

2 Cut a 22cm-long slit through the centre of both felt layers. Fold the fabric along the slit. Cut a 12cm-long slit through one double layer of fabric at right angles to the first slit as shown.

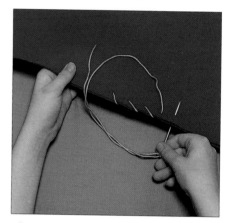

3 Use the needle and thread to sew together the sides of the tunic. Make the stitches as large as possible and be sure to leave enough space for armholes at the top.

4 Draw lots of 5cm squares in pencil on the cream calico fabric. Paint on colourful designs like the ones shown and leave them to dry. Cut out the squares and glue them to your tunic.

When the glue is dry you can try on your tunic. The original Inca tunics were brightly coloured and decorated with geometric patterns.

Medieval witch

The familiar image of a witch – dressed in ragged clothes with a broomstick and a warty face – developed from a much-feared folklore figure called the hag. Myths, from ancient Egypt through to pre-Christian Europe, tell of ugly old women who used supernatural power to bring misfortune to those around them. During medieval times, many innocent old women who looked like hags became the victims of witch hunts. They were tried and usually found guilty, then sentenced to burn alive at the stake.

YOU WILL NEED

Black cotton fabric (200 x 110cm), ruler, white pencil, scissors, needle, black thread, newspaper, stiff paintbrush, silver paint, two sheets of thin black card (42 x 59cm and 32 x 32cm), sticky tape, small piece of silver card, PVA glue and glue brush, green and black tissue paper.

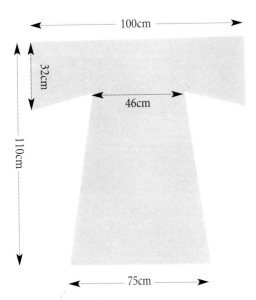

1 Fold the black fabric in half widthways. Lay it out on a flat surface. Then use the template to draw the witch's dress shape on to the fabric with a white pencil.

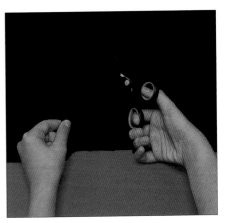

2 Cut out the dress shape. Cut a slit 24cm across in the middle of the folded edge for your neck. Then cut a second line 12cm long down the back of the fabric.

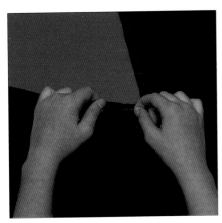

3 Turn the fabric inside out. Use a needle and some thread to sew a simple running stitch up each side of the witch's dress. Then sew under the arms of the dress.

4 Cut a jagged edge along the cuffs of each sleeve and along the bottom of the dress. Turn the dress inside out so that the fabric is right side out and the stitches are hidden.

5 Lay the dress on a sheet of old newspaper. Dip a stiff brush in silver paint. Pull the bristles back towards you and spray paint on to the fabric. When dry, spray the other side.

6 Roll the rectangle of thin, black card into the shape of a cone. Use a white pencil to draw a shape on the card to show where it overlaps and should be taped.

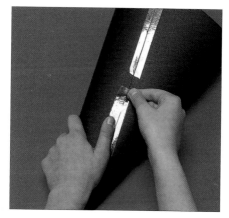

7 Cut away the excess card and roll the card back into a cone shape. Then secure it with sticky tape. Trim the bottom edge of the cone to fit the size of your head.

8 Place the hat on the square black card. Use the white pencil to draw a rough circle around the rim about 5cm away from it. Draw a second circle to fit exactly around the rim of the hat.

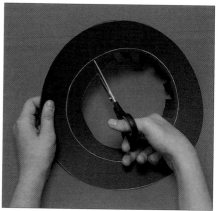

9 Cut around the outside ring. Then cut out the centre, making sure to leave an extra 3cm inside the white line ring. Make snips into the ring as far as the line to make small tabs.

10 Fit the rim of the hat on to the bottom of the cone-shaped section. Fold the tabs up inside the hat and use small pieces of sticky tape to fix the rim to the hat.

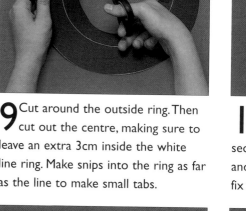

11 Draw a rectangular shape on to the silver card to make a hat buckle. Draw a second rectangle inside the first one. Cut out the buckle and glue it on to the front of the hat.

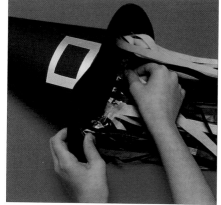

12 Cut sheets of green and black tissue into long strips to make witch's hair. Glue the strips all the way around the inside of the witch's hat, leaving a gap at the front by the buckle.

Complete the witch's look by using face paints. Paint dark lines under your eyes and around your mouth to make you look as if you have wrinkles. Black out one of your teeth. You will also need a broom, which you can make by tying twigs to an old broom handle.

Cowboy gear

The clothes of a typical cowboy had to be tough, because he spent a long time in the saddle. Overtrousers called chaps protected his legs from the cattle's horns, as well as from burn marks from throwing his lassos. High-heeled leather boots helped to keep the rider's feet in the stirrups on the saddle. The cowboy's hat was usually made from a type of hard-wearing wool called felt. A wide brim shielded his face from the sun. Hats could also double up as water carriers for horses to drink from.

Leg chaps

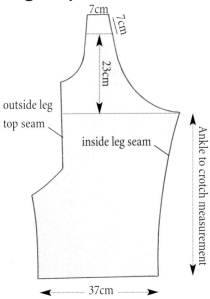

7cm 7cm
23cm
outside leg top seam
inside leg seam
Ankle to crotch measurement
37cm

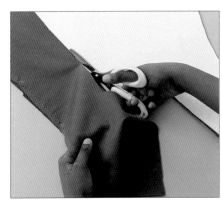

1 Cut two templates from paper. Fold the fabric in half to make a long thin piece with the right sides together. Pin the templates to the material. Cut round the fabric to make four pieces.

2 Each chap has two pieces. Pin the outside leg top seam of one of the chaps as shown. Use a running stitch to sew 1.5cm in from the cut edge. Pin and sew the inside leg seam.

3 Turn the leg the right way out. Following the top dotted line on the template, fold over the belt loops. Pin them along the bottom edge and then carefully stitch them.

4 Pin and then sew the outside part of the outside leg bottom seam 10cm in from the cut edge. Make your stitches as neat as possible, as they will be visible when you wear the chaps.

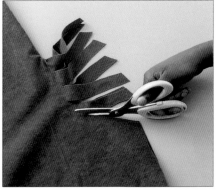

5 Cut strips into the wide flap down the outside leg to make a fringe. Try not to cut into the seam. Repeat steps 1 to 6 to make the second leg for your chaps.

Felt hat

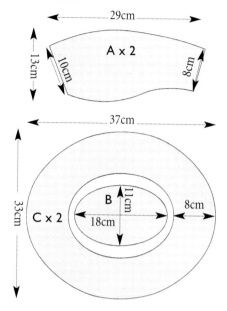

1 Make the templates from paper and pin them to the felt. Cut out. Pin and sew the two short sides of the hat (template A). Pin and sew the crown (template B) to the top of the sides.

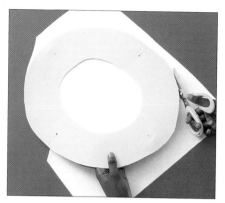

2 Take template C and pin it on to the piece of stiffened fabric. Cut around it, and then cut out the hole in the centre. The result will be used to make the brim of your cowboy hat.

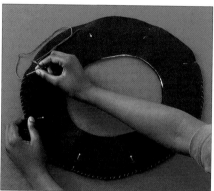

3 Sandwich the stiffened fabric between the two felt brims cut using template C and pin the two sides of the brim together. Sew the outside edge of all three pieces as shown.

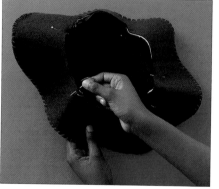

4 Turn the hat brim upside down and carefully pin it to the hat crown you have just made. This way, the seam will end up inside the hat. Sew the pieces together as shown above.

To put on your chaps, pull each leg over your jeans. Then get someone to help you thread a thick leather belt through the loops front and back. Don't forget your hat and 'kerchief!

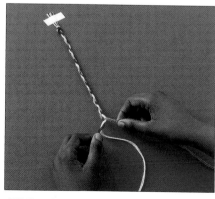

5 Cut 1m lengths from each of the three balls of coloured wool. Fold each strand of wool in half. Knot them at the top and tape them to a work surface. Then plait the wool together.

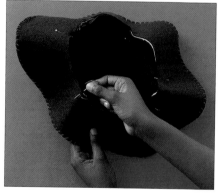

6 Finish the plait by tying a knot at each end. The plait will become the decorative band for your hat when you wrap it around the base of the crown and knot it tightly around the rim.

Hats and Headwear

Hats and headwear have been worn by men and women all over the world for thousands of years. Their original purpose was to protect the head from extremes of weather, but hats also became signs of status or official position. A crown came to indicate the authority of a king or queen, while religious and military leaders wore headgear that readily identified them and the position they held. As fashion accessories, hats and headwear have been made in bright colours, beautiful materials and all sorts of shapes. They have been decorated with feathers, beads, jewels and bows.

▲ Sun worshipper
Pharaoh Akhenaten of Egypt, shown worshipping the sun god Aten, wore a number of different crowns to indicate his many different roles as ruler of Egypt. Here, Akhenaten wears a special type of hat to show his position as high priest.

◄ A band of gold
Boudicca, queen of the Iceni tribe in Celtic Britain, wears a gold band around her head. This band is called a diadem and indicates her important position as a ruler. Rare and precious gold was considered to be the metal of royalty.

Imperial silk ▲

Puyi, the last emperor of China, ascended to the throne as a small boy. He wears richly embroidered silk robes and a small silk skullcap decorated with coloured embroidery.

▲ Mayan splendour

A mural shows two warriors from Central America standing over a captive. They wear the magnificent clothes of the Mayan nobility. The headdresses, decorated with feathers and even an animal head, indicate the importance of the two warriors.

◄ European adventurer

A Portuguese naval officer from the early 1600s wears the typical clothes of his high social position. On his head he wears a small, neat hat called a copotain, which has a narrow brim and is made of fur or felt.

▲ Practical headwear

A Saami boy from Lapland wears a traditional pom-pom hat. It is a cheerful and very practical design for the Arctic climate.

Egyptian crown

The pharaohs of ancient Egypt wore many accessories to show that they were important. Pictures and statues showed them with special badges of royalty, such as crowns, headcloths, false beards, sceptres and a crook and flail held in each hand.

The word pharaoh comes from the Egyptian *per-aa* (great house or palace). Later, the word came to mean the person, or ruler, who lived in the palace. The pharaoh was the most important person in Egypt and the link between the people and their gods. The Egyptians believed that on his death, the pharaoh became a god in his own right.

The pharaoh led a busy life. He was the high priest, the chief law-maker, the commander of the army and in charge of the country's wealth. He had to be a clever politician, too. Generally, pharaohs were men, but queens could rule if a male successor was too young. A pharaoh could take several wives. In a royal family, it was common for fathers to marry daughters and for brothers to marry sisters. Sometimes, however, pharaohs married foreign princesses to make an alliance with another country.

▲ **Royal headwear**
Thutmose III is remembered as a brave warrior king. This picture shows him wearing the headcloth that is one of the special symbols of royalty.

▲ **Crowning glory**
Rameses III was the last great warrior pharaoh. Here, Rameses is wearing an elaborate crown that is another special badge of royalty.

Templates

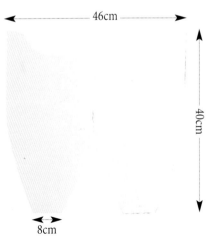

46cm

40cm

8cm

White crown of Upper Egypt

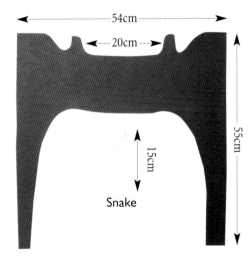

54cm

20cm

55cm

15cm

Snake

Red crown of Lower Egypt

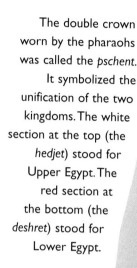

YOU WILL NEED

Two large sheets of card (red and white), pencil, ruler, scissors, masking tape, cardboard roll, bandage, tennis ball, PVA glue and glue brush, white and gold acrylic paints, water pot, paintbrush, beads, skewer.

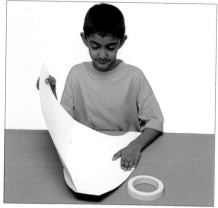

1 Make each section of the crown using the templates. Bend the white crown section into a cylinder. Use lengths of masking tape to join the two edges of the cylinder together.

The double crown worn by the pharaohs was called the *pschent*. It symbolized the unification of the two kingdoms. The white section at the top (the *hedjet*) stood for Upper Egypt. The red section at the bottom (the *deshret*) stood for Lower Egypt.

2 Tape the cardboard roll into the hole at the top of your pharaoh's crown. Plug the end of the crown with bandages or a tennis ball wedged in position and glue down the edges.

3 Wrap the white section of the crown with lengths of bandage. Paint over these with an equal mixture of white paint and glue. Leave the crown in a warm place to dry.

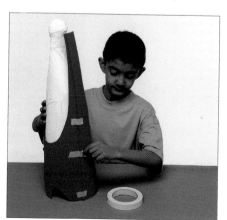

4 Now take the red crown section. Wrap it tightly around the white crown section as shown above. Hold the two sections together using strips of masking tape.

5 Paint the snake shape with gold acrylic paint and stick on beads for its eyes. When dry, score lines across its body with a skewer. Bend the body and glue it to the front of the crown.

Tribal headddress

One of the most popular images of a Native American is that of a warrior dressed in fringed buckskin and a war bonnet, and decorated with body paint and beads. That was just one style of dress, mainly used by the Plains tribes. A warrior had to earn the right to wear a headdress like the one you can make in this project. Each act of bravery during conflict earned the warrior the right to tie another feather to his headdress. Plains warriors also tied locks of their victims' hair to the front of their shirts.

YOU WILL NEED

1m x 1cm red ribbon, red upholstery tape (75 x 6cm), ruler, masking tape, needle and thread, white paper, scissors, black paint, paintbrush, water pot, 3.7m balsa dowelling, PVA glue and glue brush, six feathers, five pieces of different coloured felt, beads or sequins, pair of compasses, red paper, coloured ribbons.

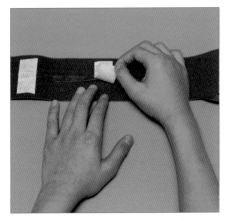

1 Lay the 1m-long red ribbon along the middle of the upholstery tape. Leave 12.5cm lengths at each end to tie the headdress on. Tape the ribbon on to the upholstery tape and sew it on.

2 Cut 26 feather shapes from the white paper, each 18cm long and 4cm wide. Paint the tips black. When the paint is dry, make tiny cuts around the edges of the paper feathers.

3 Cut the balsa dowelling into 26 lengths, each 14cm long. Carefully glue the dowelling to the centre of the back of each feather, starting just below the painted black tip.

4 Take the six real bird feathers and tie them with cotton thread on to the bottom of six of the feathers you made earlier. These will be at the front of the headdress.

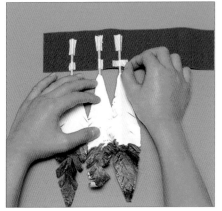

5 Glue and tape all the feathers on to the front of the red band, overlapping the feathers slightly as you go. Position them so that the six real feathers are in the centre.

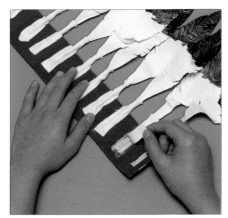

6 Measure and cut 26 lengths of white felt. Each piece of felt should be 6 x 1cm. Glue the felt strips over each piece of balsa dowelling, so that the sticks are hidden.

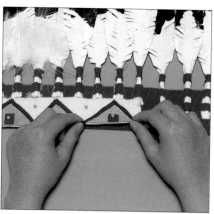

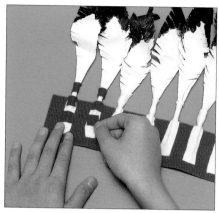

7 Cut out red felt pieces measuring 1.5 x 1cm. Cut three pieces for five feathers at each end and two pieces for the rest. Glue the red felt on to the white felt to make stripes.

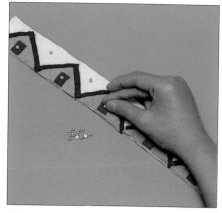

8 Cut out a 40 x 4 cm band from yellow felt. Glue on triangles of dark blue and light blue felt and small squares of red felt as shown. You can also decorate it with beads or sequins.

9 Carefully glue the decorative band on to the red band using a ruler to help you place it in the middle. Some feathers will show on either side of the band.

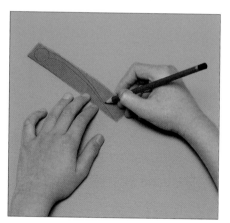

10 Draw a circle on to the red paper, 3cm in diameter. Then draw a 15cm-long tail feather starting at the circle. It should measure 1cm across and taper to a point.

11 Draw seven more of these tail feathers and cut them out. Glue them on to the ends of the feathers on the middle of the band so that the points stick into the air.

Elaborate war bonnets were kept for ceremonial occasions and not worn into battle. Jewellery, body paints and tattoos were also common.

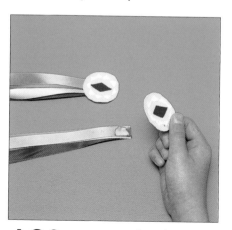

12 Cut out two circles of yellow felt, 5cm in diameter. Decorate the felt circles with red and white felt shapes. Glue the coloured ribbons to the backs of the circles.

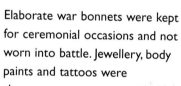

13 Finally, stick the felt circles on to the headdress on top of the decorative band. The circles should be placed so that the ribbons hang down either side by your ears.

Arctic Saami hat

Clothes in the Arctic were often beautiful as well as practical. Strips or patches of different furs were used to form designs and geometric patterns on outer clothes. Fur trimmings, toggles and other decorative fastenings added final touches to many clothes. Jewellery included pendants, bracelets, necklaces and brooches. Ornaments such as these were traditionally made of natural materials, such as bone and walrus ivory.

Inuit women from North America decorated clothes with birds' beaks, tiny feathers or porcupine quills. In Greenland, lace and glass beads were popular decorations. The clothes of the Saami from Scandinavia were the most colourful. Saami men, women and children wore blue outfits with a red and yellow trim. Men's costumes included tall hats and flared tunics. Women's clothes included flared skirts with embroidered hems and colourful hats, shawls and scarves.

▲ **Animal insulation**
In the bitter Arctic cold, people wore warm, waterproof clothing made from the skins of animals such as seals.

▲ **Colourful costumes**
A Saami herdsman in traditional dress holds aloft a reindeer calf born at the end of the spring migration.

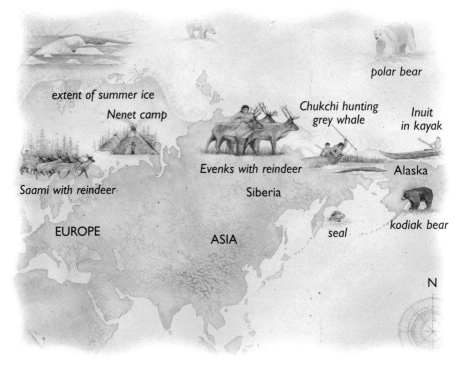

▲ **Arctic inhabitants**
This map shows some of the main groups of people who still live in the Arctic region. Many Arctic peoples, such as the Saami and Evenks, have long depended on reindeer for food and to make clothes, shelter and tools.

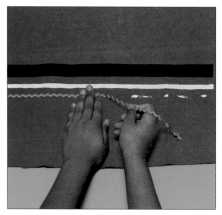

YOU WILL NEED

Red felt measuring 58 x 30cm, ruler, pencil, black ribbon measuring 58 x 2cm, PVA glue and glue brush, coloured ribbon, white felt, pair of compasses, red card, scissors, ribbon strips (red, green and white) measuring 44 x 4cm, red ribbon measuring 58 x 4cm.

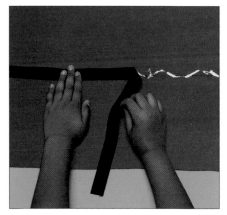

1 Use a ruler and pencil to mark out the centre of the piece of red felt along its length. Carefully glue the length of black ribbon along the centre line as shown above.

2 Continue to decorate the red felt section with pieces of coloured ribbon. You can add some strips of white felt to add to your striking Saami hat design.

3 Cut out a circle of red card with a diameter of 18cm. Draw a circle inside with a diameter of 15cm. Cut into the larger circle as far as the 15cm line to make a series of tabs.

4 Glue the ends of the decorated red felt section together as shown above. You will need to wrap this felt section around your head and measure it to ensure the hat fits properly.

The style of Saami hats varied from one place to another. In southern Norway, men's hats were tall and rounded. Further north, their hats had four points.

5 Fold down the tabs cut into the circle of red card. Dab them with glue, tuck them inside one end of the red felt section and then stick them firmly to make the top of the hat.

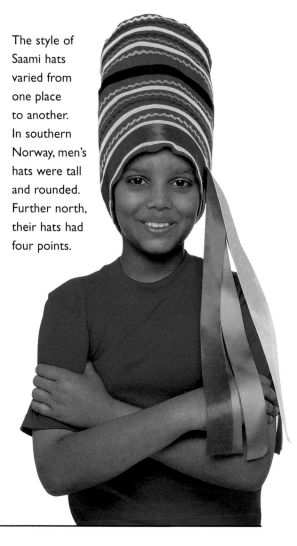

6 While the hat is drying, glue coloured ribbon strips together. Glue these strips 15cm from the end of the 58cm-long band of red ribbon. Glue this to the base of the hat.

Medieval headpiece

In the Middle Ages, noble ladies hid their hair beneath a fancy headdress. The ring-shaped chaplet you can make in this project is one of the simpler headdress styles worn in medieval times. The more wealthy, fashionable and important a lady was, the more elaborate her clothes were. Some robes were embroidered and trimmed with fur – they were extremely expensive and expected to last a lifetime. Traders came to the castle to present a choice of materials and designs. When the lady had chosen, tailors made the clothes.

▲ **Dressed to impress**
A lady needs help from a maid to put on her complicated headpiece.

YOU WILL NEED

Pencil, ruler, corrugated card, scissors, masking tape, 2m fine fabric, two sponges, 3-4m netting, string, acrylic paints, paintbrush, water pot, nylon stocking, cotton wool, ribbon, needle and thread, 1m gold braid, PVA glue and glue brush, 2 x 2cm silver card, three 7cm lengths of thin wire, beads.

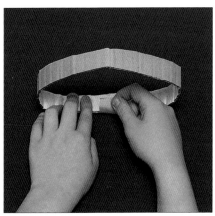

1 Cut a 4cm strip of corrugated card to fit around your head exactly, about 30cm in length. Overlap the ends of the strip and firmly secure them with masking tape.

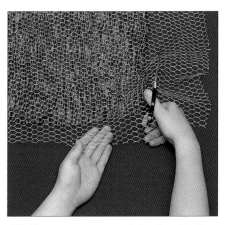

2 Cut two squares of the fine fabric, each one big enough to wrap around the sponge. Then cut two squares of netting slightly larger than the fabric squares.

3 Lay the fabric squares over the net squares. Place a sponge in the middle of each fabric square. Gather the netting and fabric over the sponges and tie them with string.

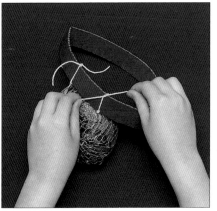

4 Paint the card circle for your head. Thread two lengths of string through each sponge and net ball. Use the string to hang one ball on each side of the card circlet.

5 Cut the bottom half leg off a coloured nylon stocking. Pack the inside tightly with cotton wool to make a firm, full sausage shape. Knot the open end to close it.

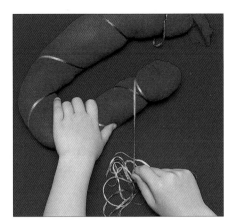

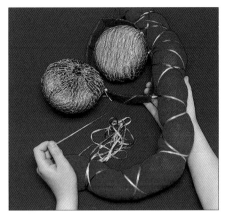

6 Tie the ribbon around one end of the sausage. Wind it diagonally along the sausage and then wind it back again to cross diagonally over the first row.

7 Thread more ribbon through the ribbon crossovers on the sausage. Then take the ribbon over and around the head circlet to join the sausage and band together.

8 Sew the two ends of the sausage shape together. Sew one end of the gold braid to cover the join. Then glue the braid around the sausage, as shown.

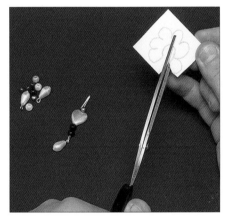

9 Cut out a flower shape from the 2 x 2cm silver card as shown above. Bend one end of the wire into a hook. Thread some beads on to the other end. Then bend the wire over.

10 Glue the flower shape on to the front of the headdress. Hook the wire beads in the middle. Glue more beads and braid around the headdress.

11 Make a double pleat in the remaining length of fabric to make the veil. Secure the veil to the inside back half of the headdress with masking tape.

A real medieval hat was called a chaplet. It was made of silk or satin fabric and held in place by a hair net. The ring-shaped chaplet fitted on top of a veil, and the veil hung down at the back of the head. Ladies often shaved the hair at the front of their heads to make their foreheads look high. For an authentic medieval look, tuck your hair out of sight under the hat.

Weaving and Sewing

The very first clothes that people wore were made from tied grasses or tree bark, or the skins of animals. The invention of the sewing needle enabled people to join different pieces of material together. Clothes became more varied and also fitted more comfortably. The weaving loom completely transformed the clothes people wore. Long lengths of cloth could be made into tents, mats and wall hangings, or cut and shaped into clothes. The weaving loom was one of the first pieces of industrial equipment to be used. The earliest known cloth was woven at least 7,000 years ago in what is now Palestine.

▲ Easy weaving

Backstrap looms were first used by the Incas around 2500BC and continue to be used in Central and South America. The upright, or warp, threads are tensioned between an upright post and a beam attached to the weaver's waist. The cross, or weft, threads are passed in between.

madder

woad

◀ Colours for cloth

Vikings used the leaves, roots, bark and flowers of many plants to dye woollen cloth fabric. For example, a wild flower called weld, or dyer's rocket, produced yellow dye. The roots of the madder plant made a dark red dye. The leaves of woad plants produced a blue dye.

◄ Silken threads

A Japanese craftworker embroiders an intricate design into woven silk using a traditional-style loom. Luxurious and highly decorated textiles were made for the robes of the wealthy. Ordinary people wore plainer clothes of dyed cottons and, occasionally, silk.

porcupine quills

glass beads

▲ Quills and beads

Native Americans have used beads to decorate anything from moccasins to shirts, and to make jewellery. Glass beads brought by traders from the 1500s replaced bone beads and porcupine quills. Quills were usually boiled, dyed and flattened, then woven together to form patterned strips.

◄ Glowing colours

This painting by Diego Rivera shows craftworkers from the region of Tarascan, Central America, dyeing the hanks of yarn before they are woven into cloth. Mesoamerican dyes were made from fruits, flowers, shellfish and the cochineal beetles that lived on cactus plants.

Mesoamerican backstrap loom

Mesoamerican homes were not just places to eat and sleep. They were workplaces, too. Weaving was a skill learned by all women in Mesoamerica and in the Andean region, and they spent long hours spinning thread and weaving it into cloth. As well as making tunics, cloaks and other items of clothing for the family, they had to give some to the State as a form of tax payment.

Cotton was spun and woven into textiles for the wealthiest citizens of Mesoamerica. Peasants wore clothes made from the woven fibres of local plants such as the yucca and maguey. Yarn was dyed before it was woven. Most dyes originated from the flowers, fruits and leaves of plants, but some were extracted from shellfish and insects such as the cochineal beetle – a tiny insect that lives on cactus plants.

▲ Skirts, tunics and cloaks
A wealthy Aztec couple sit by the fire, while their hostess cooks a meal. They are both wearing long skirts. The bright embroidery on their tunics is a sign of high rank.

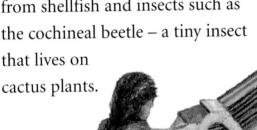

▲ Weaving fibres
Threads spun from plant fibres were woven into cloth on backstrap looms such as this one. Rough fibres from the yucca and cactus plants made coarse cloth. The wealthy had silky textiles.

Down Mexico way ▶
These Mexican women are wearing warm woollen ponchos in bright colours that would also have appealed to their ancestors.

YOU WILL NEED

Two pieces of thick dowelling about 70cm long, brown water-based paint, paintbrush, water pot, string, scissors, thick card, pencil, ruler, masking tape, yellow and red wool, needle.

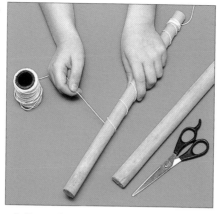

1 Paint the pieces of dowelling brown. Leave them to dry. Tie a length of string to each length of dowelling and wind it around. Leave a length of string loose at each end.

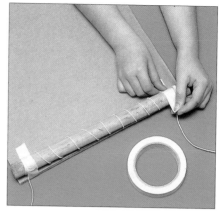

2 Cut a piece of thick card about 100 x 70cm. This is a temporary base. Lightly fix the stringed dowelling at the 70cm sides of the base using masking tape.

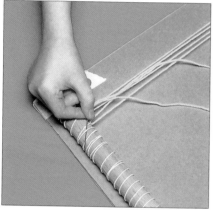

3 Now take your yellow wool. Thread the wool through the string loops using the needle and pull them through to the other end as shown above. Try to keep the yellow wool taut.

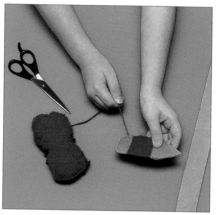

4 Cut a 300 x 35mm piece of thick card. Now cut a smaller rectangle of card with one pointed end as shown above. Wind the red wool tightly around it.

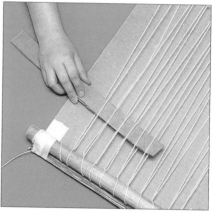

5 Slide the long card rectangle through every second thread. This device, called a shed rod, is turned on its side to lift the threads. Then tie one end of the red wool to the yellow wool.

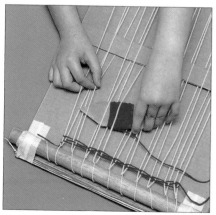

6 Turn the shed rod on its side to lift the threads and feed the red wool through the loom. Then with the shed rod flat, thread the red wool back through alternate yellow threads.

To continue weaving, take the loom off the cardboard base. Tie the loose string around your waist. Attach the other end of the loom to a post or tree with the string. Lean back to keep the long warp threads evenly taut.

Medieval needlework

In medieval Europe, most women were taught to spin and sew. Making small items, such as this medieval-style tapestry design, was a popular pastime. Before any needlework could begin, the canvas background had to be woven, and the yarns spun and dyed. Wool for spinning needlepoint yarn or weaving into cloth came from the sheep on the lord's estate. Linen for fine embroidery and cloth came from flax plants grown in the fields.

Stem stitching

1 Practise the stem stitch on a scrap of old fabric. Push the needle and thread through from the back to the front of the fabric. Hold the end of the thread at the back of the fabric.

2 Tie a double knot in the thread at the back of the fabric. Then push the needle and thread into the fabric about 5mm along from your first insertion point.

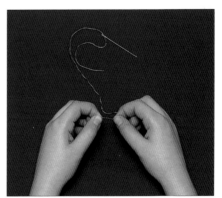

3 Pull the first stitch taut. Bring the needle up just beside the middle of the first stitch. Make a second 5mm stitch. Continue in the same way to make a line.

Medieval needlework

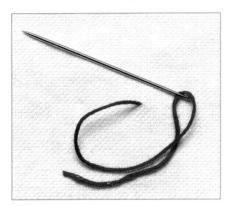

1 Use a black pen to copy the design from step nine on to the tracing paper. Turn the tracing paper over. Trace over the outline you have drawn with the soft-leaded pencil.

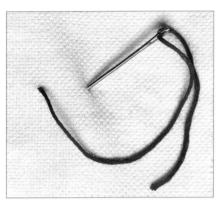

2 Tape the tracing paper (pencilled side down) on to the square of fabric. Trace over the motif once again, so that the pencilled image transfers on to the fabric.

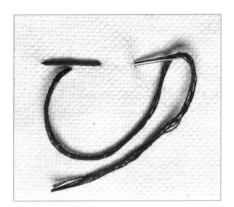

3 Cut a long piece of the orange double-stranded embroidery thread and thread the large-eyed needle. Tie a double knot at one end of the orange thread.

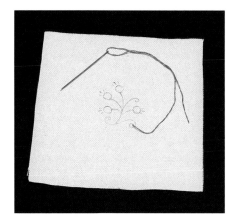

4 Start your embroidery with the scroll shape at the bottom of the design. Push the needle from the back of the fabric to the front. Pull the thread through.

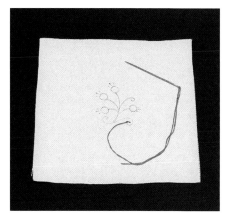

5 Push the thread through the fabric about 2mm along the line of the scroll. Pull the thread through half way along the first stitch. (See Stem stitching on the opposite page.)

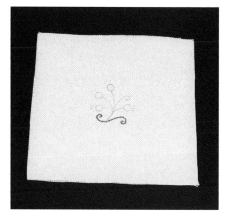

6 Carefully continue your stem stitches all the way along the scroll. The stitches should overlap so that they make a continuous and even, curved line.

7 Thread the needle with a length of green double-stranded embroidery thread. Start at the orange base of the stems and sew along each of the stems in the same way.

8 To sew the flower heads, thread the needle with a length of red embroidery thread. Sew the stem stitch in a circle. Sew a flower head at the end of every stem except one.

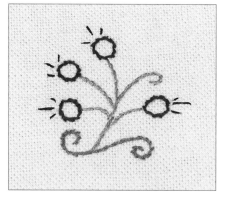

9 Thread the needle with the blue embroidery thread. Sew a single stitch for the short details on the flowers and two stitches for the longer, middle ones.

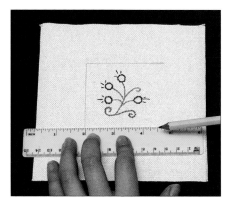

10 Mark a border in pencil 1cm from the edge of the motif. Using a long length of red embroidery thread, follow the pencil lines as a guide for your border stitches.

In medieval times, it was only girls who were taught to sew. Decorative embroidery such as this was mainly done by noblewomen since peasant women could not afford the time or the materials.

American patchwork

The earliest settlers in the USA had to be self-sufficient, because they had little money and the nearest shops were usually in towns far away. They recycled old scraps of material into patchwork designs. Large designs were often stitched on to a linen or cotton backing, with padding in between, to make a quilt. Worn out scraps were transformed into decorative, cosy and long-lasting covers. The women sometimes met up at each other's houses to make quilts. These gatherings were called quilting bees.

YOU WILL NEED

Stiff card measuring 15 x 10cm, pencil, ruler, scissors, piece of paper measuring 30 x 30cm, six pieces of patterned cotton fabric each measuring 15 x 10cm, felt-tipped pen, pins, cotton thread, needle, blue cushion cover, cushion pad.

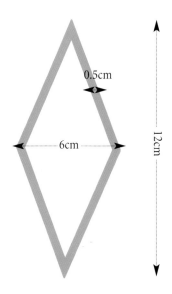

0.5cm

6cm

12cm

1 Copy the diamond-shaped template on to card and cut it out. Draw around the outside edge of the template on to paper. Contine another seven times to form the design shown above.

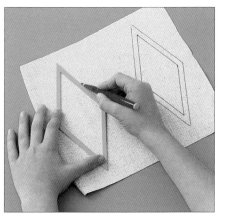

2 Choose six different patterned fabrics of the same thickness. On the back of one of the pieces of fabric, use a felt-tipped pen to draw round the inner and outer edges of the template.

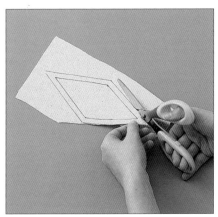

3 Mark out further diamonds on the other pieces of fabric until you have eight altogether. Then cut around the outside edges. The inner line is the edge of the seam – do not cut along it.

4 Arrange the fabric diamonds on the paper design in the way you want them to appear in the final patchwork design. Make sure you are happy with the design before you start to sew.

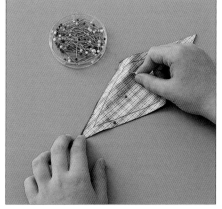

5 Take two of the diamonds that you want to go next to each other. Place one on top of the other with the patterned sides facing each other. Pin the diamonds together along one edge.

6 Sew the pinned edge of the diamond using a running stitch. Use the inner line that you drew on to the fabric with the template as a guide for the seam.

7 Repeat steps five and six to pin and sew all the diamond fabric pieces together along one of their edges. When you have finished, the fabric pieces will form a star shape.

8 Fold the free edges of the fabric diamonds in along the felt-tipped lines and pin them together. You will be left with a loose corner of fabric at each point of the star.

9 Now use a running stitch to sew down the pinned edges of the fabric diamonds. Try to make the edges as flat and the stitches as small and neat as you can.

10 Turn the star shape over and trim off the loose corners at each point. You should now have a perfect piece of star-shaped patchwork.

11 Pin the star shape carefully in the middle of the blue cushion cover. Then sew it on using small, neat stitches. When you have finished, put a pad in the cushion cover.

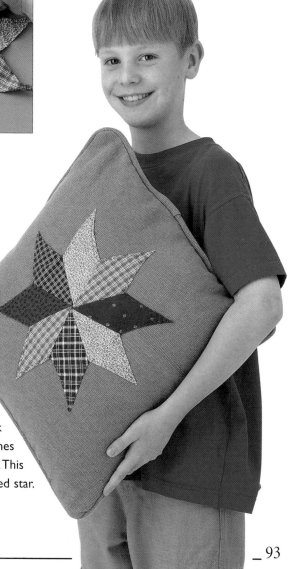

Many patchwork designs created by the early settlers became part of the American craft tradition. Patchwork patterns are often given names such as log cabin or nine patch. This one is called eight-pointed star.

Accessories

Jewellery and other decorative accessories have been worn by men and women for thousands of years. Necklaces, earrings, rings, bracelets and ankle rings were made from materials such as shells, feathers, bones, glass beads, gold and precious stones. Accessories can give a clue to the status of the person wearing them. Wealthy people could afford finely crafted ornaments made from rare and expensive materials. Monarchs, priests, warriors and officials often wore badges and other accessories that identified their rank.

▲ Shell necklaces

In ancient times, people wore necklaces made of shells and animal teeth. At this time, jewellery may have been a sign that the wearer was an important person. Necklaces like this one have been found in Asia, as well as Australia. This indicates that the two continents were once linked by a common culture.

pumice stone

ash
face pack

kohl

henna

Bead necklaces ▶

Mesopotamian necklaces sometimes had thousands of different beads on several separate strings. The large one here, found at a farming site called Choga Mami, has around 2,200 beads roughly shaped from clay.

Cosmetics ▲

In ancient Egypt, black eye kohl was made from galena, a type of poisonous lead. Later on, soot was used. Henna was painted on the nails and the soles of the feet to make them red. Popular beauty treatments included pumice stone to smooth rough skin and ash face packs.

Chinese costume ▶

Wealthy Chinese people often wore expensive and well-crafted jewellery, such as gilded pendants made from precious metals and inset with beautiful gemstones. Belt hooks and buckles became an essential part of a Chinese nobleman's clothing from about 300BC. They were highly decorated and made from bronze.

◀ Spiritual headdress

Spiritual leaders called lamas educate people in Buddhism. In Tibet, lamas sometimes wear headdresses for religious services. The one pictured here depicts the five buddhas (enlightened ones) of meditation.

Enamelled brooch ▶

Many of the barbarian invaders of ancient Rome, such as the Visigoths, Vandals and Franks, were skilled craftworkers, as can be seen from this brooch.

glass

amber

◀ Precious amber

Its beautiful shades of gold, yellow and brown made amber extremely popular with Viking jewellers. They also used plain and coloured glass for making fine bead necklaces.

Tribal necklace

Stone Age necklaces were made from all sorts of natural objects, including pebbles, shells, fish bones, animal teeth and claws, nuts and seeds. Later, amber, jade, jet (fossilized coal) and hand-made clay beads were threaded on to thin strips of leather or twine made from plant fibres. Other jewellery included bracelets made of slices of mammoth tusk. People probably decorated their bodies and outlined their eyes with pigments such as red ochre. They may have tattooed and pierced their bodies, too.

YOU WILL NEED

Self-hardening clay, rolling pin, cutting board, modelling tool, sandpaper, ivory and black acrylic paint, paintbrush, water pot, ruler, pencil, 12 x 9cm chamois leather, scissors, card, double-sided sticky tape, PVA glue and glue brush, leather laces.

1 Roll out the clay on to a board. Cut out three crescent shapes with the modelling tool. Leave to dry. Rub the crescents gently with sandpaper and paint them an ivory colour.

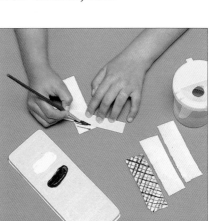

2 Cut four strips of leather to measure 9 x 3cm. Use the edge of a piece of card as a guide for your brush and make a criss-cross pattern on the strips of leather as shown.

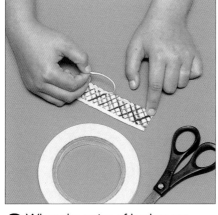

3 When the strips of leather are completely dry, fold the side edges of each strip in. Stick them securely in place with a piece of double-sided sticky tape.

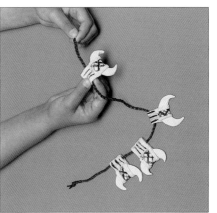

4 Brush glue on the middle of each clay crescent. Wrap a strip of leather around a crescent, leaving enough to form a loop at the top. Glue the loops in place. Paint three lines on each loop.

5 Plait three leather laces to make a thong to fit around your neck. Thread on the leopard's claws. Arrange the claws so that there are small spaces between them.

Stone Age people believed that wearing a leopard claw necklace gave them magical powers.

Egyptian mirror

The ancient Egyptians were fond of cosmetics. Cleopatra, who ruled Egypt in 51BC, used one of the first moisturisers to protect her skin from the effects of the desert sand. Both men and women wore green eyeshadow made from a mineral called malachite and black eyeliner made from a type of lead called galena. Mirrors were used by wealthy Egyptians for checking hairstyles, applying make-up or simply admiring their looks. The mirrors were made of polished copper or bronze, with handles of wood or ivory.

YOU WILL NEED

Self-hardening clay, modelling tool, cutting board, small piece of card or sandpaper, wire baking tray, small plate, mirror card, pencil, scissors, gold paint, paintbrush, water pot, PVA glue and glue brush.

1 Roll a piece of self-hardening clay into a tube. Mould the tube into a handle shape. Use the modelling tool to decorate the handle in the shape of a god or with a flower design.

2 Make a slot in the handle with a piece of card or sandpaper. Place the handle on a wire baking tray and leave it in a warm place to dry. Turn the handle over after two hours.

3 Draw round a small plate on to the mirror card. Add a pointed bit to fit in the slot in the handle. Cut the mirror shape out. When the handle is dry, insert the mirror in the slot.

4 It is now time to paint the handle. Paint one side carefully with gold paint and leave it to dry. When it has dried, turn the handle over and paint the other side.

5 Finally, you can assemble your mirror. Cover the base of the mirror card in glue and insert it into the handle slot. Now your mirror is ready to use.

The shiny surfaces and shapes of mirrors reminded Egyptians of the s°un's disc, so they became religious symbols.

Egyptian pectoral

Archaeologists know that the Egyptians loved jewellery, because so much has been unearthed in their tombs. Some are beautifully made from precious stones and costly metals. Other pieces are much simpler and are made from materials such as pottery and bone. The Egyptian original of this pectoral (necklace) was made by a technique called *cloisonné*. Gold wire was worked into a framework with lots of little compartments or *cloisons*. These were filled with coloured enamel (glass) paste. Then the piece was fired.

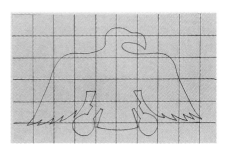

1 Take a sheet of A4 paper and draw vertical lines 2cm apart and then horizontal lines 2cm apart to make a grid as shown. Copy the design above on to the grid, one square at a time.

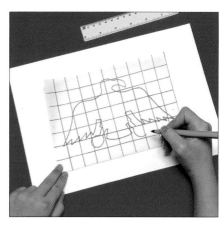

2 Place the tracing paper over the design. Use masking tape to secure it. Use a pen and ruler to trace your design and the grid on to the tracing paper. Cut out the falcon shape.

3 Place the self-hardening clay on to a cutting board. Use a rolling pin to flatten it out. Roll out the clay to measure 21 x 15cm in size with a thickness of 5cm.

4 Use masking tape to fix the tracing paper to the clay. Trace the design and then use the modelling tool to cut around the outline of the falcon. Make sure you cut right through the clay.

5 Remove the tracing paper. Use a fine modelling tool to mould the detail. Use a cocktail stick to make a 3mm hole on each wing, 2cm away from the top edge of the wing.

6 Leave the clay falcon to dry in a warm room. Use a medium-sized paintbrush and blue acrylic paint to colour body and wings of the falcon. Leave it to dry completely.

7 Use red, blue, green and gold acrylic paints to add decorative touches to the falcon as shown above. Try to make the design look as if it is really made of precious gems and gold.

8 Clean the paintbrush in water and leave the falcon to dry. Use the clean brush to apply a thin coat of wood varnish over the model. Then clean the paintbrush with white spirit.

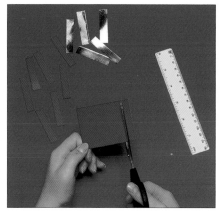

9 Paint five 5cm square pieces of plain paper blue and five pieces gold. Cut each square into strips, each 1cm wide. You will need 25 strips of each colour in total.

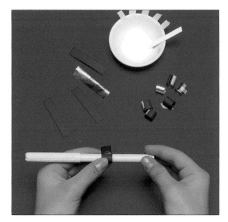

10 When the strips are dry, roll each one around a pen. Dab PVA glue on to the ends of the paper to stick them. Use masking tape to secure the ends of the paper until dry.

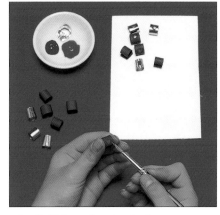

11 When the glue is dry, remove the tape and paint the paper tubes with red, blue and gold dots as shown above. You now have 50 beads to make a necklace.

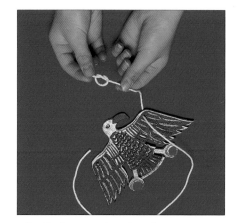

12 Cut two lengths of string, each 45cm long. Thread one end of each piece of string through the holes in the falcon's wings. Tie a knot in the strings.

13 Thread the beads on to the pieces of string. Alternate the blue and gold beads. You should thread 25 beads on to each string to make the decorative necklace.

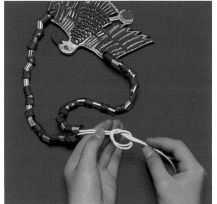

14 Finish threading all the beads on to the string. Tie the ends of the two pieces of string with a secure knot. Trim off excess string to finish off your necklace.

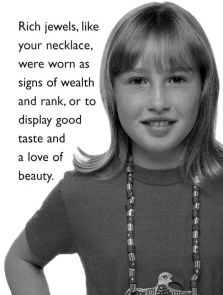

Rich jewels, like your necklace, were worn as signs of wealth and rank, or to display good taste and a love of beauty.

Chinese fan

Court dress in China varied greatly over the ages. Foreign invasions brought new fashions and dress codes. Government officials wore elegant robes that reflected their rank and social status. Beautiful silk robes patterned with *lung pao* (dragons) were worn by court ladies, officials and the emperor himself. Many people, both men and women, might carry a fan as a symbol of good upbringing as well as to provide a cool breeze in the sweltering summer heat.

fan

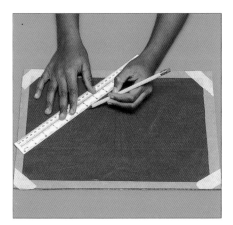

1 Tape tissue paper on to the base. Draw two semicircles (16cm radius and 7cm radius) from one side of the base. Then draw even lines about 1cm apart between the two semicircles.

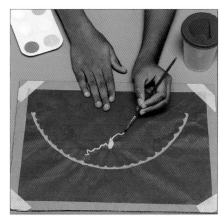

2 Draw a design on to the tissue paper. Paint in the details and leave the paint to dry. Then remove the paper from the base and cut out the fan along edges of the semicircles.

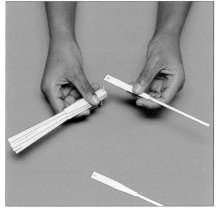

3 Use scissors to cut a slither off each side of each balsa strip for half its length. Pierce a compass hole at the wide base of the strip. Thread the strips on to a barbecue stick.

4 Fold the decorated tissue paper backwards and forwards to form a concertina. Glue each alternate fold of the paper to the narrow ends of the balsa strips as shown above.

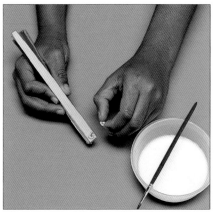

5 Paint the outer strips of the fan pink and let the paint dry. Cut out two small card discs. Glue them over the ends of the barbecue stick to secure the strips as shown above .

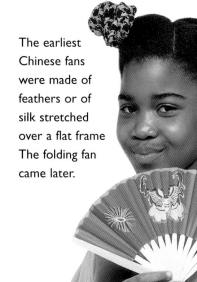

The earliest Chinese fans were made of feathers or of silk stretched over a flat frame The folding fan came later.

Japanese fan

Until 1500, Japanese court fashions were based on traditional Chinese styles. Men and women wore long, flowing robes made of many layers of fine, glossy silk, held in place by a sash and cords. Flat fans, or *uchiwa,* like the one in this project, could be tucked into the sash when not in use. In the 1500s, *kimonos* (long, loose robes) became popular among wealthy artists, actors and craftworkers. Women wore wide silk sashes called *obis* on top of their kimonos. Men fastened their kimonos with narrow sashes.

YOU WILL NEED

Thick card measuring 38 x 26cm, pencil, ruler, pair of compasses, protractor, blue felt tip pen, red paper measuring 30 x 26cm, scissors, acrylic paints, paintbrush, water pot, glue stick.

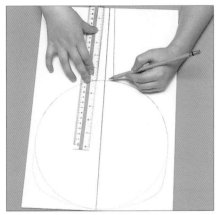

1 Draw a line down the centre of the piece of thick card. Draw a circle 23cm wide two-thirds of the way up. Add squared-off edges at the top of the circle. Draw a 15cm long handle.

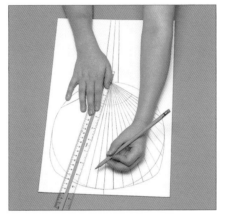

2 Place a protractor at the top of the handle and draw a semicircle around it. Now mark lines every 2.5 degrees. Draw pencil lines through these marks to the edge of the circle.

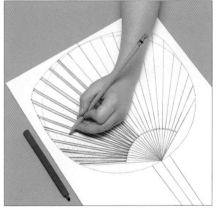

3 Draw a blue line 1cm to the left of each pencil mark. Then draw a blue line 2mm to the right of each of the pencil marks. Pencil in a rough squiggle in between the blue sections.

4 Cut out the fan. Draw around the fan shape on the red paper. Cut it out. Leave to one side. Then cut out the sections marked with squiggles on the white fan. Paint the white fan brown.

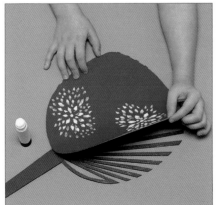

5 Leave the fan to dry. Paint the red paper with white flowers and leave to dry. Paste glue on to one side of the card fan. Stick the undecorated side of the red card to the fan.

Japanese noble ladies hid their faces in court. They used decorated fans such as this one as a screen.

Japanese netsuke fox

There is a long tradition among Japanese craftworkers of making everyday things as beautiful as possible. Craftworkers also created exquisite items for the wealthiest and most knowledgeable collectors. They used a wide variety of materials, including pottery, metal, lacquer, cloth, paper and bamboo. Ceramics ranged from plain, simple earthenware to delicate porcelain painted with brilliantly coloured glazes. Japanese metalworkers produced alloys (mixtures of metals) that were unknown elsewhere in the ancient world. Cloth was woven from many fibres in elaborate designs. Bamboo and other grasses were woven into elegant *tatami* (floor mats) and containers of all different shapes and sizes. Japanese craftworkers also made beautiful *inro*. These are little boxes, used like purses, that dangled from men's kimono sashes using a *netsuke* (carved toggle).

▲ **Keeping it safe**
Carved ivory or wooden toggles, called netsuke, were used to hold the inro in the waist sash of a kimono. Netsuke were shaped into representations of gods, dragons or living animals.

▲ **Boxes for belts**
These small boxes were originally designed for storing medicines. The first inro were plain and simple, but after about 1700 they were often decorated with exquisite designs. These inro have been lacquered (coated with a shiny substance made from the sap of the lacquer tree). Inside, they contain several compartments stacked on top of each other.

YOU WILL NEED

Paper, pencil, ruler, rolling pin, self-hardening clay, cutting board, modelling tool, balsa wood, fine sandpaper, acrylic paint, paintbrush water pot, darning needle, cord, small box (for an inro), scissors, toggle, wide belt.

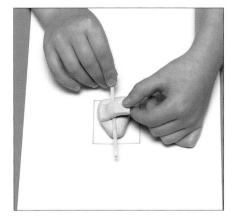

1 Draw a 5 x 5cm square on to the paper. Roll out some clay to the size of the square. Shape a point at one end. Lay a small length of balsa along the back. Secure it with a thin strip of clay.

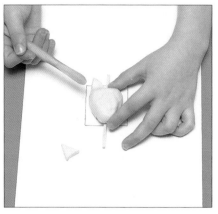

2 Turn the clay back on its right side. Cut out two triangles of clay for the ears. Join them to the head using a modelling tool. Make indentations to shape them into the ears of a fox.

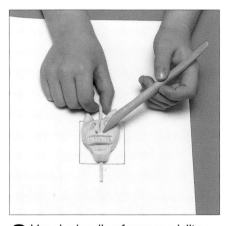

3 Use the handle of your modelling tool to make the fox's mouth. Carve eyes, nostrils, teeth and a frown line. Use the blunt end of the pencil to make holes for the fox's eyes.

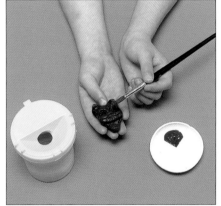

4 Leave the netsuke fox to dry. Then gently sand the netsuke and remove the balsa wood stick. Paint the netsuke with several layers of acrylic paint. Leave it in a warm place to dry.

Wear your inro dangling from your belt. In ancient Japan inro were usually worn by men. They were held in place by carved toggles called netsuke.

5 Thread some cord through four corners of a small box with a darning needle. Then thread the cord through the toggle and the hole on the netsuke left by the balsa wood.

6 Put a wide belt round your waist. Thread the netsuke under the belt. It should rest on the top of the belt as shown above. The inro (box) should hang down.

Native American anklets

Most of the wars between different Native American tribes were fought over land or hunting territory, and later over horses. As European settlers began to occupy more land, many tribes fought to stop them. Before going into battle, Native American warriors performed a war dance to ask for spiritual guidance and protection during the conflict. Ceremonial dress and body painting was a feature of these occasions. The anklets in this project are similar to the ones worn by many tribes during their war dances.

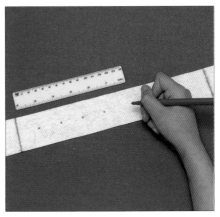

1 Mark two lines across the felt strips, 24cm in from each end. Make a series of marks in between these lines. Start 3cm away from the line, then mark at 3cm intervals.

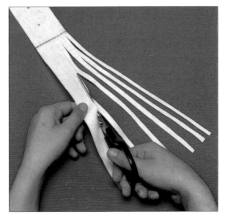

2 Create the fringing at each end of the anklet. Do this by cutting into both ends of the band up to the marked lines. Repeat the process for the other anklet.

3 Thread a large needle with strong, doubled and knotted thread. Insert the needle into the fabric and pull through until the knot hits the fabric.

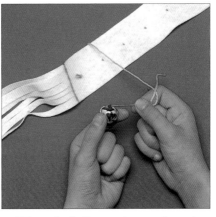

4 Thread a bell over the needle and up to the felt. Push the needle back through the felt. Knot the end on the opposite side to the bell. Trim excess thread. Repeat for the other seven bells.

Tie the anklets round your ankles. The bells of the North American Indians were sewn on to strips of animal hide. They were tied around the ankles and just under the knees and worn for ceremonial dances.

Native American necklace

Tribes in North America took pride in their appearance. As well as wearing decorative necklaces, headdresses and other jewellery, many tribes wore tattoos as a sign of status or to gain protection from spirits. Hairstyles were important, too, and could indicate that a young man was unmarried or belonged to a warrior class. Woodlands men had a distinctive hairstyle. They braided their hair at the front and decorated it with turkey feathers. Some Plains warriors shaved their heads completely, leaving a long tuft on top.

YOU WILL NEED

Thin white paper strips, PVA glue and glue brush, acrylic paints (blue, turquoise and red), paintbrush, water pot, scissors, self-hardening clay, skewer, string.

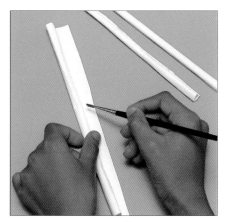

1 Roll up the strips of thin white paper into 5mm tubes. Glue down the outer edge to seal the tubes and leave them to dry. Make three of these paper tubes.

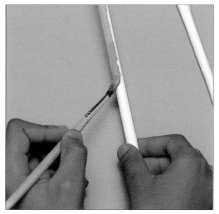

2 When the glue has dried, paint the rolls of paper. Paint one roll blue, one roll red and one roll turquoise, making sure that you cover all the white areas. Leave them to dry.

3 When they have dried, the painted paper tubes will have hardened slightly. Carefully cut the tubes to separate them into 1cm pieces. These will be the beads of your necklace.

4 Roll the clay into two large clay beads. Pierce the centres with a skewer. Leave the beads to dry and harden. When they are ready, paint both of the beads blue. Leave to dry.

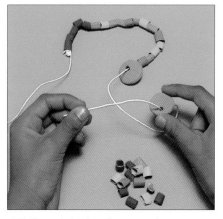

5 Thread the beads on to the string. Start with the clay beads which will hang in the centre. Then add blue either side, then turquoise, then red. Knot the ends together when you have finished.

Native Americans made beads from bone, stone and shell. Some of their bone beads were 8–10cm long. European traders introduced glass beads in the 1500s.

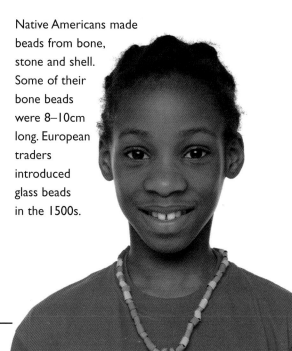

Glass bead jewellery

Native Americans were not only hunters and warriors, they were also artists and craftworkers. Tribespeople made everything they needed for themselves, from clothes and blankets to tools and weapons. The first settlers from Europe took coloured glass beads with them to the USA. Many Native American tribes bargained with traders for the beads. They developed great skill in using them to make brilliant, richly coloured patterns on dresses, trousers, shoes and many other possessions.

YOU WILL NEED

70cm piece of narrow leather thong, ruler, scissors, 165cm strong waxed thread, selection of glass and silver beads in different sizes, four brightly coloured dyed feathers, two glass and two silver beads with holes big enough to cover the knotted leather thong.

1 To make a Native American glass bead necklace, cut two strips of leather thong, each 15cm long. You will use these strips to tie the finished necklace around your neck.

2 Next, take the waxed thread and carefully cut off one long piece about 25cm long using the scissors. Then cut four smaller pieces of waxed thread, each 10cm long.

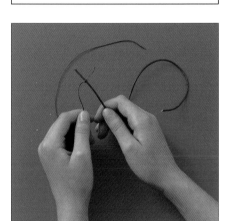

3 Knot one end of one leather strip to one end of the 25cm-long waxed thread. Thread on one of the glass or silver beads with a hole that will cover the knot you have made.

4 Thread different beads on to the long piece of waxed thread until there is about a 10cm gap left at the end. Thread the beads in a repeating pattern or randomly, as you prefer.

5 Now make the four dangling pieces of the necklace. For each one, tie one end of the 10cm-long piece of waxed thread around the quill of a brightly coloured feather.

6 Thread on some smaller beads, covering only half of each piece of waxed thread. Tie a knot to secure the beads. Again, you can thread them in a pattern if you like.

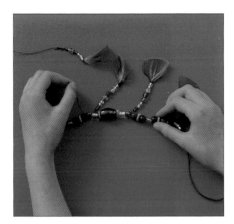

7 Tie each feathery piece on to the main necklace. Then tie on the second 15cm-long leather thong at the free end. Cover the knot with one of the glass or silver beads with a big hole.

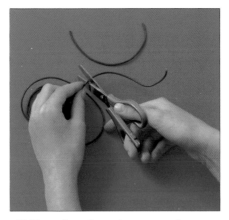

8 To make a bracelet to match your necklace, cut two 20cm long strips of leather thong. When the bracelet is finished, you will use these to tie it around your wrist.

9 Next, cut five lengths of waxed thread, each measuring about 20cm in length. These threads are going to form the main part of your beaded bracelet.

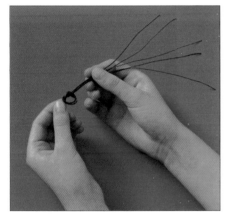

10 Take the five lengths of waxed thread, and tie a big knot at one end to join them all together. Try to make the knot as small and as neat as possible.

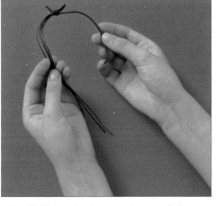

11 Take the knotted end of the waxed threads and carefully tie on one of the leather strips. Cover the knot with one of the glass or silver beads with a big hole.

Jewellery like this is still sold in the western USA. Today, Native Americans make all sorts of different jewellery items for the tourist trade.

12 Thread some beads on to one of the waxed threads, keeping some thread spare. You can make a pattern or not, as you prefer. Then tie a knot to keep the beads in place.

13 Bead and knot all five waxed threads and then tie them all together. Tie on the last leather strip and cover the knot with a large bead. Now your bracelet is ready to wear.

Arctic purse

Surviving in the Arctic was hard. Men and women had to work long hours to keep everyone warm, clothed and fed. Women looked after the domestic chores. Their work included tending the fire, cooking, preparing animal hides and looking after their children. Arctic women were also skilled at craftwork, and sewing was an extremely important job. They had to find time to make and repair all the family's clothes and bedding, as well as make items such as bags, purses and other useful containers.

YOU WILL NEED

Chamois leather (21 x 35cm), PVA glue and glue brush, pencil, ruler, scissors, shoelace (50cm long), pieces of decorative felt (red, dark blue and light blue), two blue beads.

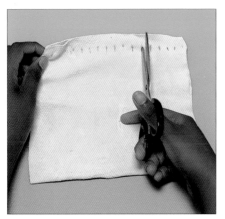

1 Fold the chamois leather in half. Glue down two sides, leaving one end open. Pencil in marks 1cm apart on either side of the open end. Make small holes at these points with the scissors.

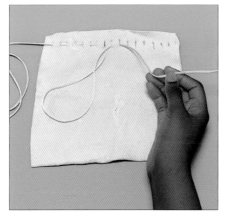

2 Thread a shoelace through the holes on both sides as shown above. Tie the ends of the shoelace together and leave an excess piece of lace hanging.

3 Carefully cut two strips of red felt 21cm long and 5cm wide. Then mark and cut a narrow fringe about 1cm deep along both edges of each red felt piece as shown.

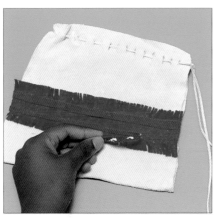

4 Glue strips of red fringing felt to either side of the purse. Add extra decoration by sticking 1cm strips of dark blue and light blue felt on top of the red fringing felt and the purse.

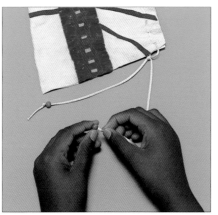

5 Tie the two blue beads securely to each of the excess shoelace. Close the purse by pulling the shoelace and tying a knot in it. Your Arctic purse is ready to use.

Drawstring purses such as this one were often made of soft deer hide called buckskin.

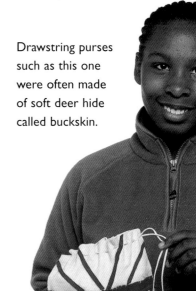

Celtic mirror

Metalworkers made many valuable Celtic items, from iron swords to the beautiful bronze handles of their mirrors. Patterns and techniques invented in one part of the Celtic world quickly spread to others. Metalworkers excelled in several different techniques. Heavy objects were cast from solid bronze using a clay mould. Thin sheets of silver and bronze were decorated with *repoussé* (pushed out) designs. The designs were sketched on to the back of the metal, then gently hammered to create raised patterns.

YOU WILL NEED

Pair of compasses, pencil, ruler, stiff gold mirror card, scissors, tracing paper, pen, self-hardening clay, cutting board, gold paint, paintbrush, water pot, PVA glue and glue brush.

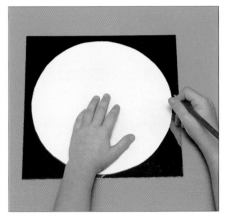

1 Use the compasses to draw a circle with a diameter of 22cm on to the gold card. Cut the gold circle out. Use this circle as a template to draw a second circle on to gold card.

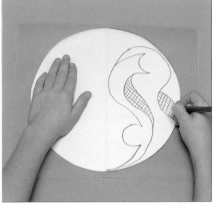

2 Cut out the second gold circle. Draw another circle on to some tracing paper. Fold the piece of tracing paper in half and draw on a Celtic pattern like the one shown above.

3 Lay the tracing paper on to one of the circles. Trace the pattern on to half of the gold circle, then turn the paper over and repeat the tracing. Go over the pattern with a pen.

4 Roll out several pieces of clay and sculpt them into a handle about 15cm long and 9cm wide. Leave to dry. Paint one side with gold paint. Leave to dry. Turn over and paint the other side.

5 Stick the two pieces of mirror card together, white side to white side, with the gold sides facing out as shown above. Glue the handle on to the side of the mirror when the paint has dried.

The bronze on a Celtic mirror would have been polished so that the owner could see his or her reflection on it.

Celtic torc

The Celts were skilled at many different crafts, including glass, jewellery, enamel and metalwork. Only wealthy people could afford items made from gold. Celtic chiefs often rewarded their best warriors with rich gifts of fine gold armbands. Heavy necklaces called torcs were also highly prized. The Celts believed that torcs had the power to protect people from evil spirits. For the same reason, the Celts often painted or tattooed their bodies with a dark blue dye taken from a plant called woad.

1 Roll out two lengths of clay about 60cm long and about 1cm thick on the cutting board. Twist the rolls together, leaving about 5cm of untwisted clay at either end.

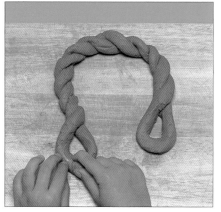

2 Make loops out of the untwisted ends of the clay torc by joining them together as shown above. Dampen the ends with a little water to help join the clay if necessary.

3 Use a ruler to measure an opening between the two looped ends. The ends should be about 9cm apart so that the torc will fit easily around your neck. Let the torc begin to dry.

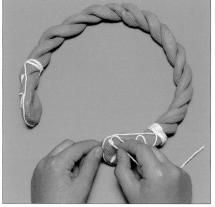

4 When the torc is partially dry, cut two pieces of string about 8cm in length. Use the string to decorate the looped ends of the torc. Glue the string securely in place.

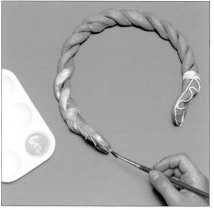

5 Allow the clay torc to dry out completely. When it is hard, cover the torc and decorative string with gold or bronze paint. Leave to dry again before you wear your torc.

Celtic torcs were made from precious metals such as iron, bronze and gold.

Celtic brooch

Looking good was important to Celtic men and women because it made people admire them. Ancient Roman reports suggest that different groups of men within Celtic society cut their hair and shaved their faces in different styles to show their status. Legends told that warriors who did not have naturally blonde hair (preferred by the Celts) bleached it with a mixture of urine and wood-ash. Jewellery was extremely important to the Celts. Bracelets, brooches and torcs were worn by all members of Celtic society.

YOU WILL NEED

Self-hardening clay, rolling pin, cutting board, modelling tool, sharp pencil, sandpaper, acrylic paints (light blue, dark blue and white), paintbrush, water pot, large safety pin, sticky tape.

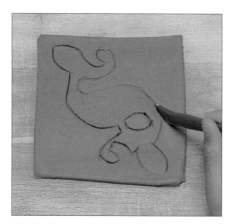

1 Roll out a 15 x 15cm square of clay on to the cutting board. It should be about 5mm thick. Copy a dragon shape on to the clay, using the finished brooch as a guide.

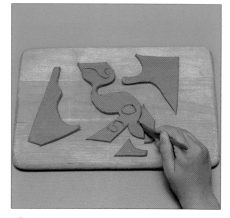

2 Cut out the dragon shape. Then use the modelling tool to draw some of the features of the dragon into the centre of your brooch as shown above.

3 Cut the centre hole out of the brooch. Add the dragon's two faces and more patterns using a modelling tool. Finish the patterns with the sharp end of a pencil. Let the brooch dry.

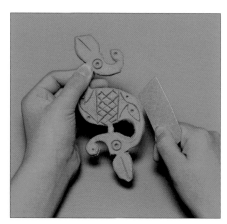

4 When the brooch has dried, gently hold it in one hand. With your other hand, sand the edges with a piece of smooth sandpaper until they are completely smooth.

5 Paint the brooch light blue. Add dark blue and white decoration as shown above. Let the brooch dry. Stick a large safety pin on the back of the brooch with sticky tape.

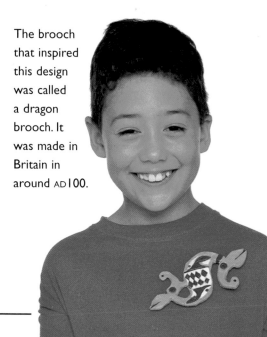

The brooch that inspired this design was called a dragon brooch. It was made in Britain in around AD100.

Viking brooches

The Vikings loved showy jewellery, especially armbands, rings and gold and silver necklaces. These were often decorated with ornate designs. Jewellery was a sign of wealth and could be used instead of money to buy other goods.

Brooches were worn by Viking women. Typical dress for Viking women and girls was a long plain shift. It was made of wool or linen. Over this they wore a woollen tunic, with shoulder straps secured by ornate brooches. Between the brooches there was often a chain or a string of beads.

YOU WILL NEED

Self-hardening clay, rolling board, ruler, string, scissors, PVA glue and brush, bronze paint, A4 sheet of white paper, water pot, paintbrush, pair of compasses, pencil, tracing paper, gold foil, card, safety pin.

1 Roll two balls of clay into slightly domed disc shapes 2-3cm across. Let them dry. Glue string borders around them. Paint them with bronze paint. Leave them to dry.

2 Use compasses to draw two circles on a sheet of white paper. Make them the same size as your brooch shapes. Draw a Viking pattern in your circle or copy the one shown above.

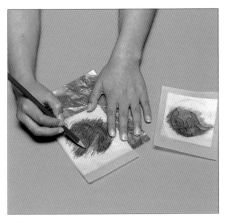

3 Use tracing paper to trace each pattern on to a piece of gold foil. Cut the patterns out in small pieces that will interlink. Take care not to tear the foil.

4 Glue each piece of the foil pattern on to the outside of one of the clay brooches. Leave the brooch to dry. Then glue the foil pattern on to the other clay brooch.

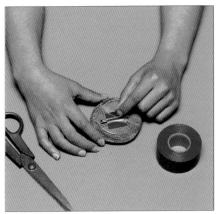

5 Cut and stick a circle of painted gold card on to the back of each brooch. Fix a safety pin on to the back of each brooch with masking tape. Your brooches are now ready to wear.

Brooches were important pieces of jewellery. They were used as fasteners for cloaks and tunics.

Viking bracelet

All Vikings turned their hand to craftwork. Men carved ivory and wood during the long winter evenings, and women made woollen cloth. Professional craftworkers worked gold, silver and bronze and made fine jewellery from gemstones, amber and jet. Other beautiful objects were carved from antlers or walrus tusks. Homes and churches had beautiful wood carvings. Patterns included swirling loops and knots, and birds and animals interlaced with writhing snakes and strange monsters.

YOU WILL NEED

Tape measure, self-hardening clay, cutting board, white cord or string, scissors, modelling tool, silver paint, paintbrush, water pot.

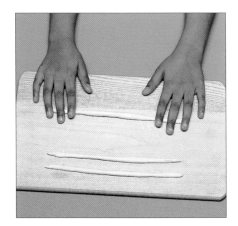

1 Measure your wrist with a tape measure. Roll three clay snakes just longer than the size of your wrist. This will ensure that the bracelet will pass over your hand but not fall off.

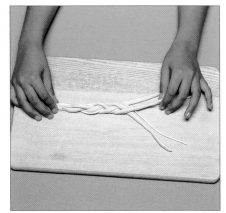

2 Lay out the clay snakes in a fan shape. Then cut two lengths of white cord a bit longer than the snakes, and plait the clay snakes and the two cords together as shown above.

3 Trim each end of the clay and cord plait with a modelling tool. At each end, press the strands firmly together and secure them with a small roll of clay as shown above.

4 Carefully curl the bracelet round so it will fit neatly around your wrist. Make sure you leave the ends open. Leave the bracelet in a safe place to dry thoroughly.

5 When the bracelet is completely dry, paint it with silver paint. Give it a second coat if necessary. Leave the bracelet to dry again. When it is completely dry you can try it on.

Vikings liked to show off their rank by wearing expensive gold and silver jewellery.

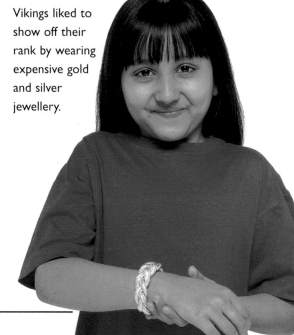

Aztec feather fan

Countless tropical birds live in Central America. Their brightly coloured feathers became an important item of trade in the Aztec world. Birds were hunted and raised in captivity for their feathers, which were arranged into elaborate patterns and designs. Skilled Aztec featherworkers wove beautiful garments, such as decorative headdresses, feather *ponchos* (shirts) and fans. Jewellery was popular, too, but it could only be worn by the ruler and the nobility. Earrings, necklaces, labrets (lip-plugs) and bracelets made of gold and precious stones were all popular items. As well as wearing jewellery, tattooing was a widespread practice in Mesoamerica.

▲ **Tax collection**
The Aztecs loved feather decoration. These pictures show items that were collected as a form of tax payment from the lands they conquered.

◀ **Feather work**
The Aztecs had an expert guild of featherworkers who used complicated methods of gluing and weaving to make items such as headdresses and fans.

YOU WILL NEED

Pair of compasses, pencil, ruler, thick card (90 x 45cm), scissors, thin red card, green paper, double-sided sticky tape, feathers (real or paper), roll of masking tape, acrylic paints, paintbrushes, water pot, coloured felt, PVA glue and glue brush, single-sided sticky tape, coloured wool, bamboo cane.

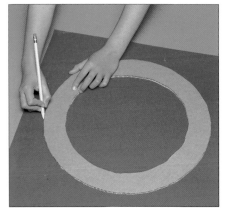

1 Use the compasses to draw two rings about 45cm in diameter and 8cm wide on thick card. Cut them out. Use a thick card ring to make another ring from the thin red card as above.

2 Cut lots of leaf shapes from green paper. Stick them around the edge of one thick card ring using double-sided sticky tape. Add some real feathers or ones made from paper.

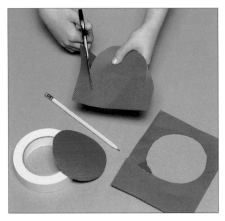

3 Cut two circles about 12cm in diameter from thin red card. Draw around something the right size, such as a roll of masking tape. These circles will be the centre of your feather fan.

4 Paint a flower on to one of the two smaller red circles and a butterfly on the other. Cut lots of v-shapes from the felt and glue them to the large red ring.

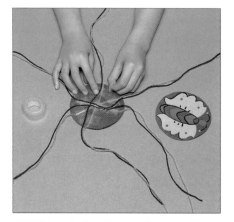

5 Using single-sided sticky tape, fix lengths of coloured wool to the back of one of the red circles as shown above. Place this red circle in the centre of the leafy ring.

6 Tape the wool to the outer ring. Glue the second card ring on top. Insert the cane in between. Stick the second red circle face up in the centre. Glue the larger, outer ring on top.

Aztec nobles and rulers were cooled with beautiful feather fans such as the one you have made.

Buckles and badges

In the Wild West, lawmen wore a metal star pinned on the front of their jackets to identify themselves. It was their job to keep law and order. The first project here shows you how to make your own sheriff's badge.

Every belt needs a buckle, and one way a cowboy could get a new one was to win it as a prize at a special contest called a rodeo. Wearing this would show his friends how skilful he was as a cowboy. The second part of this project shows you how to make a prize belt buckle of your own.

▲ **Tools of the trade**
Cowboys had tough lives and wore tough, practical clothes. This cowboy wears a gun at his belt and carries a rope lasso, or lariat, for roping cattle.

YOU WILL NEED

Self-hardening clay, rolling pin, cutting board, ruler, star-shaped pastry cutter, PVA glue and glue brush, kebab stick or sharpened pencil, water, flowerpot, modelling tool, large safety pin with flat plate, two strips of bias binding tape, 8cm long needle and thread, silver poster paint, paintbrush, water pot, permanent black marker.

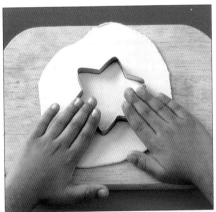

1 Roll a handful of clay out into two circles, each 5mm thick. With the star-shaped pastry cutter, press out a star from one of the clay circles. Lift the star from the surrounding clay.

2 Roll out some of the excess clay to make six tiny balls. Each one should be about half the size of your fingernail. Glue each ball on a point of the star shape.

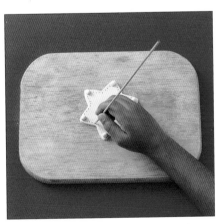

3 Use the pointed end of a kebab stick or a sharpened pencil to make a line of tiny dots around the edge of the star shape. Try to be as neat as you possibly can.

4 To give the star a curved shape, lightly brush the back of the star with water and press it on to the side of a flowerpot. Peel the star away gently. Leave it to dry overnight.

5 Roll out the second ball of clay. Use a modelling tool to cut a rectangular shape with rounded corners as shown. The rectangle should measure about 8 x 5cm.

6 Follow step 2 again to make 12 more tiny modelling clay balls with excess clay. Then carefully glue the balls around the edge of the clay buckle.

7 Once again, use the pointed end of a kebab stick or a sharpened pencil to add some decorative touches to the parts of the buckle between the balls with dots and swirls.

8 Follow step 4 again to give the buckle a curved shape. When you are happy with the shape of the buckle, peel it off gently. Then leave it to dry overnight.

9 After 24 hours, when the clay star badge is dry, glue the plate of the safety pin to the back of the star. Carefully attach the pin to the flat space in the middle of the badge.

10 When the buckle is completely dry, glue two strips of bias binding tape across the back of the buckle. Use a running stitch to sew the ends together to make two loops.

Thread a thick leather belt through the loops on the back of your buckle and pin on your sheriff's badge – you are ready to hunt down those outlaws!

11 When the glue on the badge and buckle is completely dry, you can paint them both with silver paint to give them an authentic metallic sheen.

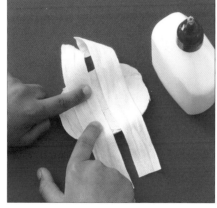

12 When the paint has dried, you can add the finishing touches using a permanent black marker. Try drawing a star shape in the middle of the badge and the buckle.

Science and Technology

Discovery, invention and progress went hand-in-hand with civilization. Systems of writing, weights and measures, currency and communication were vital to running a successful empire. Transport and travel were the key to trade and expansion of territory. The projects in this section provide an insight into the developing technologies, such as transport and warfare, that gave people the edge over their neighbours.

Inventions and Learning

H umans have striven to understand the world around them ever since they first walked on the Earth some 30,000 years ago. The earliest people lived by hunting animals and gathering fruit. Their inventions were simple tools and weapons. Farming and permanent settlements, and the subsequent development of towns and cities, made life much more complicated. This, together with increased wealth, prompted some remarkable scientific and technological breakthroughs. The world was changed dramatically by new inventions that made life ever easier and more efficient.

▲ Geometric calculations

The ancient Egyptians were skilled mathematicians and made many new discoveries in geometry. For example, they knew how to calculate the height of a pyramid by measuring the length of its shadow on the ground.

◄ A Greek philosopher

Pythagoras of Samos (560-480BC) became one of the most highly respected Greek philosophers and teachers. Pythagoras believed that numbers were the perfect basis of life. He is most famous for his theory about right-angled triangles. This showed that if you square the two sides next to the right angle, the two add up to the square of the third side. (Squaring means multiplying a number by itself.)

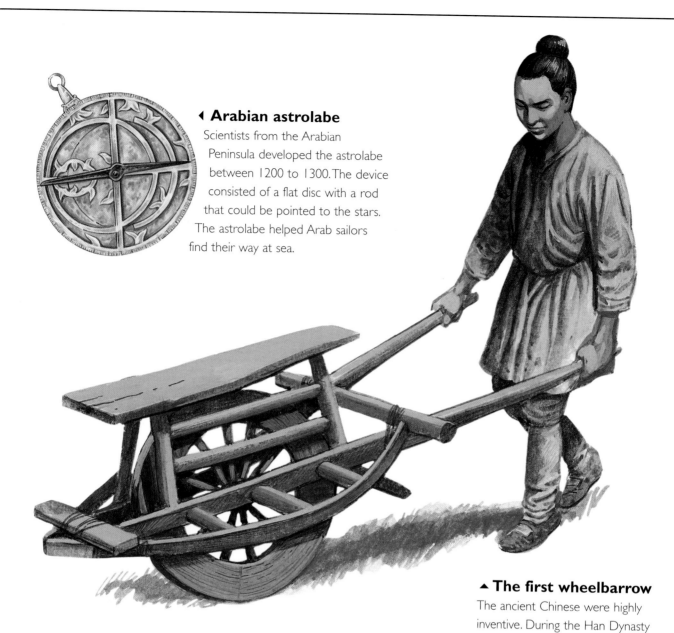

◀ Arabian astrolabe

Scientists from the Arabian
Peninsula developed the astrolabe
between 1200 to 1300. The device
consisted of a flat disc with a rod
that could be pointed to the stars.
The astrolabe helped Arab sailors
find their way at sea.

▲ The first wheelbarrow

The ancient Chinese were highly
inventive. During the Han Dynasty
(from 207BC to AD220), technological
developments included the invention
of the wheelbarrow, some 1,000 years
before people in the West.

◀ Remarkable roads

The Romans were some of the greatest
builders and engineers of the ancient
world. Their road-building methods were
unsurpassed for centuries. They began building
roads in 334BC. By the time the Roman
Empire was at its peak, at around AD117, they
had laid down more than 85,000km of roads.

Stone Age bow drill

Our ancestor, *Homo erectus,* learned to use fire at least 700,000 years ago. Early humans ate cooked food and had warmth and light at night. Fire was a useful way of keeping wild animals at bay and was also used to harden the tips of wooden spears. Hunters waving flaming branches could scare large animals into ambushes. Most archaeologists believe that *Homo erectus* did not know how to make fire but found smouldering logs after natural forest fires. Campfires were carefully kept alight, and hot ashes may have been carried to each new camp. Eventually, people learned that they could make fire by rubbing two dry sticks together. Then they found that striking a stone against pyrite (a type of rock) created a spark. By 4000BC, the bow drill had been invented. This made lighting a fire much easier.

YOU WILL NEED

Thick piece of dowelling (25cm long), craft knife, sandpaper, wood stain, paintbrush, water pot, balsa wood (8 x 8cm), modelling tool, self-hardening clay, rolling pin, cutting board, scissors, chamois leather, raffia or straw.

▼ The first match
One way early people made fire was to put dry grass on a stick called a hearth. Then they rubbed another stick against the hearth to make a spark and set the grass alight.

hearth

◄ Making dinner
Cave-dwelling *Homo erectus* people prepare to cook a meal in front of their cave. One member of the group makes stone tools, perhaps to cut up the dead animal. Another tends to the fire, and two children help an adult to dismember the carcass before it is cooked.

1 Shape one end of the piece of thick dowelling into a point with a craft knife. The blade of the knife should always angle away from your body when you cut the wood.

2 Sand down the stick and apply a coat of wood stain. Cut out the balsa wood base into a shape roughly like the one shown above. Paint the base with wood stain. Leave it to dry.

3 Use a modelling tool to gouge a small hole in the centre of the balsa-wood base. The sharpened end of the piece of dowelling should fit into this hole.

4 Roll out a piece of clay. Cut out a bone shape with a rounded end as shown above. Make a hole in each end of the bone and smooth the sides with your fingers. Let the bone shape dry.

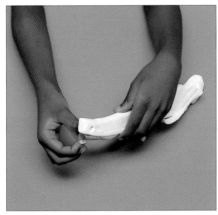

5 Use a pair of scissors to cut a thin strip of chamois leather twice as long as the bone. This will be the thong used to twist the bow drill. Tie the strip to one end of the bone.

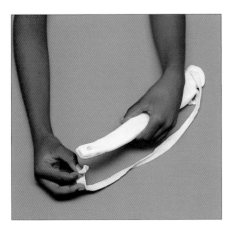

6 Thread the strip of chamois leather through the other hole. Tie a knot at the end to secure it. Now the bow piece is ready to be used with the drill you have already made.

7 Scatter raffia or straw around the balsa wood base. Wrap the leather thong around the drill piece and place the pointed end of the drill in the hole on the base.

If you like, add a wood handle to the base to help you hold it. The bow drill you have made will not light real fires but shows you how Stone Age people spun a drill to make fire.

Egyptian shaduf

The ancient Egyptians called the banks of the River Nile the Black Land. This was because the river flooded each year in June, depositing a rich, fertile, black mud. The land remained under water until autumn. During dry periods of the year, farmers dug channels and canals to carry water to irrigate their land. A lifting system called a shaduf was introduced to raise water from the river. The success of this farming cycle was vital. Years of low floodwaters or drought could spell disaster. If the crops failed, people went hungry.

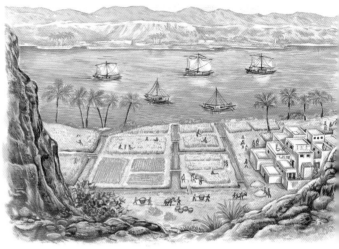

▲ Home on the Nile

Most ancient Egyptians lived close to the River Nile. The river was the main means of transport and provided water for their crops and their homes.

Templates

Cut out the pieces of card following the measurements shown.

A = irrigation channel and river bank
B = river
C = water tank

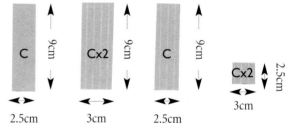

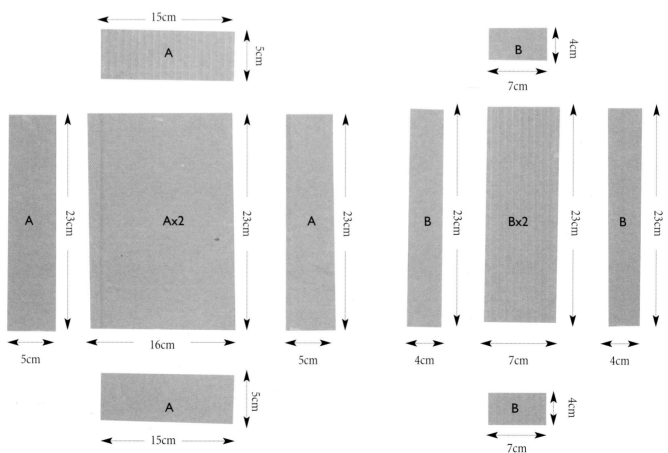

YOU WILL NEED

Card, pencil, ruler, scissors, PVA glue and glue brush, masking tape, acrylic paints (blue, green and brown), paintbrush, water pot, four balsa wood strips (two measuring 8cm and two 4cm), small stones, twig, self-hardening clay, hessian, string. Note: mix green paint with dried herbs for the grass mixture.

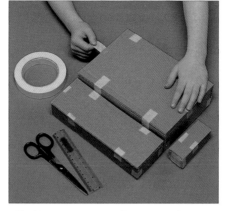

1 Glue the edges of boxes A, B and C as shown above. Secure them with masking tape until they are dry. Then paint the river section B and the water tank C blue and leave to dry.

2 Paint the box A with the green grass mixture on top, brown on the sides and the irrigation channel blue as shown. Next, get the balsa strips to make the frame of the shaduf.

3 Glue the four balsa wood strips to make a frame. Support them with masking tape on a piece of card. When dry, paint the frame brown. Then glue the stones around the water tank.

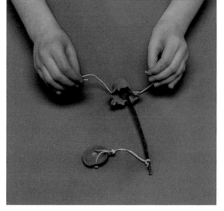

4 Use a twig for the pole of the shaduf. Make a weight from clay and wrap it in hessian. Tie it to one end of the pole. Make a bucket from clay, leaving two holes for the string.

The shaduf was invented in the Middle East and brought into Egypt about 3,500 years ago. It has a bucket on one end of a pole and a heavy weight on the other. First, the weight is pushed up, lowering the bucket into the river. As the weight is lowered, it raises up the full bucket of water.

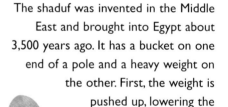

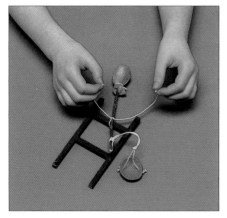

5 Using string, tie the bucket to the pole. Tie the pole, with its weight and bucket, to the frame of the shaduf. Glue the frame to the water tank, and then glue the tank to the riverbank section.

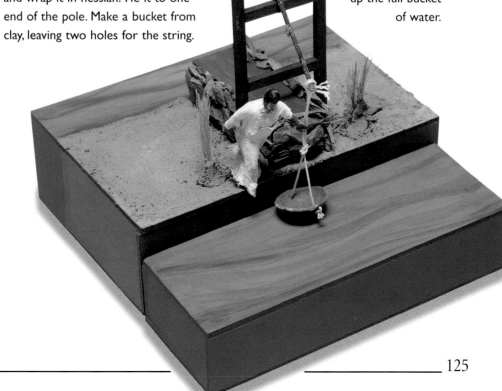

Archimedes' screw

The Greeks could afford to devote time to studying and thinking because their civilization was both wealthy and secure. They learned astrology from the Babylonians and mathematics from the Egyptians. They used their knowledge to develop many practical inventions, including water clocks, cogwheels, gearing systems, slot machines and steam engines. However, these devices were not widely used because there were many slaves to do the work instead.

Archimedes was the world's first great scientist. He came up with theories that could be proved or disproved by practical experiment or mathematical calculation. One of his most famous inventions, the screw pump, is still used in some places in the Middle East almost 2,000 years after this scientific breakthrough. The device is used to lift water from irrigation canals and rivers on to dry fields.

▲ **Great inventor**
Archimedes of Syracuse in Sicily was born around 285BC and spent most of his life in the city studying mathematics. He was killed when the Romans invaded Syracuse in 211BC.

◀ **Variable weight**
One of Archimedes' great breakthroughs was the discovery that an object weighs less in water than in air. This is why you can lift quite a heavy person in a swimming pool. The reason for this buoyancy is the natural upward push, or upthrust, of the water.

weight

weight balanced by upthrust of water

◀ **Pump it up**
Archimedes' screw is a very simple but effective pump. Inside a tube is a spiral, which scoops up the water as someone turns the handle at the top.

YOU WILL NEED

Clean plastic bottle, scissors, self-hardening clay, strong tape, length of clear plastic tubing, bowl of water, blue food colouring, empty glass bowl.

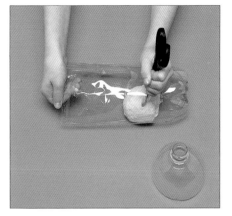

1 Cut off the top of the bottle. Put a lump of clay on the outside of the bottle, about 5cm from the end as shown. Punch a hole here with scissors and cut off the bottom of the bottle.

2 Cut a strip of strong tape about the same length as the bottle. Tape along the length of the cut bottle as shown above. The tape will give the plastic tubing extra grip later on.

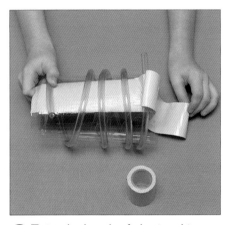

3 Twist the length of plastic tubing around the bottle from one end to the other as shown above. Secure the length of tubing in place with another piece of tape.

4 Place a few drops of blue food colouring into a bowl of water. Add the food colouring slowly and stir thoroughly so that the colour mixes evenly with the water.

The invention of the Archimedes' screw made it possible for farmers to water their fields from irrigation channels. It saved them having to walk back and forth between the river and fields with their buckets.

5 Place one end of the bottle and tubing construction into the bowl of coloured water. Make sure that the tube at the opposite end is pointing towards an empty bowl.

6 Twist the bottle around in the bowl of blue water. As you do so, you will see the water start to travel up the tube and gradually fill up the empty bowl.

Roman groma

The Romans were great builders and engineers. As the legions conquered foreign lands, they built new roads to carry their supplies and messengers. The roads were very straight, stretching across hundreds of kilometres. Romans used a groma to measure right angles and to make sure roads were straight. The roads were built with a slight hump in the middle so that rainwater drained off to the sides. Some were paved with stone. Others were covered with gravel or stone chips.

Roman engineers also used their skills to carry water supplies to their cities by building aqueducts. They built great domes, arched bridges and grand public buildings all across the Roman Empire, making use of whatever local materials were available. The Romans were also the first to develop concrete, which was cheaper and stronger than stone.

▲ ▼ Travel in the Empire
The Romans built strong stone bridges to carry roads high above rivers. Where ground was liable to flooding, they built embankments called aggers. Roman legions could move around the Roman Empire with astonishing speed thanks to the road system.

◄ Building a road
The Romans laid a deep solid foundation of large stones for their roads. They covered this with a smooth surface of flat stones, with a raised centre, or crown, so that rainwater could drain off at either side. They also dug ditches along the sides of the road to carry the water away.

YOU WILL NEED

Large piece of strong corrugated card, ruler, pencil, scissors, balsa wood pole, masking tape, card square, PVA glue and glue brush, non-hardening modelling material, aluminium foil, string, large sewing needle, broom handle, acrylic paints, paint brush, water pot.

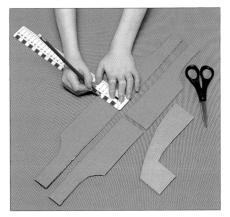

1 Cut three pieces of card, two measuring 20 x 6cm and one 40 x 6cm. Cut another piece at 15 x 12cm for the handle of the groma. Cut them into the shapes shown above.

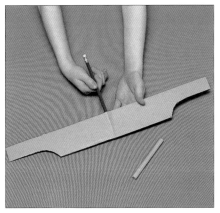

2 Measure to the centre of the long piece of card and use a pencil to make a slot here between the corrugated layers. The slot is for the balsa wood pole.

3 Slide the balsa wood pole into the slot and tape the card pieces in a cross. Use the card square to ensure the four arms of the groma are at right angles. Glue and secure with tape.

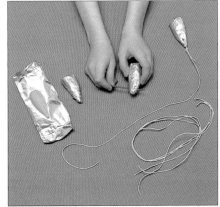

4 Roll lumps of modelling material into four small cones and cover each of them with aluminium foil. Then thread string through the tops of the cones to complete the plumblines.

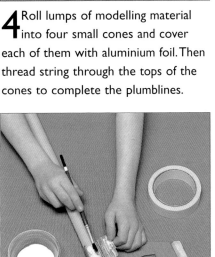

5 Make a hole at the end of each arm of the groma. Tie on the four plumblines. The cones must all hang at the same length – 20cm will do. If the clay is too heavy, use wet newspaper.

6 Split the top of the corrugated card handle piece. Wrap it around the balsa wood pole and glue it in place as shown. Split and glue the other end to the broom handle. Now paint the groma.

Slot the arms on to the balsa wood pole. Use the plumb lines as a guide to make sure the pole is vertical. The arms can be used to line up objects in the distance.

Viking coin and die

The Vikings were successful merchants. Their home trade was based in towns such as Hedeby in Denmark, Birka in Sweden and Kaupang in Norway. As they settled new lands, their trading routes began to spread far and wide. In about AD860, Swedish Vikings opened up new routes eastwards through the lands of the Slavs. Merchants crossed the Black Sea and the Caspian Sea and travelled to Constantinople (Istanbul), capital of the Byzantine Empire, and to the great Arab city of Baghdad. Viking warehouses were full with casks of wine from Germany and bales of woollen cloth from England. There were furs and walrus ivory from the Arctic and timber and iron from Scandinavia. Vikings also traded in wheat from the British Isles and rye from Russia.

beeswax

Viking coin

silk

▲ Trade exchange
The Vikings used coins for buying and selling goods at home, but they bartered items with their trading partners. In the East, the Vikings supplied furs, beeswax and slaves in exchange for silk, jewellery and spices.

▲ Trading nations
The routes taken by the Viking traders fanned out south and east from Scandinavia. Trade networks with the East linked up with older routes such as the Silk Road to China. Everyday items such as pottery and wool were brought back from western Europe.

YOU WILL NEED

Self-hardening clay, cutting board, rolling pin, pencil, thin card, pair of compasses, scissors, PVA glue and glue brush, bronze and silver paint, paintbrush, water pot, modelling tool.

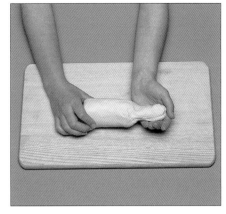

1 Roll out a large cylinder of clay on to a cutting board and model a short, thick handle at one end. This will be the die. Leave the die to dry and harden in a warm place.

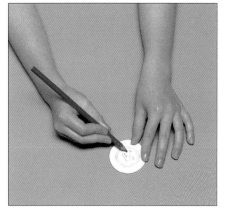

2 Draw a circle on a piece of thin card and cut it out. It should be about the same size as the flat end of the die. Use a pencil to draw a simple shape on the card circle.

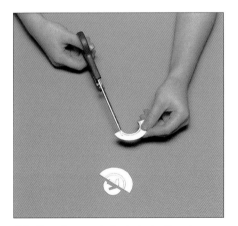

3 Cut the card circle in half and then cut out the shape as shown above. If you find it hard to cut out your coin design, you could ask an adult to help you.

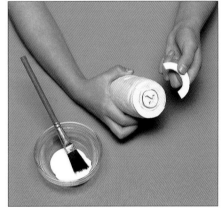

4 Glue the paper pieces on to the end of the die with PVA glue as shown above. You may need to trim the pieces if they are too big to fit on to the end.

5 Viking dies would have been made of bronze or some other metal. Paint your die a bronze colour to look like metal. Make sure you give the die an even coat of paint. Leave to dry.

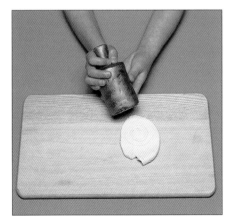

6 Roll out some more clay. Use the die to stamp an impression on to the clay. Use a modelling tool to cut around the edge of the circle, let the coin dry and then paint it silver.

A die is a metal stamp used to punch the design on to the face of a coin. The first coins showing Viking kings were made in England.

Mayan codex

The Maya were the first, and only, Native American people to invent a complete system of writing. They wrote their symbols in folding books called codices. These symbols were also carved on buildings, painted on pottery and inscribed on precious stones. Maya writing used glyphs (pictures standing for words) and also picture-signs that represented sounds. The sound-signs could be joined together – similar to the letters of our alphabet – to spell out words and to make complete sentences.

▼ Names of days

These symbols represent some of the names of the 20 days from the farmers' calendar. The 20 days made one month, and there were 13 months in a year. These symbols were combined with a number from one to 13 to give the date, such as 'Three Vulture'. Days were named after familiar creatures or everyday things, such as the lizard or water. Each day also had its own god. Children were often named after the day on which they were born.

eagle	motion	rain	dog
serpent	monkey	reed	deer
grass	jaguar	vulture	rabbit
house	lizard	death's head	water

YOU WILL NEED

Thin card, ruler, pencil, scissors, white acrylic paint, large paintbrush, water pot, eraser, tracing paper (optional), acrylic paints, palette, selection of paintbrushes.

1 Draw a rectangle measuring 100 x 25cm on to the piece of thin card and cut it out. Cover the rectangle with an even coat of white acrylic paint. Leave it to dry.

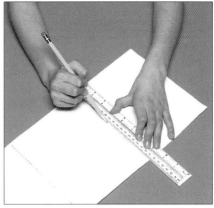

2 Using a pencil and ruler lightly draw in four fold lines, 20cm apart on the painted card, as shown above. This will divide the card into five equal sections.

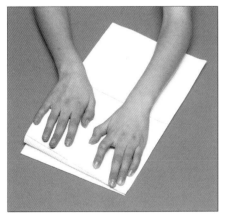

3 Carefully fold along the pencil lines to make a zig-zag book as shown in the picture above. Unfold the card and rub out the pencil lines with an eraser.

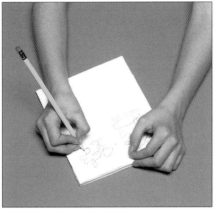

4 To decorate your codex you could trace or copy some of the Maya codex drawings from these pages. Alternatively, you could make up your own Mesoamerican symbols.

5 Paint your tracings or drawings using bright acrylic paints. Using the Maya numbers on this page as a guide, you could add some numbers to your codex, too.

zero

one

four

five

eleven

eighteen

▲ Maya numbers

The Maya number system used only three signs – a dot for one, a bar for five and the shell symbol for zero. Other numbers were made using a combination of these symbols.

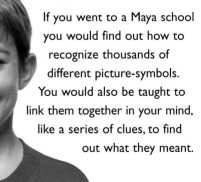

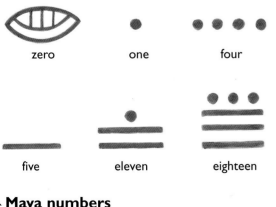

If you went to a Maya school you would find out how to recognize thousands of different picture-symbols. You would also be taught to link them together in your mind, like a series of clues, to find out what they meant.

Inca quipu

Inca mathematicians used a decimal system (counting in tens). One way of recording numbers and other information was on a quipu. Knots on strings may have represented units, tens, hundreds, thousands or even tens of thousands. To help with their arithmetic, people also placed pebbles or grains of maize in counting frames.

The Incas worked out calendars of twelve months by observing the Sun, Moon and stars as they moved across the sky. They knew that these movements marked regular changes in the seasons. Inca farmers used the calendar to tell them when to plant crops. Inca priests set up stone pillars outside the city of Cuzco to measure the movements of the Sun.

As in Europe at that time, astronomy, which is the study of the stars, was linked with astrology, which is the belief that the stars and planets influence human lives. Incas saw the night sky as being lit up by mythical characters. On dark nights, Inca priests looked for the band of stars that we call the Milky Way. They called it Mayu (Heavenly River) and thought its shape mirrored that of the Inca Empire.

▲ **Star gazer**
An Inca astrologer observes the position of the Sun. He is using a quipu. The Incas believed that careful watching of the stars and planets revealed their influence on our lives. They named one constellation (star pattern) the Llama. It was believed that it influenced llamas and those who herded them.

YOU WILL NEED

Waste paper, rope and string of various thicknesses, long ruler or tape measure, scissors, acrylic paints, paintbrush, water pot, 90cm length of thick rope.

1 Cut the rope and string into about 15 lengths, each measuring between 15cm and 80cm. Paint them in bright colours such as red, yellow and green. Leave them to dry.

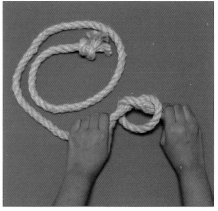

2 To make the top part of the quipu, take another piece of thick rope, measuring about 90cm in length. Tie a firm knot at each end of the rope as shown above.

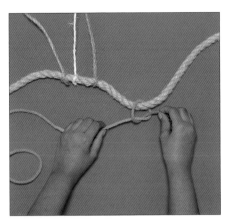

3 Next, take some thinner pieces of rope or string of various lengths and colours. Tie each one along the thicker piece of rope, so that they hang down on the same side.

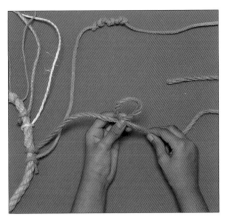

4 Tie knots in the thinner pieces of rope or string. One kind of knot that you might like to try begins by making a loop of rope as shown in the picture above.

5 Pass one end of the rope through the loop. Pull the rope taut but do not let go of the loop. Repeat this step until you have made a long knot. Pull the knot tight.

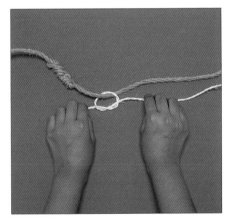

6 Make different sizes of knots on all the ropes and strings. Each knot could represent a family member, school lesson or other important details of your life.

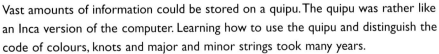

7 Now add some more strings to the ones you have already knotted. Your quipu may be seen by a lot of people, but only you will know what the ropes, strings and knots mean.

Vast amounts of information could be stored on a quipu. The quipu was rather like an Inca version of the computer. Learning how to use the quipu and distinguish the code of colours, knots and major and minor strings took many years.

Illuminating letters

Before a way of printing words was invented in the late 1400s, the only way to have more than one copy of a book was to write it out by hand again. This was a time-consuming process and made books very valuable and rare. The pages were often beautifully illustrated with decorated letters like the one in this project. In Christian countries, many noble households had only one book, the Bible. Most books were kept in monastery libraries. In the 1500s, the only people who could read and write well were usually monks, priests or nuns. Kings and queens were also well educated.

▲ **Lasting letters**
Many books were written on parchment, which was longer lasting than paper.

YOU WILL NEED

Pair of compasses, pencil, ruler, 16 x 16cm white art paper, eraser, acrylic paints, fine-tipped artist's paintbrushes, water pot, scissors, gold paint, PVA glue and glue brush, 26 x 26cm richly coloured mounting card.

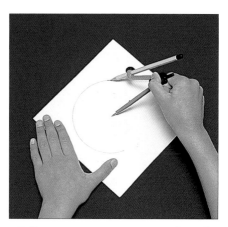

1 Set your compasses to a radius of 6cm. Place the point at the centre of the 16 x 16cm white art paper and carefully draw a 12cm-diameter circle as shown above.

2 Keep the compasses at the same radius. Place the point 2cm away from the centre of the first circle. Then draw a second circle so that it overlaps with the first.

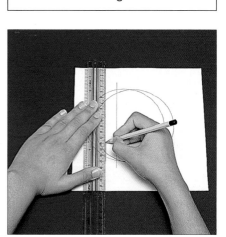

3 Place the ruler on the left-hand side of the overlapping circles. Draw two vertical lines from the top to the bottom of the circles. The lines should be around 2cm apart.

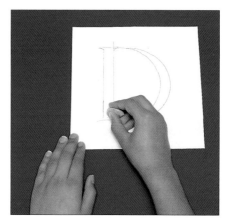

4 Rub out the lines of the circles to the left of the ruled lines. Use the ruler to draw two short lines to cap the top and the bottom of the vertical stem of the letter 'D'.

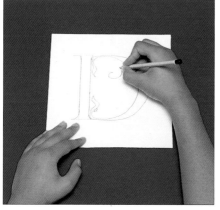

5 Extend the inner curve of the D into two squiggles at the top and bottom of the stem. Draw two simple spirals in the centre of the D as shown in the picture above.

6 Use the spirals to help you to fill in the rest of your letter design. Double the curving lines to make stems and leaves and add petals. Look at the picture above as a guide.

7 Draw two lines to the left of the vertical stem of the letter 'D'. Add a squiggle and leaves at the top and bottom and also some decorative kinks as shown above.

8 Use a pencil and ruler to draw a border around the letter about 1.5cm wide. Leave the right-hand side until last. See how the curve of the D tips out of the border.

9 First paint the border using a bright colour. Carefully fill in the whole design using other colours. Make sure that each colour is dry before you fill in the next one.

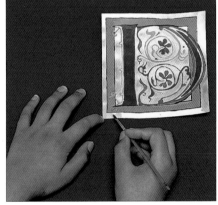

10 When the paint is dry, use a ruler and scissors to trim the whole artwork to a 15cm square. Then colour in the gold background. Leave it to dry on a flat surface.

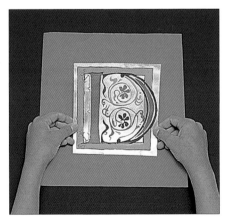

11 Spread PVA glue over the back surface of the artwork. Then carefully place it squarely in the centre of the mounting card to add a richly coloured border to the letter.

In days gone by, there was lots to do before work could start. Animal skins were soaked, scraped and dried to make parchment. Feathers were sharpened into quills, and inks were mixed. Take time to draw and paint your illuminated letter. Monks and scribes were fast workers, but they still only managed to do two or three drawings a day. A mistake meant that the scribe would have to start again.

Pirate map

The area chosen for this map is the Spanish Main, which was a hotbed of pirates from the 1620s to the 1720s. When the Spanish first explored the Americas in the late 1400s, much of the surface of the Earth was unmapped territory. Consequently, many countries sent out naval expeditions to draw up detailed charts of distant waters for use by their trading ships. Most pirates had to make do with jotting down the details of the islands, coral reefs, coastlines and river mouths as they sailed by.

Sometimes the pirates were lucky enough to capture a ship with up-to-date charts. Bound volumes of detailed nautical charts, known as waggoners, were a valuable prize for any pirate captain. When sailing into an unknown harbour, ships had to take a local guide or pilot on board – at the point of a sword if necessary.

YOU WILL NEED

Thick art paper, ruler, pencil, scissors, strong black tea left to cool, paintbrush, fine black felt-tipped pen, eraser, colouring pencils, large and small bottle tops.

1 Measure a rectangle on the paper, measuring 35 x 27cm. Cut it out, making the edges of the rectangle wavy and uneven to give the map an authentic aged and worn appearance.

2 Scrunch up the paper rectangle tightly into a ball. Then open and smooth it out on a flat surface. The creases will remain in the paper, giving the final map a used look.

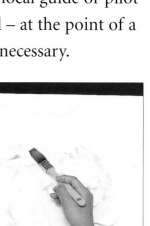

3 Paint cold, strong tea on to the scrunched-up paper. The tea will stain the paper brown to look like old, worn parchment. Then leave the paper until it is completely dry.

4 Smooth out the paper again. Stain the edges darker by brushing on more tea all the way around, from the outside inwards. Leave the paper to dry completely.

5 Copy the coastline from the finished map in step 12 using your pencil. If you prefer, you could make up your own map or trace a map from another book and use that instead.

6 Carefully draw over the coastline with your fine black felt-tipped pen. Make sure that you do not smudge the ink with your hand. Rub out the pencil lines with an eraser.

7 Colour the land green and the sea blue with your pencils. Graduate the colours, making them a little darker along the coastline and then fading inland or out to sea.

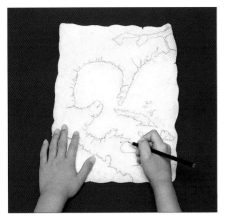

8 Choose three landmarks such as bays or headlands. Use the pencil and ruler to draw lines from the landmarks to a spot in the sea. This will mark your ship's position.

9 Use the ruler and a black pencil to draw straight lines across this position, or co-ordinate, as shown above. The resulting lines will look like the spokes of a wheel.

10 Draw around the large bottle top to make a circle on part of the map. Then draw an inner circle with the small bottle top to make a compass shape as shown.

The best maps for pirates would show safe ports and harbours, creeks and inlets. They also needed to show where there were dangerous coasts, currents and rocks. Maps had to be looked after so that they did not wear out with heavy use and in the damp conditions at sea.

11 Draw small, elongated triangles pointing outwards from the inner circle along the co-ordinate lines. Use bright colouring pencils to fill in the triangles on the compass.

12 You can add more decorative details, such as arrow points on the compass, dolphins in the sea and treasure chests on the land. Your pirate map will then be complete.

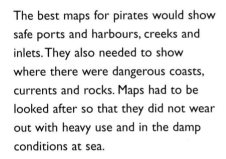

Transport

People have often had to travel long distances for basic needs such as building materials, food and water. At first, everything had to be carried by foot, but the task was made much easier with the domestication of animals such as oxen and horses. These animals could be used to transport people and their goods. The invention of the wheel and of boats also revolutionized transport. Early vehicles, such as carts and sailing boats, enabled people to travel much greater distances across land and by sea. Heavy loads could be transported much more quickly, too.

▲ Speed boat

An Arctic hunter paddles his kayak. Sea kayaks were used to hunt sea mammals such as seals and walruses. These sleek, light one-person vessels were powered and steered by a double-bladed paddle. The design was so successful that kayaks are still used today.

▲ Riding without stirrups

Celtic leader Vercingetorix, seen here mounted on his horse. Big, strong horses were introduced into western Europe from the lands east of the Black Sea. These mounts gave Celtic hunters and warriors a great advantage over their enemies.

◀ Camel caravan

Arab merchants blazed new trails across the deserts. They traded in luxuries such as precious metals, gemstones and incense. The trading group, with its processions of camels, is known as a caravan. Camels are well-suited to life in the desert. They have enlarged, flexible foot pads, which help to spread their weight across the soft desert sand. Camels also have one or two humps on their backs, which contain fat and act as a food reserve.

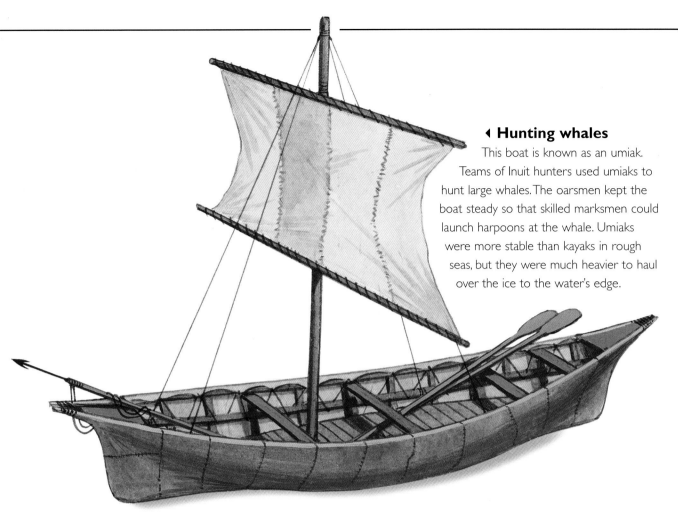

◀ Hunting whales

This boat is known as an umiak. Teams of Inuit hunters used umiaks to hunt large whales. The oarsmen kept the boat steady so that skilled marksmen could launch harpoons at the whale. Umiaks were more stable than kayaks in rough seas, but they were much heavier to haul over the ice to the water's edge.

▼ Icemobile

A modern-day Inuit of the Arctic drives his scooter across the ice and snow. Scooters have largely replaced the traditional sledges pulled by dogs. For most present-day Arctic people, life is a mix of ancient and modern ways. Many Arctic groups use the new technologies of the developed world while holding on to the traditions and culture of their ancestors.

▲ High and mighty

A Mayan nobleman is carried in a portable bed known as a litter. This one is made from the hide of a wildcat called the jaguar. Spanish travellers reported that the Aztec emperor was carried in a litter, too. Blankets were also spread in front of the emperor as he walked, to stop his feet touching the ground.

Sumerian coracle

The ancient region of Mesopotamia was situated on the Tigris and Euphrates rivers and their tributaries. The rivers formed a vital transport and communications network around the country. The Sumerians lived in the south of Mesopotamia around 6,000 years ago. Later on, the land in north Mesopotamia became known as Assyria. The boat in this project is modelled on a Sumerian coracle. These boats were made from leather stretched over a wooden frame.

◄ Rowing the boat
The Phoenicians lived by the Mediterranean Sea to the west of Mesopotamia. They were the great sailors and shipbuilders of the time. Their ships were large and many-oared, and the sailors worked out how to navigate using the stars.

▲ Built on the banks
The ancient city of Nimrud, on the banks of the River Tigris, was part of the Assyrian Empire. Archaeologists have found the remains of several palaces and temples here.

1 Make a dish shape using the self-hardening clay. It should be about 14cm long, 11cm wide and 4cm deep. Make a mast hole for the dowelling mast. Attach it to the base.

2 Trim the excess clay around the top of the boat to smooth it out. Use a cocktail stick to make four small holes through the sides of the boat. Let the clay dry out completely.

3 When it is dry, paint the boat a light brown base colour. Cover the work surface with paper. Then use a brush and your fingers to flick contrast colours and create a mottled effect.

4 Put a drop of glue inside the mast hole. Put more glue around the end of the dowelling mast and then push it into the hole. The mast should stand upright in the centre of the clay boat.

5 Wait until the glue has dried and the mast stands firm. Then paint a layer of water-based varnish all over your boat. Let the first layer dry and then paint another layer over it.

6 Take two lengths of string about 60cm long. Tie the end of one piece through one of the holes you made earlier, around the top of the mast and into the opposite hole.

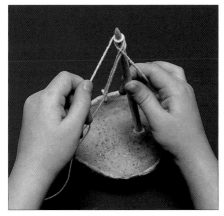

7 Complete the rigging of the boat by tying the other piece of string through the empty holes and around the top of the mast as before. Trim off the excess string.

Coracles, such as the one you have made, had a mast for a light sail. It was probably steered using oars or a punt pole. Small boats such as these are still used today on the River Euphrates.

Assyrian chariot

The wooden wheel was first used as a means of transport around 5,500 years ago in what is now the Middle East, and the news spread fast in neighbouring regions. In Sumerian times (3000–2000BC), wild asses hauled chariots, while oxen and mules were used for heavy loads. By about 900BC, the time of the Assyrian Empire, spoked wheels had replaced the earlier wheels made from a single piece of solid wood.

Roads varied in quality through the Assyrian Empire. Local paths were little more than tracks, but there were good roads between the main towns. These were well-maintained so that messengers and state officials could reach their destination quickly. The Assyrians also perfected the art of chariot warfare, which gave them a big advantage over enemies who were fighting on foot. They could attack their enemies from above, and were able to move around the battlefield quickly.

▲ Unstoppable warriors
Chariots were mainly used by Assyrian kings and their courtiers when hunting and in battle. At rivers, the chariots were dismantled and carried across on boats, and people swam across using inflated animal skins as life belts.

▲ Wheeled procession
An artist's impression of a Sumerian funeral procession shows the solid wood wheel design of the early chariots in Mesopotamia. Rituals involving death and burial were an important part of Sumerian life.

▲ Education of a prince
Learning to drive a chariot and fight in battle were part of King Ashurbanipal's education as crown prince of Assyria. He was also taught foreign languages, how to ride a horse and hunt.

YOU WILL NEED

Thick card, pair of compasses, ruler, pencil, scissors, pen, masking tape, newspaper, two card tubes, flour and water (for papier mâché), cream and brown acrylic paints, paintbrush, water pot, two pieces of dowelling measuring 16cm long, needle, four cocktail sticks.

1 Measure and cut out four card circles, each one measuring 7cm in diameter. Carefully use the scissors to make a hole in the centre of each circle. Enlarge the holes with a pen.

2 Cut out two sides for the chariot, 12cm long and 7.5cm wide as shown, one back 9 x 7.5cm, one front 15 x 9cm, one top 9 x 7cm and one base 12 x 9cm.

3 Trim the top of the front to two curves as shown above. Stick the side pieces to the front and back using masking tape. Then stick on the base and the top of the chariot.

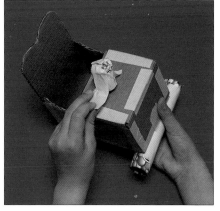

4 Roll up a piece of old newspaper to make a cylinder shape about 2.5cm long and tape it to the chariot as shown above. Attach the card tubes to the bottom of the chariot.

The solid-wheeled chariot you have made is based on a very early chariot design made in northern Mesopotamia around 4,000 years ago. When the spoked wheel replaced the solid wheel, chariots became lighter, faster and easier to steer.

5 Mix a paste of flour and water. Dip newspaper strips into the paste to make papier mâché. Cover the chariot with layers of papier mâché until the card underneath is hidden. Let it all dry.

6 Paint the chariot. Use a needle to make a hole at each end of a piece of dowelling. Insert a cocktail stick, add a wheel and insert into the tube. Secure another wheel at the other end. Repeat.

Chinese sampan

From early in China's history, its rivers, lakes and canals were its main highways. Fisherfolk propelled small wooden boats across the water with a single oar or pole at the stern. These were often roofed with mats, like the sampans still seen today. Large wooden sailing ships, which we call junks, sailed the open ocean. They were either keeled or flat-bottomed, with a high stern and square bows. Their sails were made of matting stiffened with strips of bamboo.

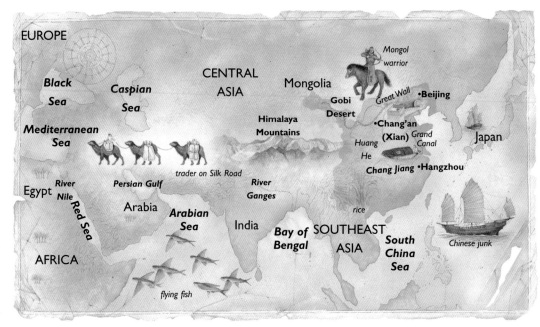

▲ Trading places

The map shows the extent of the Chinese Empire during the Ming Dynasty (1368–1644). Merchants transported luxury Chinese goods along the Silk Road, from Chang'an (Xian) to the Mediterranean Sea. Chinese traders also sailed across the South China Sea to Vietnam, Korea and Japan.

Templates

Cut templates B, C, D and G from thick card. Cut templates A, E and F from thin card.

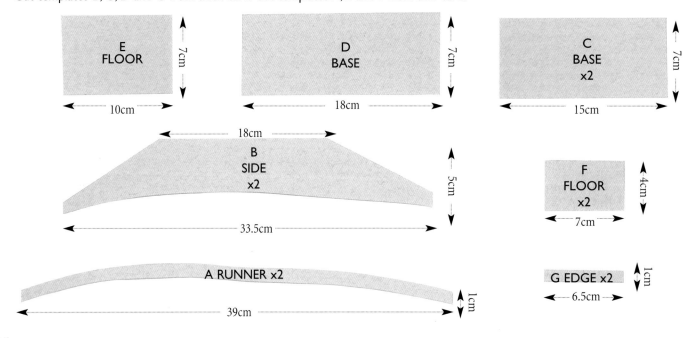

E FLOOR — 7cm — 10cm

D BASE — 7cm — 18cm

C BASE x2 — 7cm — 15cm

B SIDE x2 — 18cm — 5cm — 33.5cm

F FLOOR x2 — 4cm — 7cm

A RUNNER x2 — 39cm — 1cm

G EDGE x2 — 1cm — 6.5cm

YOU WILL NEED

Thick card, thin card, ruler, pencil, scissors, PVA glue and glue brush, masking tape, seven wooden barbecue sticks, string, thin yellow paper, acrylic paints (black and dark brown), paintbrush and water pot.

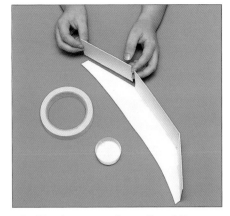

1 Glue base templates C and D to side template B as shown. Hold the pieces together with strips of masking tape while the glue dries. When dry, remove the masking tape.

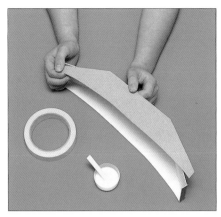

2 Glue the remaining side B to the boat. Stick the runner A pieces to the top of the sides and secure with masking tape. Make sure the ends jut out at the front and back of the boat.

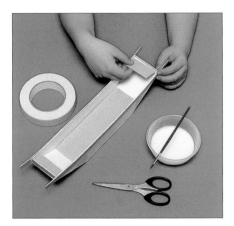

3 Glue floor E to the centre of the base. Add the floor F templates to the ends of the base. Stick the edge G templates in between the edge of the runners and leave to dry.

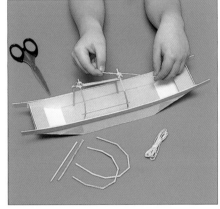

4 Bend two barbecue sticks into arches. Cut two sticks into struts. Tie struts to the sides and top of the arches. Make a second roof by bending three barbecue sticks into arches.

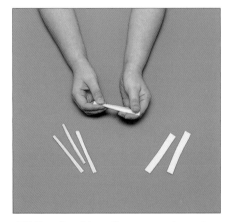

5 Cut the thin yellow paper into strips, each measuring 10 x 1cm. Fold the strips in half as shown. The strips will make the matting for the two boat roofs.

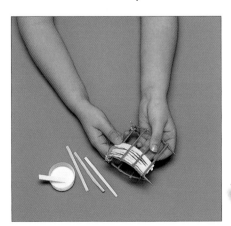

6 Paint the boat and the roof sections and allow them to dry. Glue the roof matting strips to the inside of the roofs. When the glue is dry, place the roofs inside the boat.

To add the finishing touch to your sampan, make a boatman with an oar and rowlock to propel the vessel.

Native American canoe

Many tribes native to North America were nomadic. At first, walking was their only form of transport across the land. Hunting and trade were the main reasons for travelling. Infants were carried in cradleboards, while Inuit babies in the Arctic were put into the hoods of their mothers' parkas. Carrying frames called travois were popular among those living on the Plains. Dogs dragged these frames at first, but horses replaced them in the late 1600s. Tribes could then travel greater distances to fresh hunting grounds.

Much of North America is covered with rivers, streams and lakes, and tribespeople were also skilled boatbuilders. There were bark canoes in the woodlands, large cedar canoes on the Northwest Coast and kayaks in the Arctic.

Templates

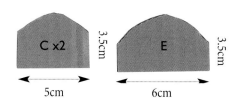

C x2 — 5cm — 3.5cm

E — 6cm — 3.5cm

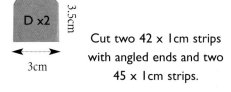

D x2 — 3cm — 3.5cm

Cut two 42 x 1cm strips with angled ends and two 45 x 1cm strips.

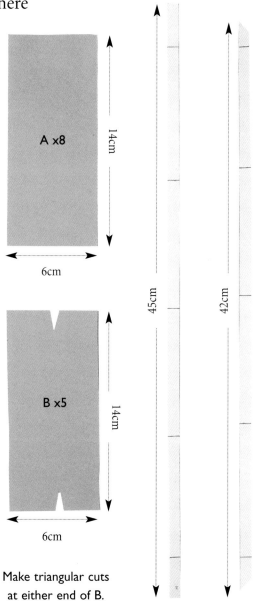

A x8 — 14cm — 6cm

B x5 — 14cm — 6cm

45cm

42cm

Make triangular cuts at either end of B.

▲ **Into America**

The first Native Americans probably came from Siberia. They crossed land bridges at the Bering Strait around 13,000BC.

Arctic Ocean

N

Siberia

Bering Strait

Bering Sea

Alaska

Pacific Ocean

Northwest Coast

Thick card (templates C, D and E), brown paper (templates A and B), cream paper (strips), pencil, ruler, scissors, PVA glue and glue brush, needle and thread, brown acrylic paints, paintbrush, water pot.

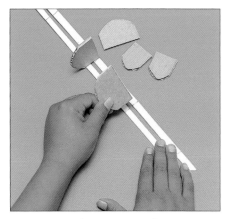

1 Cut out the templates. Starting at the centre, mark five evenly spaced lines on one 45cm strip and one 42cm strip. Glue the side of the E template across the centres of the strips.

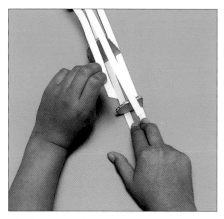

2 Glue the C template either side of the E template and the D templates either side of those. Line up the other two strips and glue those to the other sides of the C, D and E templates.

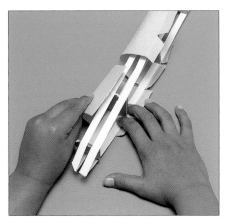

3 Glue the two 45cm strips and the two 42cm strips at both ends. Glue templates B to the frame, making sure that the cuts at either end fit over the C, D and E templates as shown.

4 Tidy up the ends by gluing the excess paper around the frame of the canoe. Place four A templates over the gaps, and glue them to the top of the frame as shown above.

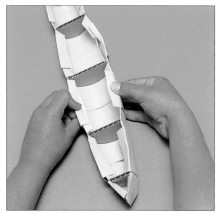

5 Stick the remaining A templates over the inside of the boat until the entire frame is covered. Carefully fold over and glue the tops of the paper around the top edge of the boat.

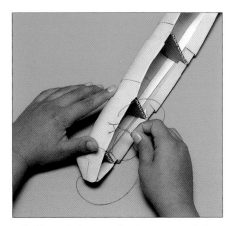

6 Thread the needle. Sew around the top edge of the boat to secure the flaps. Paint your boat brown and add detail. Make two paddles from thick card and paint them dark brown.

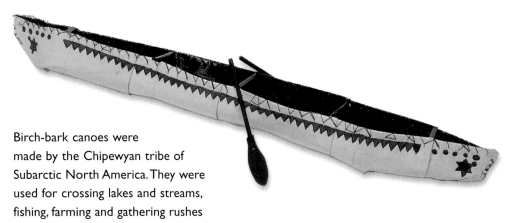

Birch-bark canoes were made by the Chipewyan tribe of Subarctic North America. They were used for crossing lakes and streams, fishing, farming and gathering rushes and wild rice.

Viking longship

The Vikings were excellent seafarers and were among the most skilful shipbuilders the world has ever seen. One of the most famous Viking vessels was the longship. It could be up to 23m in length. This long sailing ship was used for ocean voyages and warfare, and it was shallow enough to row up a river. The longship had an open deck without cabins or benches. The rowers sat on hide-covered sea chests that contained their possessions, weapons and food rations.

Templates

Ask an adult to cut out the card and balsa wood templates following the measurements shown.

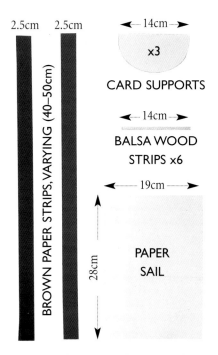
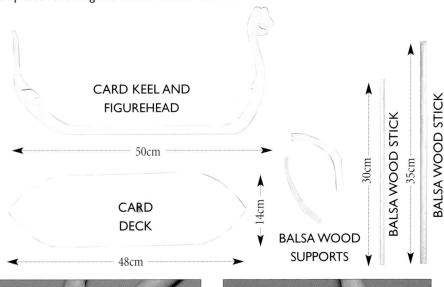

CARD KEEL AND FIGUREHEAD

50cm

CARD DECK

14cm

48cm

BALSA WOOD SUPPORTS

30cm

BALSA WOOD STICK 35cm

BALSA WOOD STICK

2.5cm 2.5cm

BROWN PAPER STRIPS, VARYING (40–50cm)

14cm
x3
CARD SUPPORTS

14cm
BALSA WOOD STRIPS x6

19cm
28cm
PAPER SAIL

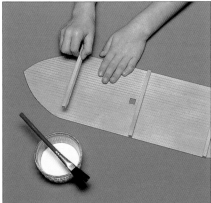

1 Paint the deck shape black on one side and brown on the other. Use a pencil to mark planks 5mm apart on the brown deck. Pierce a hole for the mast. Glue on three of the 14cm balsa strips.

2 Glue three 14cm balsa wood strips to the other side of the deck as in step 1, matching them with the planks on the other side. Then glue on the three card supports as crossbeams.

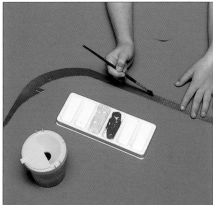

3 Carefully paint one side of the keel and figurehead template using bright red acrylic paint. Leave it to dry, turn it over and paint the other side of the card using the same colour.

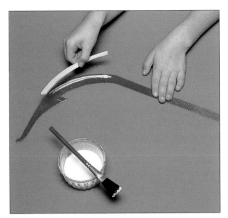

4 When the paint is completely dry, glue the two balsa wood supports either side of the curved parts of the keel as shown. These will strengthen the keel and figurehead section.

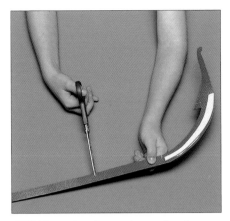

5 When the glue is dry, make three marks along the length of the keel, each one at a point that matches up to the crossbeams of the deck section. Use scissors to cut slots as shown.

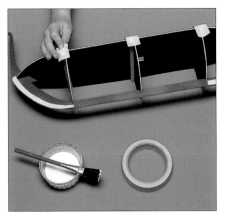

6 Slide the deck crossbeams into position on the keel slots and glue them in place. Use masking tape to make sure the joins are firm while the glue is drying.

7 Use varying lengths of pale and dark brown paper strips for the planks, or 'strakes', along each side of the keel. Carefully glue each strip into position along each side.

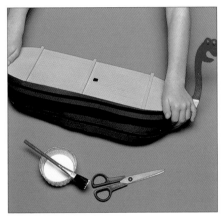

8 Continue gluing the strips into place. Alternate pale and dark brown strips to finish. Trim the excess off each strip as they get lower so that they form a curve.

9 Make a mast using the 30cm long balsa wood and the 35cm long stick. Glue the two pieces firmly together and bind them with string as shown above.

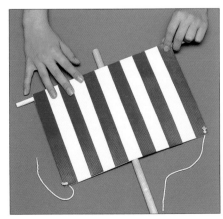

10 Paint the sail with red and white stripes. Glue the sail to the 30cm cross beam. Attach string as rigging at the bottom of the sail. Add card eyes to the dragon on the figurehead.

A longship put to sea with a crew of around 30 fighting men. Each one knew how to fight as well as how to man the oars. The round shields of the warriors were slotted along the side of the ship. An awning of sailcloth could be erected to keep off the sun or rain.

Celtic wagon

After around 200BC, the Celts began to build fortified settlements as centres of government, craftwork and trade. Some grew up around existing hill forts or villages; others occupied fresh sites. The Romans called them *oppida* (towns). Some of the oppida were very large. For example, Manching, in southern Germany, covered about 380ha, and its protective walls were over 7km long.

Travel between the settlements was slow and difficult compared with today. There were no paved roads, although the Celts did build causeways of wood across marshy ground. Overland journeys were on foot or horseback, and only the wealthiest chieftains could afford to drive a chariot. The Celts used wooden carts pulled by oxen to transport heavy loads of farm produce, timber or salt. Oxen were very valuable and were the main source of wealth for many farmers.

YOU WILL NEED

White card, pencil, ruler, scissors, felt-tipped pen, PVA glue and glue brush, balsa wood, masking tape, sandpaper, pair of compasses, drawing pins, leather thong, silver paint, paintbrush, water pot.

▼ Linking up

European trade routes followed great river valleys or connected small ports along the coast, from Ireland to Portugal. The Celts spread far and wide and, by 200BC, had even attacked and defeated the Romans in various parts of Europe and had attacked Greece's holy temple of Apollo at Delphi.

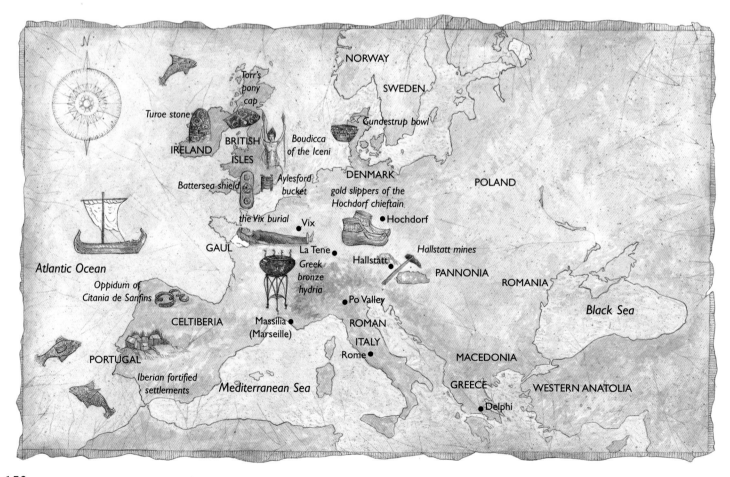

1 Measure and cut out a piece of white card to 29 x 16cm. Using a ruler and felt-tipped pen, draw lines to make a border 2cm in from the edges of the card as shown above.

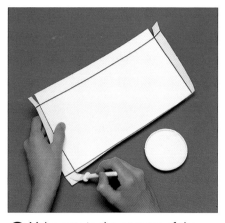

2 Make cuts in the corners of the card as shown above. Score along each line and then fold the edges up to make a box shape. This will be the body of the wagon.

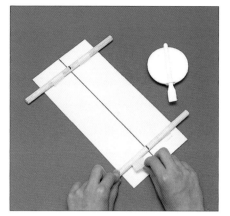

3 Measure and cut out another piece of card to 27 x 12cm. Take two lengths of balsa wood, each measuring 20cm. Glue and tape the balsa across the card 4cm in from the two ends.

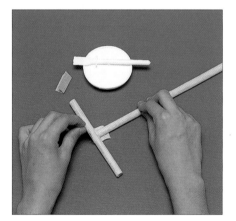

4 Take two sticks of balsa , one 26cm in length and the other 11cm. Sand the end of the long stick to fit against the shorter piece. Glue the pieces together. Secure with tape until dry.

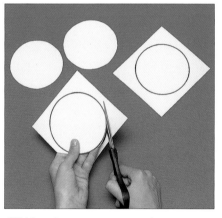

5 Use the compasses to draw four circles on four pieces of card, each measuring 10cm in diameter. Then carefully cut the circles out as shown above.

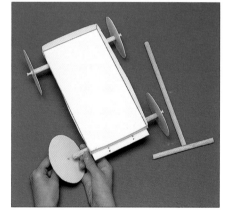

6 Glue the wagon body on to the card with balsa attached. Fix the wheels to the balsa wood shafts by pressing a drawing pin through the centre of each wheel.

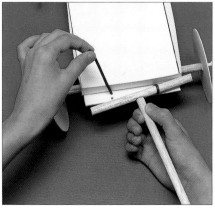

7 Pierce two holes in the front of the wagon. Thread the leather thong through the holes and tie it to the T-shaped steering pole you made in step 4. Paint the wagon silver.

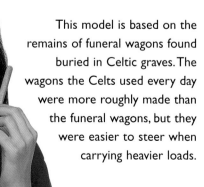

This model is based on the remains of funeral wagons found buried in Celtic graves. The wagons the Celts used every day were more roughly made than the funeral wagons, but they were easier to steer when carrying heavier loads.

Arctic sledge

The surface of the Arctic Ocean is partially frozen throughout the year and in winter snow covers the land. In the past, sledges were the most common way of travelling over ice and snow. They were made from bone or timber and lashed together with strips of animal hide or whale sinew. They glided over the snow on runners made from walrus tusks or wood. Arctic sledges had to be light enough to be pulled by animals, yet strong enough to carry an entire family and its belongings. In North America, the Inuit used huskies to pull their sledges. In Siberia and Scandinavia, however, reindeer were used to pull sledges. In ancient times, Arctic peoples often used skis to get around. They were made of wood and the undersides were covered with strips of reindeer skin. The hairs on the skin pointed backwards, allowing the skier to climb up hills.

▲ Getting around

Today, petrol-driven snowmobiles make for quick and easy travel across the Arctic ice. In the past, Arctic people relied on animals to pull sledges across the frozen landscape.

YOU WILL NEED

Thick card, balsa wood, ruler, pencil, scissors, craft knife, PVA glue and glue brush, masking tape, pair of compasses, barbecue stick, brown acrylic paint, paintbrush, water pot, string, chamois leather, card box.

▼ Travelling companions

Huskies are well adapted to life in the harsh Arctic cold. Their thick coats keep the animals warm in bitterly cold temperatures as low as −50°C, and they can sleep peacefully in the fiercest of blizzards. The snow builds up against their fur and insulates them.

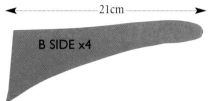

Templates

Draw the shapes on card (use balsa wood for template C) and cut them out. Glue two A templates together. Repeat this for the other two A templates. Do the same for all four B templates. Cover all the edges with masking tape.

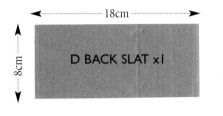

6.5cm

A RUNNERS x4

54cm

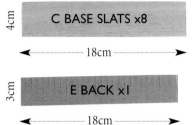

4cm

C BASE SLATS x8

18cm

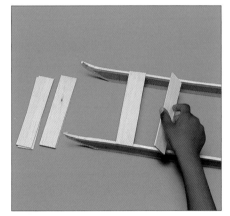

18cm

8cm

D BACK SLAT x1

8cm

21cm

B SIDE x4

3cm

E BACK x1

18cm

1 Using a small pair of compasses, make small holes along the top edge of the glued A templates. Use the end of a barbecue stick to make the holes a little larger.

2 Glue the balsa wood slats C in position over the holes along the A templates as shown above. You will need to use all eight balsa wood slats. Glue back slat D in position.

3 Carefully glue the B templates and the E template to the edge of the sledge as shown above. Allow the glue to dry completely before painting the model sledge.

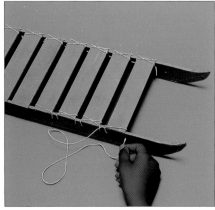

4 Thread lengths of string through the holes to secure the slats on each side. Decorate the sledge with a chamois-covered card box and secure it to the sledge.

Inuit hunters used wooden sledges pulled by huskies to hunt for food over a large area. The wood was lashed together with animal hide or sinew.

Military Technology

People have always needed to defend themselves or fight for more land. The development of weaponry runs alongside the growth of the earliest civilizations. Weapons were needed, not just for hunting, but for defence and attack. From the very beginning, there were two distinct types of weapon – missiles such as the spear, which could be thrown from a distance, and strike weapons such as the club, which could be used at close quarters. Stone Age people used sharpened flints for daggers and spears. As time passed, these early weapons were eventually replaced by steel swords, heavy artillery and pistols.

▲ War chariot

The Hittites controlled much of Anatolia (modern-day Turkey) and parts of Mesopotamia and Syria. Much of their military success came from their skill as charioteers. Hittite chariots held up to three people, one to drive the horses and two to fight. Hittite charioteers were feared by their enemies.

◄ Light cavalry

The horse of this Persian warrior is not protected by armour so it needs to be fast and nimble. The warrior carries only a short spear so that he can make a quick strike against the enemy and then retreat.

◀ Crow's beak

The Romans developed a grappling weapon called a corvus, which looked rather like a crow's big beak. (*Corvus* is the Latin word for crow.) It was a hinged gangplank with a spike that sank into the enemy ship's deck. Twin-hulled siege vessels carried fighting towers to the enemy.

◀ Warriors of Japan

Japanese warriors were called samurai. They fought with deadly, two-handed swords and were dressed in padded armour and helmets. The armour consisted of bamboo plates sewn on to a padded jacket. Mythical motifs decorated the helmet.

Top heavy ▶

This Asian soldier carries an array of different weapons – a sword, a dagger, bow and arrows, an axe and a shield. The sword was heavier at the tip, which gave it greater weight when he swung it down on his enemy.

Greek sword and shield

When the Greeks went to war, it was usually to engage in raids and sieges of rival city states. Major battles with foreign powers were rare, but the results could be devastating. Army commanders chose their ground with care and relied heavily on the discipline and training of their troops. The core of a Greek army consisted of foot soldiers called hoplites. Their strength as a fighting force lay in their bristling spears, singled-edged swords, overlapping shields and sheer weight of numbers.

YOU WILL NEED

String, pencil, pair of compasses, ruler, thick card, scissors, PVA glue and glue brush, gold paper, silver paper, masking tape, black acrylic paint, paintbrush, water pot, aluminium foil.

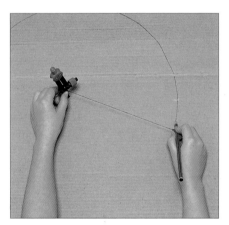

1 Tie a 22cm length of string to a pencil and compasses. Draw a circle on to the card as shown above. Carefully cut around the edge of the circle using your scissors.

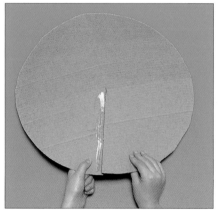

2 Make a cut into the centre of the circle as shown above. Line the edges of the cut with glue. Overlap the edges by 2cm, and stick them together so that your shield is slightly curved.

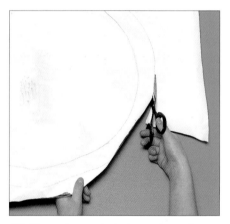

3 Place the card circle on to a piece of gold paper and draw around it. Draw another circle 2cm larger than the first. Cut out the larger gold circle as shown above.

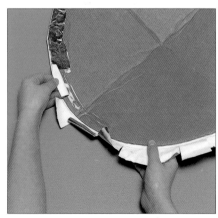

4 Glue the gold circle on to your card circle. Make small cuts along the edges of the gold paper. Fold the edges over the circle and glue them to the back of the card circle.

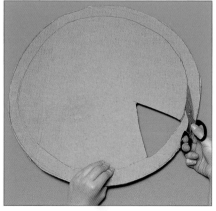

5 Use the string and compasses to draw another 22cm circle on to a piece of card. Draw another circle 2cm smaller than the first. Cut out the inner circle in stages with scissors.

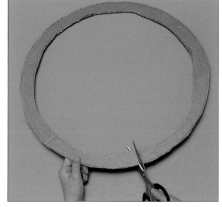

6 Cut through the ring of card in one place as shown above. Cover the ring with silver paper. Wrap the silver paper around the card and glue it down securely.

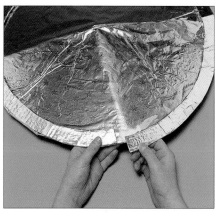

7 Glue the silver ring around the edge of the gold shield as shown above. You will have to overlap the ends of the silver disc to fit it neatly around the shield.

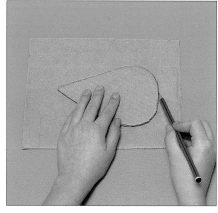

8 Draw a teardrop shape measuring about 12 x 8cm on to a piece of thick card. Cut the teardrop shape out. Make four more teardrops using the first one as a template.

9 Cover and glue silver paper to three teardrops and gold paper to two teardrops. Then glue the teardrops on to the gold shield, keeping them evenly spaced, as shown above.

Greek swords were mostly short, single-edged blades made of iron. They were designed for close hand-to-hand fighting. Sometimes blades were curved, but more often they were straight and broad.

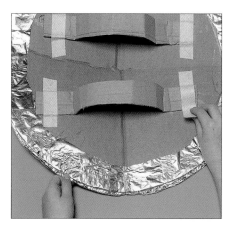

10 Cut out two strips of card 25 x 3cm. Curve the strips. Glue them on to the back of the shield to make a pair of handles big enough for your arm to fit through. Secure with masking tape.

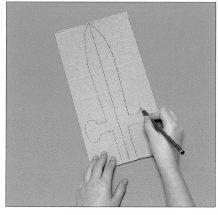

11 Cut out a rectangle of thick card measuring 30 x 15cm. Draw a line down the centre of the card as a guide. Draw a sword shape on to the card.

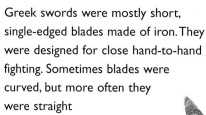

12 Cut out the sword shape from the card. Paint one side of the handle with black paint. When the paint is dry, turn the sword over and paint the other side of the handle.

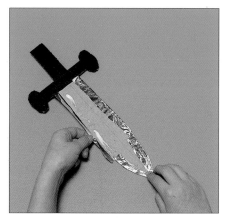

13 Finally, cover both sides of the blade of the sword with aluminium foil and neatly glue it down. The aluminium foil will give the blade of your sword a shiny surface.

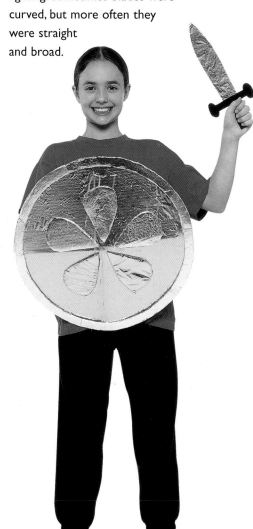

Greek warrior greaves

Greek men of fighting age were expected to swear allegiance to the army of the city in which they lived. In Sparta, the army was on duty all year round. In other parts of Greece, men gave up fighting in autumn to bring in the harvest and make wine. The only full-time soldiers in these states were the personal bodyguards of a ruler or mercenaries who fought for anyone who paid them.

Armies consisted mainly of hoplites (foot soldiers) and cavalry (soldiers on horseback). The cavalry was less effective in war because the riders had no stirrups. The cavalry was mainly used for scouting, harassing a beaten enemy and carrying messages. The hoplites, who engaged in hand-to-hand combat, were the most important fighting force. The hoplites' armour consisted of a shield, helmet, spear, sword and metal shin protectors called greaves.

copper

tin

▲ Raw materials

Tin and copper were smelted to make bronze, the main material for Greek weaponry and armour. Bronze is harder than pure copper and, unlike iron, does not rust. As there was no tin in Greece, it was imported.

◄ Show of strength

The fighting force known as the hoplites was made up of middle-class men who could afford the weapons. The body of a hoplite soldier was protected by a bronze cuirass (a one-piece breast- and backplate). The cuirass was worn over a leather tunic. Their bronze helmets were often crested with horsehair. Shields were usually round and decorated with a symbol.

YOU WILL NEED

Clear film, plaster bandages, bowl of water, sheet of paper, kitchen paper, scissors, cord, gold paint, paintbrush, water pot.

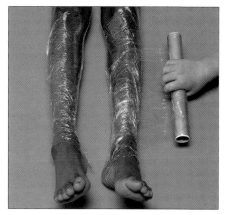

1 Ask a friend to help you with the first three steps. Loosely cover both of your legs (from your ankle to the top of your knee) in clear film as shown above.

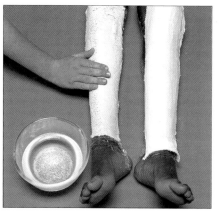

2 Soak each plaster bandage in water. Working from one side of your leg to another, smooth the bandage over the front of your leg. You will need to use several layers of plaster bandage.

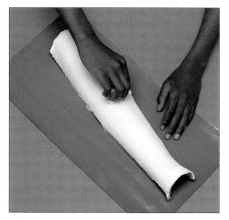

3 When you have finished, carefully remove each greave. Set them out on a sheet of paper. Dampen some kitchen paper and use it to smooth the greaves down. Let them dry.

4 Trim the edges of the greaves with scissors to make them look neat. Measure four lengths of cord to fit around your legs – one below each knee and one above each ankle.

Greaves were attached to the lower legs to protect them in battle. Real greaves were made of bronze and would have been very heavy.

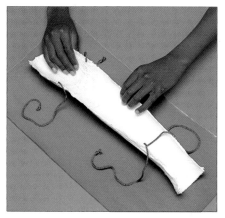

5 Lay the first cord in place on the back of the greaves where you want to tie them to your legs. Fix the cord in place with more wet plaster bandages. Repeat with the other three cords.

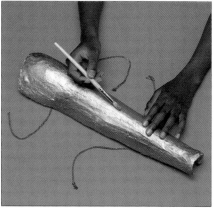

6 Let the plaster bandages dry with the cord in place. Now paint each greave with a layer of gold paint. Once they are dry, tie the greaves around your legs.

Roman armour

Soldiers in the Roman Empire were well equipped for fighting. A legionary was armed with a *pugio* (dagger) and a *gladius* (short iron sword) for stabbing and slashing. He also carried a *pilum* (javelin) of iron and wood. In the early days, a foot soldier's armour was a mail shirt, worn over a short, thick tunic. Officers wore a cuirass – a bronze casing that protected the chest and back. By about AD35, plate armour replaced the mail shirt. The iron plates (sections) were joined by hooks or leather straps. Early shields were oval, and later ones were oblong with curved edges. They were made of layers of wood glued together, covered in leather and linen. A metal boss over the central handle could be used to hit an enemy who got too close.

▲ Overseas duty
Roman soldiers were recruited from all parts of the enormous empire, including Africa. They were often sent on duty far away from their home. This was to make sure they did not desert.

▲ Highlight of the games
The chariot was not used a great deal by the Roman army. However, it was a popular sight at the public games held in Rome and other major cities. Most chariots held two people. If there was only one rider, he would tie the reins around his waist. This kept his hands free so he could use his weapons.

YOU WILL NEED

Tape measure, A1 sheets of metal-coloured card (one or two, depending on how big you are), pencil, scissors, PVA glue and glue brush, 2m length of cord, pair of compasses.

1 Measure the size of your chest. Cut out three strips of card, 5cm wide and long enough to fit around your chest. Cut out some thinner strips to stick the three main ones together.

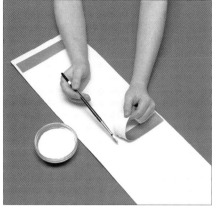

2 Lay the wide strips flat and glue them together with the thin strips you cut. Let the glue dry. The Romans would have used leather straps to hold the wide metal pieces together.

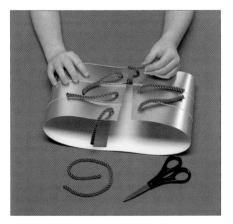

3 Bend the ends together, silver side out. Pierce a hole in the end of each strip using scissors. Cut 6 pieces of cord and pull through, knotting the cord at the back.

4 Cut a square of card as wide as your shoulders. Use a compass to draw a 12cm-diameter circle in the centre. Cut the square in half and cut away the half circles.

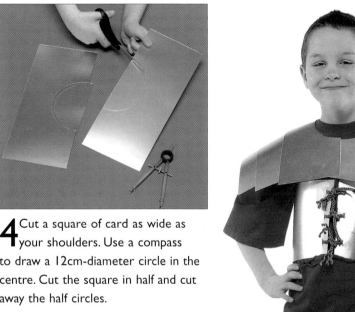

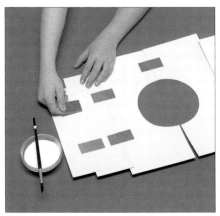

5 Use smaller strips of card to glue the shoulder halves together but leaving a neck hole. Cut out four more strips, two a little shorter than the others. Attach them in the same way.

Put the shoulder piece over your head and tie the chest section around yourself. Now you are a legionary ready to do battle with the enemies of Rome. Metal strip armour was invented during the reign of Emperor Tiberius (AD 14–37). Originally, the various parts of metal strip armour were hinged and joined together either by hooks or by buckles and straps.

Japanese samurai helmet

During the Japanese civil wars, between 1185 and 1600, emperors, shoguns (governors) and daimyo (nobles) all relied on armies of samurai (warriors) to fight their battles. Samurai were skilled fighters. Members of each army were bound together by a solemn oath, sworn to their lord, who gave them rich rewards. The civil wars ended around 1600, when the Tokugawa Dynasty of shoguns came to power. After this time, samurai spent less time fighting, and served their lords as officials and business managers.

YOU WILL NEED

Thick card, pin, string, ruler, felt-tipped pen, scissors, tape measure, balloon, petroleum jelly, PVA glue, water, bowl, newspaper, pencil, self-hardening clay, bradawl, plain paper, gold card, acrylic paints, paintbrush, water pot, glue brush, masking tape, split pins, two 20cm lengths of cord.

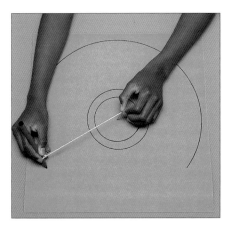

1 Draw an 18cm-diameter circle on to a piece of thick card using the pin, string and felt-tipped pen. Draw two larger circles 20cm and 50cm in diameter as shown above.

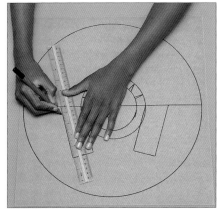

2 Draw a line across the centre of the three circles using a ruler and felt-tipped pen. Draw lines for tabs in the middle semicircle. Add two flaps either side as shown above.

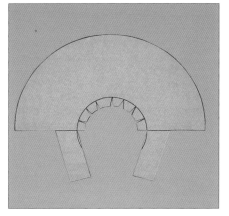

3 Cut out the neck protector piece completely to make the shape shown above. Make sure that you cut carefully around the flaps and along the lines between the tabs.

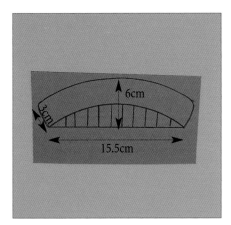

4 Draw the peak of the helmet on to another piece of card, using the measurements on the template above. Cut out the peak. Then blow up a balloon to the size of your head.

5 Cover the balloon with petroleum jelly. Tear newspaper into strips and add three layers of papier mâché (with two parts PVA glue to one part water) on the top and sides of the balloon.

6 When the papier mâché is dry, pop the balloon and trim the edges of the papier mâché cast. Ask a friend to make a mark with a pencil on either side of the helmet by your head.

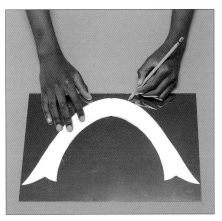

7 Place a piece of self-hardening clay under the pencil marks. Make two holes – one above and one below each pencil mark – with a bradawl. Repeat on the other side of the helmet.

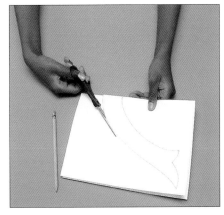

8 Fold a piece of A4 paper in half and draw a horn shape on to it using the design shown above as a guide. Cut out the shape so that you have an identical pair of horns.

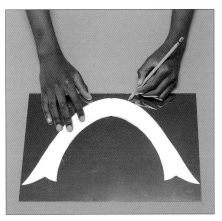

9 Take a piece of A4 gold card. Using the paper horns you have drawn as a template, draw the shape on to the gold card. Carefully cut the horns out of the card.

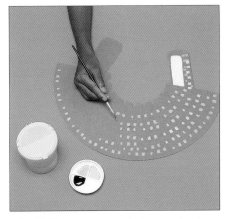

10 Paint a weave design on both sides of the neck protector and a cream block on each flap as shown above. Paint your papier mâché helmet brown. Leave the paint to dry.

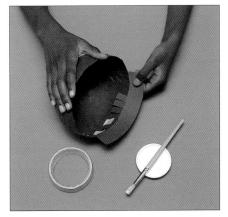

11 Cut and bend back the tabs on the peak of the helmet. Making sure the peak is at the front, glue the tabs to the inside as shown above. Secure the tabs with masking tape.

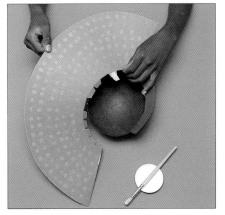

12 Now bend back the front flaps and the tabs of the neck protector and glue them to the helmet as shown above. Leave the helmet to dry completely.

13 Glue the gold card horns to the front of the helmet as shown above. Secure the horns with split pins. Use more split pins to decorate the ear flaps.

14 To wear your helmet, thread a piece of cord through one of the holes in the side of the helmet and tie a knot in the end. Thread the other end of the cord through the second hole. Repeat on the other side. Samurai helmets were often decorated with lacquered wood or metal crests mounted on the top of the helmet.

Viking shield

Norse warriors wore their own clothes and brought their own equipment to battle. Most wore caps of tough leather. Where metal helmets were worn, these were usually conical, and they sometimes had a bar to protect the nose. Viking raiders wore their everyday tunics and breeches and cloaks to keep out the cold. A rich Viking jarl (chieftain) might have a *brynja,* which was a shirt made up of interlinking rings of iron. Vikings also carried spears of various weights, longbows, deadly arrows and long-shafted battle axes on board the longship. The most prized weapon of all was the Viking sword. The blades of the swords were either made by Scandinavian blacksmiths or imported from Germany. A heavy shield, about 1m across, was made of wooden planks. It had an iron boss (central knob) and a rim of iron or leather.

◄ **Mass attack**
Viking raiders disembark from their longships and race into action armed with their single-headed war axes. The Vikings used various axes for hacking the enemy at close range or for throwing from a distance. These iron-bladed weapons were often elaborately decorated.

1 Use the compasses to draw a small circle in the centre of a large piece of card. Then use a length of string tied to a pencil to draw a big circle for the shield as shown above.

2 Cut out the large circle. Then draw on a big, bold design such as the one shown in this project. Paint the shield with red and gold paint. Let the paint dry completely.

3 Use an upside down paper party bowl for the shield's central boss, or knob. Scrunch up some newspaper into a flattened ball and use masking tape to fix it to the top of the bowl.

4 Spread PVA glue over the bowl and then cover it with aluminium foil. In Viking times, an iron boss would have strengthened the shield and protected the warrior's hand.

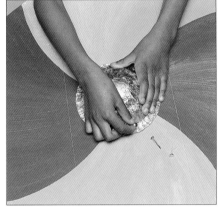

5 Glue the boss to the centre of your shield. Secure the boss with brass split pins punched through its edge and through the card of the shield.

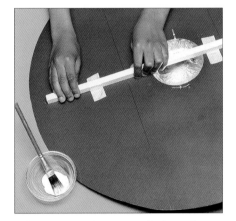

6 Ask an adult to cut a hole in the back of the shield where the boss is. Glue the strip of wood to the back of the shield and secure with strips of tape as shown above.

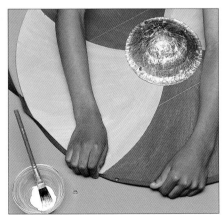

7 Attach the bias binding all the way around the rim of the shield using some brass split pins or small dabs of glue. Your shield is now ready for use in a Viking battle!

Give your shield its own Viking-style name, such as 'Fist of Thor' or 'Swordbreaker'.

Knight's helmet

A helmet protected the eyes and head of a soldier in battle. A flat-topped helmet was introduced in the 1100s, but it did not deflect blows as well as a rounded helmet. The basinet helmet of the 1300s had a moveable visor over the face. The introduction of hinges and pivots in the 1400s meant that a shaped helmet could be put on over the head and then closed to fit securely. From the 1500s, lighter, open helmets were worn. These were more comfortable, and soldiers could move around freely in battle.

YOU WILL NEED

Pencil, ruler, two large sheets of silver card, craft knife, cutting board, one large sheet of gold card, scissors, stapler and staples, PVA glue and glue brush, masking tape, pair of compasses, brass split pins.

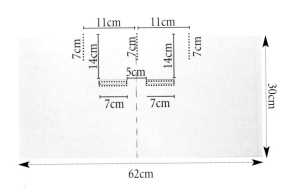

1 Using a pencil and the picture above as your guide, draw the template for your knight's helmet on to one large sheet of silver card. Measure and mark all the dotted lines as shown.

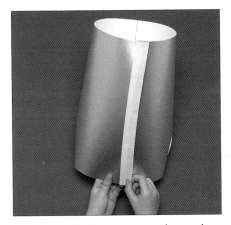

2 Use a craft knife, ruler and cutting board to cut out the eye slits. Cut a 62 x 4cm strip of gold card. Place it beneath the slits and draw the slits on the gold card. Cut them out.

3 Cut along the three 7cm dotted lines on the silver card template. Fold the card inwards as shown above to make the helmet curve. Staple the top of each overlapping section.

4 Curve the helmet into a long tube shape as shown. Glue and staple the tube together at the top and bottom. Secure the join with masking tape until the glue dries.

5 Set the compasses to 10cm and draw a circle (diameter 20cm) on the remaining silver card. Then set the compasses to 9cm and draw an inner circle with a diameter of 18cm.

6 Cut around the larger circle. Make cuts at 4cm intervals to the line of the inner circle. Bend them inwards and overlap. Fix tape on the back of the silver card to hold them in place.

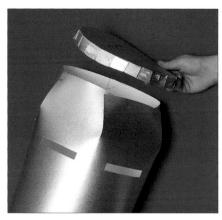

7 Put spots of glue on the outside top rim of the helmet. Hold the body of the helmet with one hand and carefully glue the top of the helmet on to the body with the other.

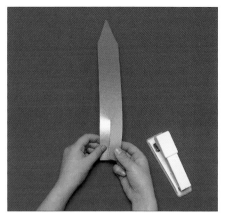

8 Cut a 30 x 4cm strip of gold card. Cut a point on one end of the strip. Cut a 7cm slit down the middle of the other end. Overlap the two flaps by about 1cm and staple.

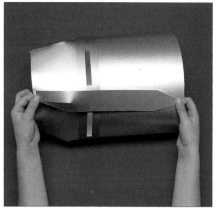

9 Staple the gold eye-slit strip into a circular band. Slip this over the helmet so that the eye slits match up. Glue it into position. Staple the nose piece in place between the eye slits.

10 Cut a 62 x 2cm strip of gold card. Put spots of glue at intervals along the back of the card strip. Carefully stick the gold band around the top of the helmet.

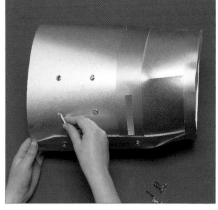

11 Use the pointed end of the compasses to pierce four holes on each 'cheek' of the helmet. Then make three holes along the nose piece. Push a brass split pin into each hole.

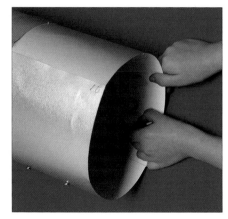

12 Split the pins and then cover the back of each one with strips of masking tape so that it does not scratch your face when you wear the helmet.

The Christian knights who fought in the Crusades wore helmets rather like the one you have made. Between 1095 and 1272, European knights fought Muslim countries for control of the Holy Land. The Crusaders wore a chainmail shirt, called a hauberk, with a cloth surcoat over the top. European armourers picked up some design ideas from their Muslim enemies, who were well-known for their skills in forging steel.

Medieval trebuchet

It took careful planning to mount a siege attack. Giant catapults played a vital role at the beginning of a siege. Their job was to weaken the castle defences before the foot soldiers moved in close. A deadly fire of boulders and flaming ammunition killed and maimed the fighters inside the castle walls. In the 1100s, powerful siege machines called trebuchets were developed to launch larger rocks over the castle walls. Decaying animals were also thrown over in the hope of spreading disease among the people inside.

YOU WILL NEED

Card, pencil, ruler, craft knife, cutting board, two 28cm and two 16cm strips of balsa, wood glue, pair of compasses, 32cm and 22cm length balsa dowelling, two 20 x 3.5 x 0.5cm pieces of balsa, scissors, four 25cm lengths square balsa dowelling, string, self-hardening clay, matchbox, acrylic paints, paintbrush, water pot.

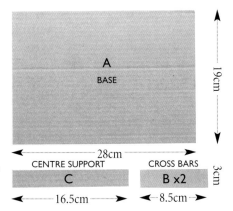

Copy the templates shown in the picture above on to a piece of thick card. Use a craft knife, cutting board and ruler to cut the pieces out.

1 Lay the base template A on to the work surface. Use wood glue to stick the two 28cm lengths and two 16cm lengths of balsa wood along each edge of the base section.

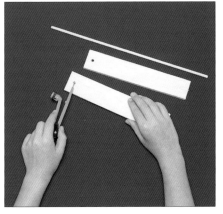

2 Use a sharp compass point to pierce a hole through the end of each of the 20cm lengths of balsa wood for side supports as shown in the picture above.

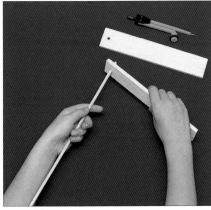

3 Use the sharp end of a pencil to make the hole a little bigger. Then push one of the pieces of balsa dowelling through each of the holes to make them the same diameter.

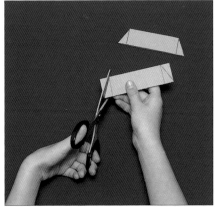

4 Use a pencil and ruler to draw two lines, 1cm from each end of the two crossbar sections B. Make a diagonal cut from the corners to the lines to make slanting edges.

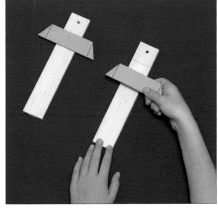

5 Lay the 20cm balsa wood side supports on to the work surface. Glue the crossbars into position below the holes, about 3.5cm below the top of the side supports as shown above.

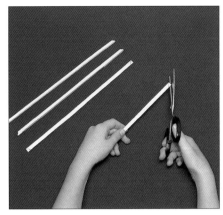

6 Place the four 25cm lengths of balsa wood dowelling on to the work surface. Ask an adult to help you cut both ends of the dowelling diagonally at an angle of 45 degrees.

7 Glue the supports mid-way along each long side of the base section. Glue the 25cm long balsa strips 2.5cm from the corners to form a triangle over the top of the support as shown.

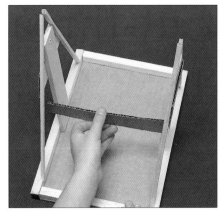

8 Glue along the ends on one side of the 16.5cm long centre support section. Stick it into place on the side supports, about 9cm from the base, as shown above.

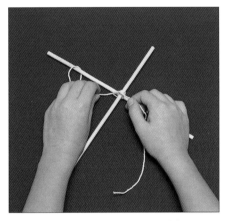

9 Make a 'T' shape with the 32cm and 22cm lengths of round dowelling with the shorter cross piece about 9cm from the top. Bind the pieces together tightly with string.

10 Roll some small pieces of clay in the palm of your hands. Mould one big ball about 5cm in diameter and some smaller balls. Leave the clay balls to one side to dry.

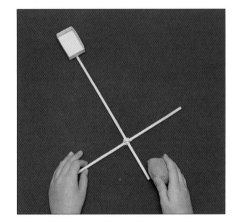

11 Glue the back of the inside of a matchbox. Stick this to the bottom of the long arm of the cross piece. Stick the big clay ball on to the other end.

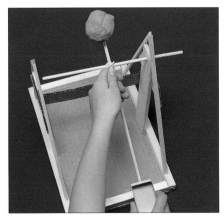

12 Fit the arms of the cross piece into the holes in the balsa wood side supports so that the matchbox is at the bottom. Finally, paint the model with acrylic paints.

Put some clay balls into the matchbox and raise the big ball. Drop it to let the missiles fly! The clay missiles fired from your trebuchet are unlikely to do much damage. However, with its long weighted arm and open support frame, the model trebuchet operates in much the same way as the real thing. The word trebuchet comes from a French word for a similar device that was used for shooting birds.

Cut-throat cutlass

The swords carried by pirates have varied greatly over the ages. Ancient Greek pirates fought with a 60cm-long, leaf-shaped blade or with a curved cut-and-thrust blade called a kopis. Their Roman enemies fought with a short sword called a gladius. Viking swords were long and double-edged for heavy slashing. The rapier, introduced in the 1500s, was a light sword with a deadly, pointed blade, but it was too long and delicate for close-range fighting on board ship. The cutlass was the ideal weapon for that.

▲ **Pirate sword**
The most common and useful pirate weapon was probably the cutlass, used from the 1600s onwards.

YOU WILL NEED

Two pieces of stiff card measuring 45 x 5cm, pencil, scissors, PVA glue and glue brush, newspaper, masking tape, one piece of stiff card (30 x 10cm), one cup of flour, half a cup of water, mixing bowl, spoon, sandpaper, brown and silver acrylic paint, two paintbrushes, water pot, black felt-tipped pen, ruler, wood varnish.

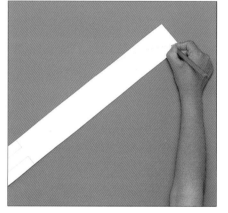

1 Take one piece of the stiff card measuring 45 x 5cm. Carefully pencil in an outline of a cutlass blade and hilt on to the piece of card as shown above.

2 Use a pair of scissors to cut the shape out. Use this as a template to lay on the second piece of card. Draw around the template and then cut out a second cutlass shape.

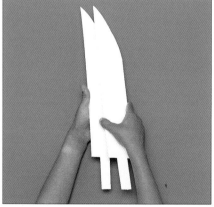

3 Lay the two matching sections of the cutlass on top of each other as shown above. Glue them together. The double thickness gives the finished cutlass extra strength.

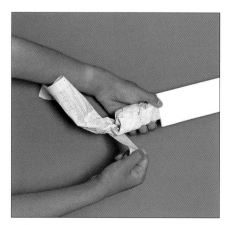

4 Twist a piece of newspaper into thick strips to wind around the hilt. The newspaper should be thick enough to make a comfortable handgrip. Bind the newspaper with masking tape.

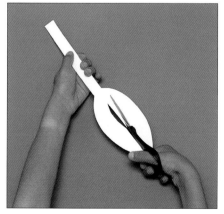

5 Draw the shape of a cutlass handle on to the stiff piece of 30 x 10cm card and cut it out. Make a cut down the middle of the wide end to about 2.5cm short of the stem as shown.

6 Tape the narrow stem of the handle to the end of the cutlass hilt. Bend the rest of the handle around to slot over the curved edge of the blade as shown above.

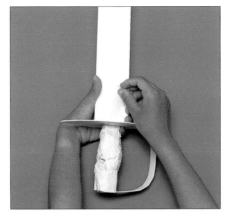

7 Make sure the oval lies flat against the hilt of the cutlass to form the hand guard. Use masking tape to seal the slit and to secure the handle of the cutlass to the blade.

8 Pour the flour into a mixing bowl and slowly add the water, a spoon at a time, mixing as you go. The mixture should form a smooth, thick paste similar to pancake batter.

9 Tear newspaper into short strips and coat these with the paste. Cover the cutlass with three layers of papier mâché. Leave the cutlass in a warm place for several hours.

10 When the cutlass is dry, smooth it down using sandpaper. Paint the cutlass with acrylic paint as shown. Allow the first coat to dry thoroughly and then apply another coat of paint.

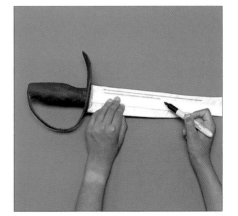

11 When the second coat of paint is completely dry, use a black felt-tipped pen and ruler to add fine details on the blade of the cutlass as shown above.

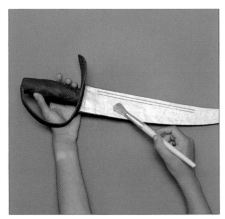

12 Finally, use a clean paintbrush to apply a coat of wood varnish to the blade and hilt. This will toughen the cutlass as well as giving it a menacing glint.

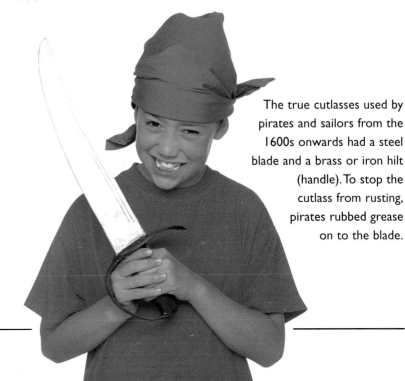

The true cutlasses used by pirates and sailors from the 1600s onwards had a steel blade and a brass or iron hilt (handle). To stop the cutlass from rusting, pirates rubbed grease on to the blade.

Customs, Arts and Entertainment

Once the necessities of survival were mastered, people could turn their attention to spiritual and creative matters. In this section you will discover that many artefacts and customs were inspired by religious beliefs and rituals. You will also find early versions of sports, games, toys and entertainment that are still enjoyed by people today.

Arts and Crafts

N o other species on the Earth has shown the ability to express itself in the same artistic way as humans. Archaeological evidence has shown that, over 50,000 years ago, the earliest humans decorated their bodies, tools and shelters with simple patterns and symbols. People then began to portray the world around them by painting images on the walls of caves. As society evolved, so did the art and culture. This is charted in history – from the early treasures of the Egyptian tombs, through the Golden Age of Greek art and Roman architecture, to the Renaissance – the revival of art and culture that formed the transition from the Middle Ages to our modern world.

▲ Cave paintings
Paintings of animals made more than 17,000 years ago have been found painted on the walls deep inside caves in Europe. They often show animals that were hunted at that time.

▲ Horse of stone
An early Egyptian stone carving of a horse's head, dating from around 1500BC. In Egyptian society, skilled artists and craftworkers formed a middle class between the poor labourers and rich officials and nobles.

◄ Skilled ironworkers
Metalworkers were some of the most important members of Celtic society. They made many of the items that Celtic people valued most, such as this magnificent iron axe head. It took many years for a metalworker to learn all the necessary skills, first to produce the metal from nuggets or lumps of ore, and then to shape it.

▲ Buried treasures

This Greek wine serving bowl, or krater, was found in a wood-lined burial chamber at Vix in eastern France. The tomb belonged to a Celtic princess, who was buried around 520BC. The princess was wearing a torc, or necklace, made of almost half a kilogram of pure gold.

Monster watch ▶

The entrance to an Assyrian palace in Mesopotamia was guarded by statues of huge monsters called lamassus. Lamassus were strange creatures with the bodies of lions or bulls, the wings of mighty birds, human heads and caps to show they had divine powers. Lamassus had five legs. The extra limb was so that they did not appear one-legged if seen from the front.

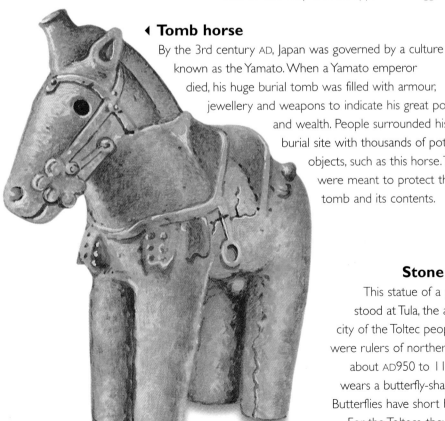

◀ Tomb horse

By the 3rd century AD, Japan was governed by a culture known as the Yamato. When a Yamato emperor died, his huge burial tomb was filled with armour, jewellery and weapons to indicate his great power and wealth. People surrounded his burial site with thousands of pottery objects, such as this horse. They were meant to protect the tomb and its contents.

Stone warrior ▶

This statue of a proud warrior stood at Tula, the ancient capital city of the Toltec people. The Toltecs were rulers of northern Mexico from about AD950 to 1160. The warrior wears a butterfly-shaped breastplate. Butterflies have short but brilliant lives. For the Toltecs, they were a symbol of brave warriors and early death.

Stone Age hand art

From about 37,000BC, early humans began to carve marks on bones and use pebbles to count. Days may have been counted on calendar sticks. Experts have noticed dots and symbols in some cave paintings, which may be counting tallies or the very beginnings of a writing system. By 7000BC, tokens with symbols to represent numbers and objects were being used by traders in the Near East. Such tokens may have led to the first written script. This developed in about 3100BC and was a form of picture-writing called cuneiform.

YOU WILL NEED

Self-hardening clay, rolling pin, cutting board, modelling tool, fine sandpaper, red and yellow acrylic paints, water, two spray bottles.

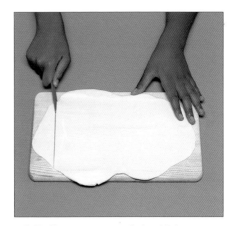

1 Roll out a piece of clay. Make sure it has an uneven surface similar to a cave wall. Use a modelling tool to trim the edges into a rough rectangle to look like a stone tablet.

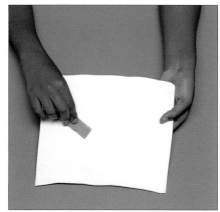

2 Leave the clay to dry. When the tablet is completely hard, rub it with fine sandpaper to get rid of any sharp edges and to make a smooth surface for your cave painting.

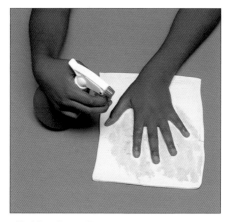

3 Mix the yellow paint with some water and fill a spray bottle. Mix the red paint in the same way. Put one hand on top of the clay tablet and spray plenty of yellow paint around it.

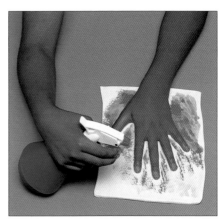

4 Keeping your hand in exactly the same position, spray on the red paint from the other bottle. Make sure you spray enough paint to leave a clear, sharp background.

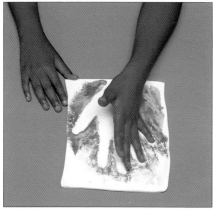

5 When you have finished your spray painting, carefully remove your hand. Take care not to smudge the paint, and then leave the tablet to dry. Wash your hands thoroughly.

This project is based on a Stone Age painting found in a cave in Argentina. The original artist blew paint through a reed or even spat paint on to the wall.

Stone Age cave painting

The earliest Stone Age cave paintings date from around 40,000BC and were etched on rocks in Australia. In Europe, the oldest works of art are cave paintings from about 28,000BC. Some caves in southwestern France and northern Spain are covered with paintings and engravings of animals, but show very few human figures. They were probably part of religious rituals. Stone Age artists also carved female figures, called Venus figurines, and decorated their tools and weapons with carved patterns and animal forms.

<table>
<tr><td>

YOU WILL NEED

Self-hardening clay, rolling pin, cutting board, modelling tool, fine sandpaper, acrylic paints, paintbrush, water pot.

</td></tr>
</table>

1 Roll out a piece of clay. Make sure it has an uneven surface similar to a cave wall. Then use a modelling tool to trim the edges into a neat rectangle shape.

2 Leave the clay to dry. When it is completely hard, rub it with fine sandpaper to get rid of any sharp edges and to make a smooth surface for your painting.

3 Paint the outline of an animal, such as this reindeer, using black acrylic paint. Exaggerate the size of the most obvious features, such as the muscular body and antlers.

4 When the outline is dry, mix black, red and yellow acrylic paints to make a warm, earthy colour. Use the colour you have mixed to fill in the outline of your chosen animal.

5 Finish your painting by highlighting some parts of the animal's body with reddish brown paint mixed to resemble red ochre. This is how Stone Age artists finished their paintings.

Stone Age artists used pigments from minerals and plants. Black, white and earthy shades of red were common.

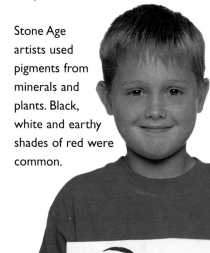

Egyptian wall painting

The walls of many Egyptian tombs were covered with colourful pictures, which were very carefully made. First, the wall was coated several times with plaster. Then it was marked out in a grid pattern to make sure that each part of the design fitted neatly into the available space. Junior artists sketched the picture in red paint. Senior artists made corrections and went over the outlines in black ink. Finally, the outlines were filled in with paint. The step-by-step panel below shows you how to draw figures the Egyptian way.

YOU WILL NEED

Paper, pencil, black pen, ruler, red pen, piece of card, mixing bowl, plaster of Paris, water, wooden spoon, petroleum jelly, coarse sandpaper, acrylic paints, paintbrushes, water pot, 25cm length of string, scissors, white fabric, PVA glue and glue brush.

Step 1   Step 2

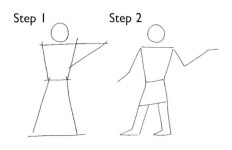

To draw figures without a grid, start with simple lines and circles. Then add simple lines for limbs and draw a tray on the shoulder. Round off the lines for the arms and legs.

Step 3

Step 4

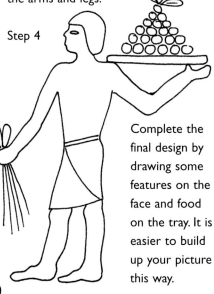

Complete the final design by drawing some features on the face and food on the tray. It is easier to build up your picture this way.

1 Draw a pencil design similar to the one shown in the final picture. Go over it with a black pen. Then use a red pen and ruler to draw vertical and horizontal lines in a 2cm-square grid.

2 Measure the maximum length and maximum width of your design. Draw a rectangular box of the same size on a piece of card, and then draw a wavy shape inside the box.

3 Mix the plaster of Paris and water in a bowl using a wooden spoon. The plaster of Paris should have a firm consistency, and the mixture should drop from the spoon in thick dollops.

4 Smear a little petroleum jelly over the piece of card. This stops the plaster from sticking to the card. Then pour the plaster of Paris to cover the wavy shape you drew earlier.

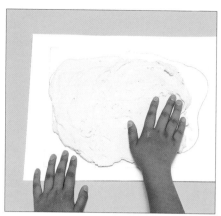

5 Spread the plaster mixture to a depth of about 8mm. Then smooth the surface with your hand. Leave this shape to dry in a warm room for at least two hours.

6 When it is dry, gently rub the plaster with coarse sandpaper. Smooth the sandpaper over the rough edges and all over the surface and sides of your slab of plaster.

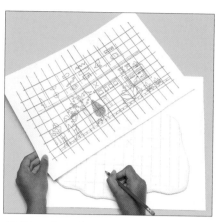

7 Use the ruler and pencil to draw another 2cm-square grid on the surface of the plaster. Carefully remove the piece of plaster from the card by lifting one edge at a time.

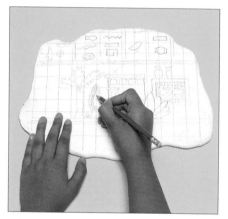

8 Transfer the design on the paper grid on to the plaster grid. Begin at the centre square and work outwards, copying one square at a time.

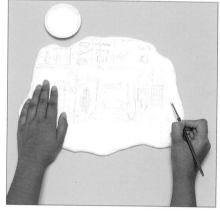

9 Use a fine paintbrush to paint the background of the plaster a cream colour. Then paint around the design itself. Leave the paint to dry for at least an hour before adding other colours.

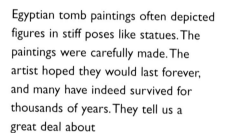

Egyptian tomb paintings often depicted figures in stiff poses like statues. The paintings were carefully made. The artist hoped they would last forever, and many have indeed survived for thousands of years. They tell us a great deal about how ancient Egyptians lived.

10 When the background is dry, add the details of the Egyptian painting using a fine paintbrush. Paint the border using red, blue, yellow, black, white and gold acrylic paints.

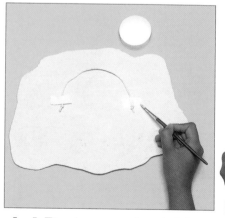

11 Tie a knot at each end of the piece of string. Cut two small pieces of fabric and glue them over the string as shown above. When the glue is dry, you can hang your painting.

Greek vase

The artists and craftworkers of ancient Greece were admired for the quality of their work. They used a range of materials, such as metals, stone, wood, leather, bone, horn and glass. Most goods were made on a small scale in workshops surrounding the *agora* (marketplace). A craftsman might work on his own or with the help of his family and a slave or two. In larger workshops, slaves laboured to produce bulk orders of popular goods. These might include shields, pottery and metalwork, all of which were traded around the Mediterranean Sea for a large profit.

YOU WILL NEED

Balloon, PVA glue, water, mixing bowl, newspaper, two rolls of masking tape, black pen, scissors, sheet of paper measuring 42 x 30cm, thick card, pencil, black and cream acrylic paints, paintbrush, water pot.

▲ **Work of art**
A good vase painter was a highly respected artist, and many signed their works. The export of vases was a major source of income for Athens.

▶ **Storage space**
Huge storage jars were used by the ancient Greeks to store food and drink. One jar could contain hundreds of litres of wine, olive oil or cereal. Handmade from clay, they kept food and drink cool in the hot Mediterranean climate.

1 Blow up a balloon. Soak strips of newspaper in one part PVA glue to two parts water to make papier mâché. Cover the balloon with two layers of papier mâché. Leave it to dry.

2 Using a roll of masking tape as a guide, draw and cut out two holes at the top and bottom of the papier mâché balloon. Discard the burst balloon.

3 Roll the 42 x 30cm sheet of paper into a tube. Make sure it will fit through the middle of the roll of masking tape. Glue the paper tube in place and secure with masking tape.

4 Push the tube through the middle of the papier mâché shape. Tape the tube into place. Push a roll of masking tape over the bottom of the paper tube and tape as shown above.

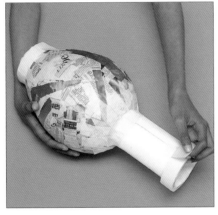

5 Attach the second roll of masking tape to the top of the paper tube. Make sure that both rolls of tape are securely fixed at either end of the paper tube.

6 Cut two 15cm strips of card. Fix them to either side of the vase for handles as shown above. Cover the entire vase with more papier mâché and leave to dry. Paint the vase cream.

7 When dry, use a pencil to copy the pattern above, or design a simple geometric pattern like the pots on the left. Paint over the design in black acrylic paint. Leave the vase to dry.

Greek vases such as the one you have made were called amphorae. They were given out as prizes at the Panathenaic games and were decorated with sporting images.

Chinese silhouettes

Paper fine enough to write on, or to make cut-out patterns, such as the one in this project, was invented in China about AD105. Arts flourished as the Empire became more stable during the Seng Dynasty (AD960-1279) and the Ming Dynasty (1368-1644). Paintings appeared on walls, screens, fans and scrolls of silk and paper. Sometimes just a few brush strokes could capture the spirit of a subject. Chinese artists also produced beautiful woodcuts (prints made from a carved wooden block).

YOU WILL NEED

Thick A4 coloured paper, pencil, small sharp scissors.

1 Take a piece of brightly coloured paper and lay it flat out on a hard work surface. Fold it in half widthways and make a firm crease along the fold as shown above.

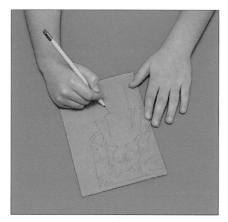

2 Use a pencil to draw a Chinese-style design on to the paper. Make a solid border around the non-folded edges. All the shapes in the design should touch the border or the fold.

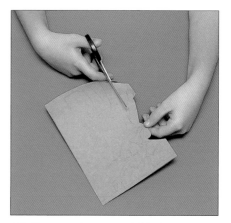

3 Keeping the paper folded, cut out the shapes you have drawn. Make sure not to cut along the edges of the shapes on the fold. Cut away areas you want to discard in between the shapes.

4 Open up the paper, taking care not to tear it. To add details to the cut-out figures, fold each figure in half separately. Pencil in the details to be cut along the crease.

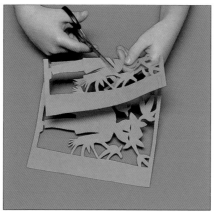

5 Carefully cut out the details you have marked along the crease. The cut-out details will be matched perfectly on the other side of the figure when you open the paper.

Display the design by sticking it to a window so that light shines through. In China, paper cut-outs are believed to bring luck and good fortune.

Japanese paper

The Japanese picked up paper-making skills from China around AD610 and improved on them. Mulberry and hemp were planted throughout the country and were used to make paper as well as textiles. Japanese paper was stronger and finer textured than Chinese paper. Soon there were many different colours and textures. Making paper was a work of art in itself. Calligraphy, the art of elegant writing, developed at the same time. Letter writers were judged on the paper they chose and their handwriting, as well as their words.

YOU WILL NEED

Eight pieces of wood (four at 33 x 2 x 1cm and four at 28 x 2 x 1cm), nails, hammer, muslin (35 x 30cm), staple gun and staples, electrical tape, scissors, waste paper, water, mixing bowl, potato masher, washing up bowl, petals, soft cloth, newspaper.

1 Ask an adult to help you make two wooden frames. Staple muslin tightly over one of the frames. Cover the stapled edges with electrical tape to make the screen as shown above.

2 Put some scraps of paper into a bowl of water and leave the paper to soak overnight. Then mash the paper into a pulp with a potato masher. The pulp should look like porridge.

3 Tip the pulp into a washing up bowl and half fill with cold water. Mix in some petals. Place the open frame on top of the screen, put it in the bowl and scoop some pulp into it.

4 Pull the screen out of the pulp, keeping it level. Gently move it from side to side over the bowl to allow a layer of pulp to form on the screen. Shake off the excess water.

5 Remove the frame. Lay the screen face down on a cloth placed on layers of newspaper. Mop away the excess water. Peel away the screen and leave to dry for at least six hours.

Peel away the cloth to reveal your paper. This heavily textured paper is suitable for painting on.

Japanese ikebana

Although the word *ikebana* roughly translates as 'flower arrangement', the Japanese incorporate all sorts of other organic things in their designs. Driftwood, rocks and shells can all be brought into use. In an ikebana arrangement, the vase or pot represents the Earth, and the plants set in it should be arranged as if they are growing naturally.

This idea is carried through to Japanese gardens which are often small but create a miniature landscape. Each rock, pool or gateway is positioned where it forms part of a balanced and harmonious arrangement. Japanese designers create gardens that look good during all the different seasons of the year. Zen gardens sometimes have no plants at all – just rocks, sand and gravel.

▲ Tiny tree

Bonsai is the Japanese art of producing miniature, but perfectly formed, trees such as this maple. This is achieved by clipping the roots and branches of the tree and training it with wires.

◄ The art of elegance

Japanese flower arrangements are often very simple. Flowers have been appreciated in Japan for hundreds of years. In the 8th century AD, thousands of poems were collected together in one book. About a third of the poems were about plants and flowers.

YOU WILL NEED

Twig, scissors, vase filled with water, raffia or string, two flowers (one with a long stem; one shorter), branch of foliage, two stems of waxy leaves.

Cut the twig so that it can be wedged into the neck of the vase. The twig will provide a structure to build on and will also control the position of the flowers.

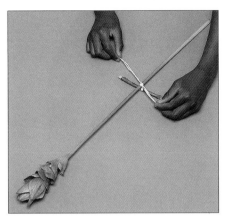

2 Remove the twig from the vase. Next, using a piece of string or raffia, tie the twig tightly on to the stem of the longest flower. Make the knot about halfway down the stem.

3 Place the flower stem in the vase. As you do this, gently slide the twig back into the neck of the vase so that it is wedged into the same position as it was before.

4 Add the flower with the shorter stem to the vase. Position this flower so that it slants forwards and to one side. Carefully lean this flower stem towards the longer one.

5 Slip the branch of foliage between the two stems. It should lean outwards and forwards. The foliage should look as if it is a naturally growing branch.

6 Position some waxy leaves at the neck of the vase. Ikebana is the arrangement of anything that grows, so the foliage is just as important as the flowers in your arrangement.

7 Add a longer stem of waxy leaves at the back of the vase to complete the arrangement, which is typical of the kinds that Japanese people use to decorate their homes.

The three main branches of this arrangement represent heaven, the Earth and human beings. Even the leaves and other material are arranged in a carefully balanced way.

Celtic manuscript

By around AD1, the Celtic lands of mainland Europe were part of the Roman Empire. Over the next 400 years, Celtic languages and artistic traditions were gradually absorbed into the Roman Empire.

In the British Isles, the situation was different, as they were more isolated and many parts were never conquered by Rome. Languages and traditions survived, creating a final flowering of Celtic culture, particularly in the Christian monasteries. There, the monks were making careful copies of sacred Christian texts. They decorated their manuscripts with plaited and spiralling Celtic designs in rich colours. In this way, the new and quite distinctive form of Celtic illumination was developed. Some manuscripts had notes scribbled in the margins such as "The ink is bad ... the day dark."

▲ Irish saint

A missionary called St Patrick took the Christian faith to Ireland. Irish monks made beautifully illuminated manuscripts. Their love of nature was obvious in their lively pictures of animals and birds.

▲ Beautiful border

The *Book of Durrow* is a Christian book decorated with Celtic designs. It was made on the Scottish island of Iona.

▲ Stone marker

Celtic standing stones were often turned into Christian crosses to mark burials, preaching places or holy ground.

YOU WILL NEED

Piece of thin card measuring 60 x 40cm, ruler, pencil, felt-tipped pen, selection of paints and paintbrushes, water pot, eraser.

I Use a pen to draw a 57 x 37cm rectangle on the thin card. Draw lines 1cm in from the long sides and 1.5cm in from the short sides. Then draw lines 9.5cm in from each end.

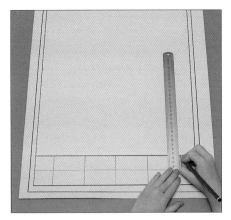

2 Divide the border at the top of the card into two horizontal sections. Now mark vertical sections 3.5cm in from each end. Then add three more vertical lines 7cm apart.

3 Begin at the top right-hand corner of the top section of the border. Place your pencil at the intersection of the first four squares. Draw a design similar to the one shown above.

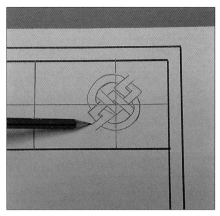

4 Add two outer circles to your design as shown above. Join the circles to the open ends of your Celtic border to create a design known as an endless knot.

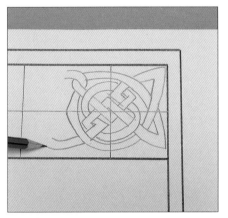

5 Add two even larger circles and the corner designs to your endless knot as shown above. Extend the open ends on the left of the design to begin a second knot.

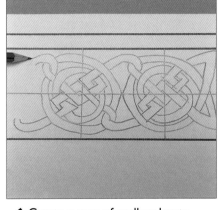

6 Create a row of endless knots. Repeat these steps to create an endless knot design in the border along the bottom of the card.

7 Paint the different strands of knot using typical Celtic colours, such as green and red. When the border is completely dry, carefully rub out the pencil grid.

You could write a few Gaelic words on to your manuscript. The words shown here mean 'And pray for Mac Craith, King of Cashell'. Interlaced designs such as this one are found in manuscripts decorated in Celtic style.

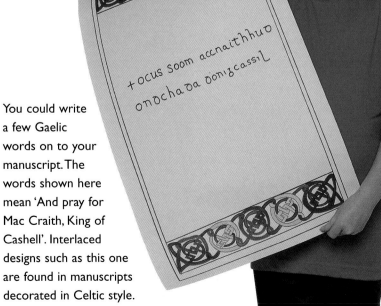

Inca tumi knife

The whole region of the Andes had a very long history of metalworking. Incas often referred to gold as 'sweat of the Sun' and to silver as 'tears of the Moon'. These metals were sacred to the gods and also to the Inca rulers and priests – the gods on Earth. At the Temple of the Sun in Cuzco, there was a whole garden made of gold and silver, with golden soil, golden stalks of maize and golden llamas. Imagine how it must have gleamed in the sunlight! Copper, however, was used by ordinary people. It was made into cheap jewellery, weapons and everyday tools. The Incas' love of gold and silver eventually led to their downfall, for it was rumours of their fabulous wealth that lured the Spanish to invade the region in the 1400s.

▲ **Copper ore**
The Incas worked with copper, found in rocks like this one, and knew how to mix it with tin to make bronze. The Incas also used gold, silver and platinum, but not iron or steel.

YOU WILL NEED

Card, pencil, ruler, scissors, self-hardening clay, cutting board, rolling pin, modelling tool, PVA glue and glue brush, toothpick, gold paint, paintbrush, water pot, blue metallic paper.

▲ **Tumi knife**
A ceremonial knife with a crescent-shaped blade is known as a tumi. Its gold handle is made in the shape of a ruler.

▲ **Precious blade**
The handle of this Inca sacrificial knife is made of wood inlaid with gemstones, shells and turquoise.

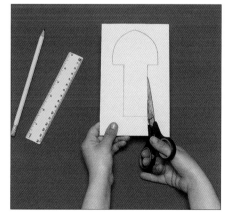

1 Draw the shape of the knife blade on a piece of card and cut it out as shown above. The rectangular part measures 9 x 3.5cm. The rounded part is 7cm across and 4.5cm high.

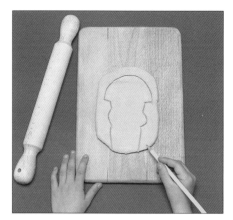

2 Roll out a slab of clay to a thickness of 1cm. Pencil in a tumi shape as shown above. It should be about 12.5cm long and measure 9cm across the widest part at the top.

3 Use the modelling tool to cut around the clay shape you have drawn. Put the leftover clay to one side. Make sure the edges of the tumi handle are clean and smooth.

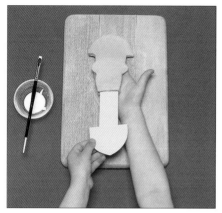

4 Use the modelling tool to cut a slot in the bottom edge of the tumi handle. Lifting it carefully, slide the card blade into the handle. Use glue to join the blade and the handle firmly.

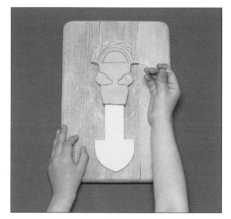

5 Use a modelling tool to mark on the details of the tumi. Use a toothpick for the fine details. Look at the finished knife (*right*) to see how to do this. Leave everything to dry.

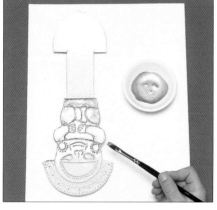

6 When the clay is dry, give one side of the tumi and blade a coat of gold paint. Leave it to dry completely before turning it over and painting the other side.

7 The original tumi knife would have been decorated with pieces of turquoise. Glue small pieces of blue metallic paper on to the handle for turquoise as shown in the picture.

The Chimú gold and turquoise tumi was used by priests of the Chimú people at religious ceremonies. It may even have been used to kill sacrifices to the gods.

Customs

▲ Urn for ashes

In some ancient societies, people cremated their dead by burning the bodies on a funeral pyre. The ashes, and sometimes the bones, of the dead person were placed in pottery urns such as the one above. The urn was then placed in a burial chamber.

Today, many aspects of life are similar from one side of the world to the other. People wear the same sort of clothes, drive similar cars and live and work in the same sort of houses and apartment blocks. This has not always been the case. For thousands of years, customs and lifestyles varied greatly between different continents and even between countries and regions. There were differences in how people dressed, what they ate and how they greeted each other.

Many customs are very closely related to religion, such as Ramadan (a Muslim period of fasting) and the barmitzvah (a coming-of-age ceremony for Jewish boys). Some ancient customs are still practised today, but a great many have been forgotten and lost forever.

▲ Crying a river

Osiris was the Egyptian god of farming. After he was killed by his jealous brother, Seth, Osiris became a god of the underworld and the afterlife. The ancient Egyptians believed that the yearly flooding of the River Nile marked the anniversary of Osiris's death when his queen, Isis (*above*), wept for him.

Symbol of hope ▶

The water lily, or lotus, is a symbolic flower in Buddhism. It represents enlightenment, which can come out of suffering just as the beautiful flower grows from slimy mud.

◀ Elephant god

The elephant god Ganesh is the Hindu lord of learning and remover of all obstacles. His parents were Shiva and Parvati. According to Hindu mythology, Shiva mistook his son Ganesh for someone else and beheaded him. Shiva realized his mistake and replaced his son's head with one from the first creature he saw – an elephant.

▲ Gateway to beyond

Many people in Japan practise the Shinto religion. Every Shinto religious shrine can only be entered through a gate called a *torii*. The torii separates the holy shrine from the ordinary world outside. It can be some distance from the shrine itself.

Pathway to Allah ▲

Islamic law schools like this one are found all over the world. Islamic law is known as the *Shari'ah* – an Arabic word meaning a track that leads camels to a waterhole. In the same way, Muslims who obey the Shari'ah will be led to Allah (God).

Stone Age wooden henge

The first stone monuments were built in Europe and date back to around 4200BC. They are called megaliths, from the Greek word meaning 'large stone'. Some of the first megaliths were made up of a large flat stone supported by several upright stones. They are the remains of ancient burial places, called chambered tombs. Others are called passage graves. These were communal graves where many people were buried. Later, larger monuments were constructed. Stone or wood circles called henges, such as Stonehenge in England, were built. No one knows why these circles were made. They may have been temples, meeting places or giant calendars, since they are aligned with the Sun, Moon and stars. The monuments were sometimes altered. Some stones were removed and others were added.

YOU WILL NEED

Card, ruler, pair of compasses, pencil, scissors, self-hardening clay, rolling pin, cutting board, modelling tool, 1cm- and 5mm-thick dowelling, acrylic paint, paintbrush, water pot, fake grass, PVA glue and glue brush, scissors, sandpaper, varnish, brush.

▲ Stone circle

The megalithic monuments of Europe have stood for thousands of years, but they have not always looked the same. Archaeologists have found many holes in the ground where additional stones and wooden posts once stood. These sites were once even more complex than they are today.

▸ The heavy work

Stonehenge in Wiltshire, England, was built with the simplest technology. The builders probably used sleds or rollers to move the stones, each weighing about 40 tonnes, about 25km to the site. Ropes and levers were then used to haul them into place.

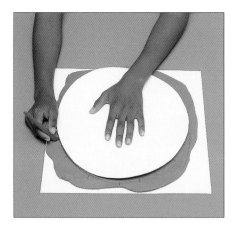

1 Cut out a card circle about 35cm in diameter. Roll out the clay, place the card circle on top and score around the card. Use a modelling tool to mark about 18 points around the circle.

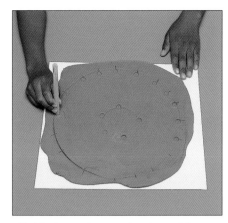

2 Mark another circle, about 10cm across, inside the first circle. Mark five points around it for posts. Press a 1cm-thick stick into each point. Repeat for the outer circle.

3 Make sure all the holes for the posts are evenly spaced. When you have finished, leave the clay base to dry. Then smooth over the base with fine sandpaper and paint it brown.

4 Roughly cover the clay base with pieces of fake grass. Glue them into position as shown above. Be careful not to cover up the holes for the posts you made earlier.

5 Cut seven long and 16 short sticks from the 1cm-thick dowelling. These will make the posts. Cut 17 short pieces from the 5mm-thick dowelling for the lintels. Varnish the sticks.

6 When the sticks are dry, glue them in place using the post holes and the picture above as a guide. Then glue the lintels on top of the outer posts to complete your wooden circle.

Wood henges had up to five rings of timber posts increasing in height towards the centre. People started building wooden henges around 3000BC. They became centres of religious and social life.

Egyptian canopic jar

Mummy-makers in Egypt removed the body's internal organs and stored them in containers called canopic jars. There was one jar each for the lungs, intestines, liver and stomach. A jackal-headed jar such as the one you can make in this project would have held the stomach. Organs could not be thrown away because people believed they might be used by an evil magician in a spell. Some mummy-makers filled the space where the organs had been with fragrant herbs and spices, clay, sand, salt, cloth or straw.

YOU WILL NEED

Ruler, pencil, thin white card, black marker pen, scissors, masking tape, old newspaper, sheet of paper, mixing bowl, plain flour, water, fork, three paper cups, fine sandpaper, cloth, white emulsion paint, acrylic paints, gold paint, paintbrushes, water pot, clear wood varnish.

1 Use a ruler and pencil to draw a rectangle measuring 26 x 6cm on to the thin white card. Trace over the outline with a black marker pen and then carefully cut out the rectangle.

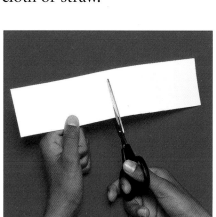

2 Use a ruler and pencil to lightly mark 1cm spaces along one of the longer sides of the rectangle. Make a cut at each mark about 4cm into the card. This will make a row of tabs.

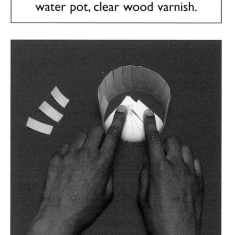

3 Tape the ends of the card together and bend the tabs inwards to make a dome shape as shown above. Stick each tab to the next one using small fingertip-sized pieces of masking tape.

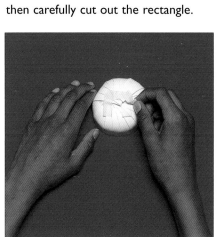

4 When you have bent and stuck all the tabs down to make the dome shape, secure the top of it using some more masking tape. This dome will form the lid of your canopic jar.

5 Take a piece of old newspaper and tear it into small strips. Scrunch them up into a ball with a diameter of 4cm (about the size of a golf ball). Cover the ball with masking tape.

6 Cut out small card triangles for ears, about 4 x 2.5cm. Roll a strip of newspaper into a tube to make the muzzle. Then use pieces of masking tape to fix these pieces to the head.

7 Hold the base of the lid firmly in one hand. With the other hand, stick strips of masking tape over the head and dome. The jackal's head is now ready for pasting.

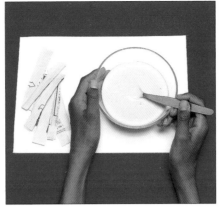

8 Cover the work surface with some paper. Put 250g of plain flour into a bowl. Pour in some water to make a paste, stirring with a fork as you pour. Tear some more newspaper into strips.

9 Dip the newspaper into the paste. Cover the jackal's head with three layers, leaving it to dry between layers. Then stack three paper cups together and cover them with the papier mâché.

10 When both the jar and jackal's head lid are completely dry, sand the outsides down with fine sandpaper until the surface is smooth. Dust them both with a cloth.

11 Paint the inside and outside of the lid and jar with white emulsion. When dry, paint the outside of the jar with cream acrylic paint, leaving a white rim of emulsion at the top.

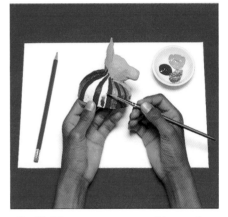

12 Mix up some green, blue and white paints to make turquoise. Use this to paint the head. Paint blue and gold stripes on the dome of the lid. Then draw a face on the head.

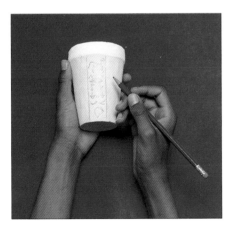

13 Draw a spell on the body of the jar using a pencil. You can copy the design shown here or you can look for references to other spells in books on Egypt.

14 Paint over your pencil design in black and paint the face of the jackal in black and white. Paint the top rim gold and leave it to dry completely. Then varnish the jar and lid.

Jars with different shaped lids were used to store the body's organs. For example, human-headed jars held the liver.

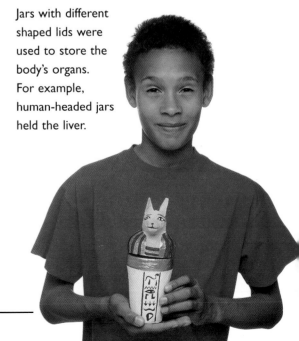

Egyptian udjat eye

When pharaohs died, everything possible was done to make sure that they completed their journey to the gods in safety. During the New Kingdom, the ruler's coffin, containing his mummy, would be placed on a boat and ferried from Thebes to the west bank of the River Nile. The funeral procession was spectacular. Priests scattered milk and burned incense, and women wept. After the ceremony, the coffin was placed in the tomb with food, drink and charms such as the udjat eye you can make in this project.

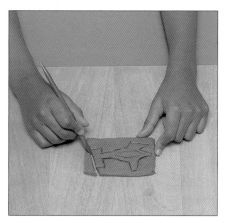

1 Use a rolling pin to roll out some clay on to a cutting board. Use the modelling tool to cut out the pattern of the eye pieces. Refer to step 2 for the shape of each piece.

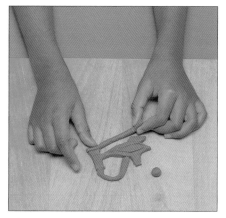

2 Remove the excess clay from the eye pieces and arrange them on the cutting board. The eye is meant to represent the eye of the falcon-headed Egyptian god called Horus.

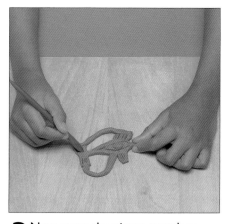

3 Now press the pieces together until you have the full shape of the eye. You may need to use the modelling tool to secure all the joins. When you have finished, leave the eye to dry.

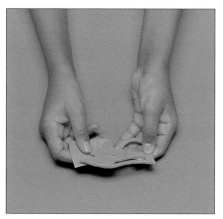

4 When it is dry, smooth the surface of the eye with fine sandpaper. Then wipe it with a soft cloth to remove any dust. The eye of Horus is now ready for painting.

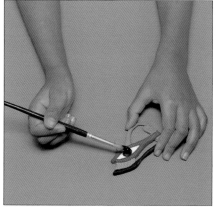

5 Paint in the white of the eye and add the eyebrow and pupil. Next paint in the red liner. Finally, paint the rest of the eye charm blue. Let each colour dry before adding the next.

Horus lost his eye in a battle with Seth, the god of chaos. Udjat eyes were thought to be lucky in ancient Egypt.

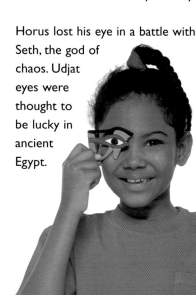

Roman temple

Many splendid temples were built to honour the gods and goddesses of the Roman Empire. The Pantheon in Rome was the largest. Special festivals for the gods were held during the year, with processions, music and animal sacrifices. The festivals were often public holidays. The mid-winter celebration of Saturnalia lasted up to seven days. It honoured Saturn, the god of farmers. As the Empire grew, many Romans adopted the religions of other peoples, such as the Egyptians and the Persians.

YOU WILL NEED

Thick card for the template pieces, pencil, ruler, pair of compasses, scissors, newspaper, balloon, PVA glue and glue brush, thin card, masking tape, drinking straws, non-hardening modelling material, acrylic paints, paintbrush, water pot.

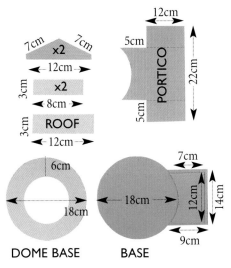

Cut the templates out of thick card, following the measurements above.

1 Glue layers of paper to half of a balloon. When dry, burst the balloon and cut out a dome. Make a hole in the top. Put the dome on its card base. Bind the pieces together as shown.

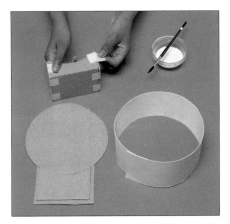

2 Cut a 12cm wide strip of thin card, long enough to fit around the base circle. Secure it with masking tape and then glue it to the base. Tape the portico section together as shown.

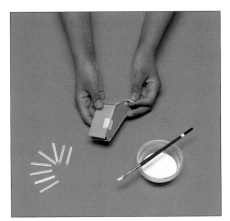

3 Cut some straws into eight pieces, each one 6cm long. These are the columns for the entrance of the temple. Glue and tape together the roof pieces for the entrance to the temple.

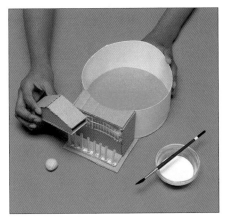

4 Glue everything together as shown and secure with tape. Fix each straw column with a small piece of modelling material at its base. Glue on the roof and the dome. Paint the model.

The Pantheon in Rome was built from AD118 to AD128. It was a temple to all the Roman gods. The Pantheon was built of brick and then clad in stone and marble. Its high dome, mosaic floor, and interior columns remain exactly as they were built.

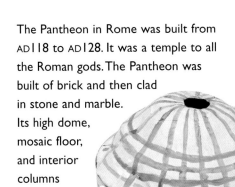

Hindu flower garland

Buddhism was the dominant religion in India until about AD200. Gradually Hinduism became more widely practised. Hinduism has remained the dominant religion in India ever since.

Hindus have many festivals to honour the gods. At many, garlands of leaves and fresh flowers are used to decorate the body and hair. Garlands are also used to decorate images of Hindu gods in the practice of puja (worship).

Flowers have been very important in India throughout its history. During the Mughal Empire (1526–1758), wealthy nobles created courtyards and gardens filled with pools and flowering plants. The Mughal rulers were Muslims. Their gardens often had a symbolic significance, because they were viewed as a miniature map of paradise. Mughal kings divided their gardens into four parts called charbhags. Each part was separated by water channels that represented the rivers of paradise.

▴ Nowhere to hide

Brahma is the Hindu god of creation. After he created the first woman, he fell in love with her. She hid herself away, so Brahma grew three more heads so that he could see her from every angle.

YOU WILL NEED

Tissue paper (orange, yellow, red, blue, pink and white), pencil, scissors, PVA glue and glue brush, length of string, darning needle.

▴ Hindu wanderer

Wandering priests or holy men are called sadhus. They give up worldly pleasure and wander from place to place begging for food.

Priestly caste ▸

Brahmin priests were one of three castes (social classes) that made up the native Aryan people in India. Each caste played a different role in important Aryan ceremonies. The Aryan customs and writings formed the basis of the Hindu religion.

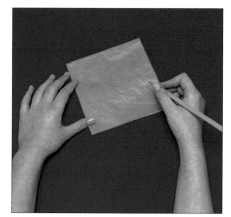

I Draw simple flower shapes on to the sheets of coloured tissue paper. If you like, you can put the sheets of coloured paper in layers, one on top of the other.

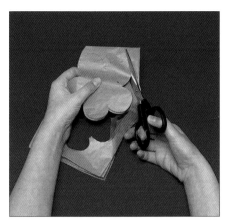

2 Carefully cut out the flower shapes using a pair of scissors. Take care not to tear the tissue paper as you cut around the outline. Cut the same number of flowers in each colour.

3 Scrunch up the tissue flower shapes with your hands to make them creased. Uncrumple each flower as shown, making sure not to smooth the flower out too much.

4 Glue the separate flower shapes together in loose layers to make larger, single flowers. Use eight layers of different coloured tissue paper for each finished flower.

5 When each flower is dry, gently fluff up the layers of tissue paper with your fingers. Try not to tear the paper as you go. Your flowers will now look much more realistic.

6 Measure a length of string to fit around your neck and hang down to the level of your waist. Start to thread each flower on to the string using the darning needle.

Indians are fond of flowers like mango blossom, ashoka flower and jasmine. They use them in many garlands. Another favourite flower is the lotus (water lily), a symbol of spirituality.

7 Thread all the tissue flowers on to the length of string. When you have finished, firmly tie a double knot in the string to secure the flowers. Your garland is now ready to wear.

Viking lucky charm

The Vikings believed the universe was held up by a great tree called Yggdrasil. There were several separate worlds. Niflheim was the snowy, cold underworld. The upper world was Asgard, home of the gods.

There were many Viking gods. Odin, the father of the gods, rode through the night sky and his son, Baldr, was god of the summer Sun. Thor, the god of thunder, carried a two-headed hammer. Vikings were superstitious and wore lucky charms, such as one in the shape of Thor's hammer, to protect themselves from evil.

▲ **Take it with you**
Vikings were buried with the weapons and treasures that they would need for the next life. Even quite poor Vikings were buried with a sword or a brooch.

YOU WILL NEED

Thick paper or card, pencil, scissors, self-hardening clay, cutting board, rolling pin, modelling tool, felt-tipped pen, fine sandpaper, silver acrylic paint, paintbrush, water pot, length of cord, piece of wire.

▲ **Pick me, Odin!**
Vikings believed that after a battle, Odin and his servants, the Valkyries, searched the battlefield. They carried dead heroes to a Viking heaven called Valholl, or Valhalla.

I Draw the outline of Thor's hammer on to thick paper or card using the final project picture as your guide. Cut it out. Use this card hammer as the pattern for making your lucky charm.

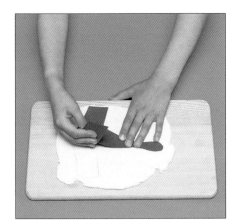

2 Roll out a piece of clay to a thickness of 5mm on the cutting board. Press the card hammer pattern into the clay so that it leaves the outline of the hammer in the clay.

3 Remove the card. Use the modelling tool to cut around the imprint. Mark lines around the edge of the hammer and draw on a pattern. Make a line at the end of the hammer for a handle.

4 Pierce a hole through the end of the handle. Cut off the handle end and turn it upright. Then join the handle back up to the main part of the hammer. Make the join as smooth as possible.

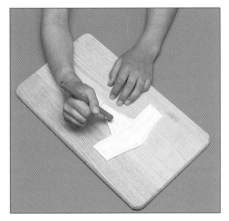

5 Use the end of a felt-tipped pen to make some more impressions on the clay hammer as shown above. When you have finished, leave the clay to dry and completely harden.

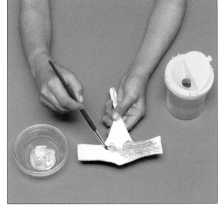

6 When your lucky charm is dry, smooth any rough edges with the sandpaper. Then paint one side silver. Leave it to dry before painting the other side of the lucky charm.

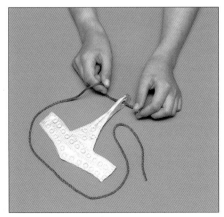

7 When the paint is dry, take a length of cord to fit around your head. Thread the cord through the hole in the hammer. Cut off any excess with the scissors and tie a firm knot.

You could add a loop of wire between the hammer and the cord for extra decoration. Many Viking charms, such as this hammer, honour the god Thor.

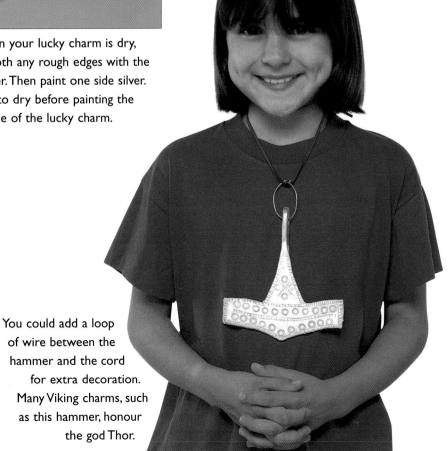

Tribal dance wand

Dancing was an important part of Native American life. Some of the sacred dances were performed before or after great events such as births, deaths, marriages, hunts or battle, but the occasion was more than just a big party. The Green Corn Dance was held at the Creek New Year and celebrated agricultural growth, and the Arikara Bear Dance aimed to influence the growth of maize and squash crops. Dancers often wore costumes. Cheyenne Sun dancers painted their upper body black (for clouds) with white dots (for hail). Assiniboine Clown dancers often danced and talked backwards and wore masks with long noses.

▲ **Fierce dance**
This is a member of the Huron tribe. He dances in his feathered headdress, brandishing his tomahawk.

▲ **Winter help**
This Woodlands tribe is performing a Snowshoe Dance. Winter was a hard time and food was scarce with few animals around to hunt. The dance asked the spirits for help to survive.

▲ **Mourning dress**
A ghost dance shirt worn by the Sioux during a dance to mourn their dead. European settlers mistakenly saw the dance as provocation to war.

YOU WILL NEED

White paper, pencil, ruler, scissors, acrylic paints, paintbrush, water pot, eight 20cm lengths of 3mm-thick balsa wood, PVA glue and glue brush, pair of compasses, thick card, red and orange paper, 75cm-long stick (1cm thick), string.

I Cut out eight 29cm-long feather shapes from white paper. Make cuts on the top edges, and paint the tips of the feathers black. Glue sticks 12cm from the top of the feathers as shown.

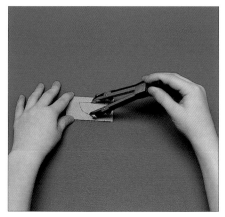

2 Use the compasses and a ruler to measure and draw two semicircles, each with a diameter of 5cm, on to the thick card. Use a pair of scissors to cut out both shapes.

3 Hold the feathers by the sticks. Glue the bottom end of each of the feathers between the two card semicircles. Arrange them around the curved edge of the card as shown.

4 Draw and cut out twelve 6cm-long feather shapes from the red and orange paper. Make another eight red feathers, each 2.5cm long. Make feathery cuts along the top edges.

5 Divide the 6cm-long feathers in two, and glue them to each end of the 75cm-long stick. Secure them with a piece of string tied around the bottom of the feathers as shown.

6 Paint the semicircles cream and then leave them to dry. Bend back the two straight edges. Place the flaps either side of the centre of the stick. Glue the flaps firmly in place.

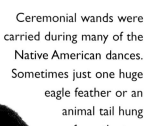

Ceremonial wands were carried during many of the Native American dances. Sometimes just one huge eagle feather or an animal tail hung from the top.

7 Glue the 2.5cm-long red feathers to the outside tips of each black feather. Leave the dance wand to dry completely. Your wand will then be ready, so let the dance begin.

Chancay doll

Archaeologists have found many burial sites in the Andes Mountains. As early as 3200BC, Andean peoples had learned how to mummify (preserve) bodies. Respect for ancestors was an important part of the civilizations in the Andes. The Chancays were an ancient people who lived on the coast of central Peru. They were conquered by the mighty Incas in the 1500s. Dolls such as the one you can make in this project were placed in the graves of the Chancays to help them in the afterlife.

Final resting place ▶
The body of an Inca noble wrapped in cloth is carried to a *chulpa* (tomb). Chulpas were tall stone towers used to bury important people in ancient Peru.

1 Draw two rectangles 16 x 11cm on cream calico fabric to make the doll's body. Then draw two shield shapes 7 x 8cm for the head. Paint the body and one head as shown. Cut them out.

2 Cut 35 strands of black wool, each measuring 18cm in length. These will make the doll's hair. Glue each wool strand evenly along the top of the unpainted head shape as shown.

3 Cut a piece of wadding slightly smaller than the head shape. Glue the wadding on top of the hair and the head piece below. Then glue the painted face on top as shown. Leave to dry.

4 For each arm, take five pipe cleaners and cut each one 11cm long. Twist the pipe cleaners together to within 1.5cm of one end. Splay the open end to make the doll's fingers.

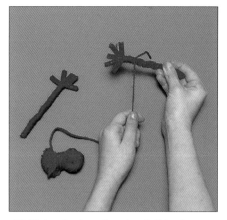

5 Make the legs for the doll in the same way, but this time twist all the way down and bend the ends to make feet. Wind red wool around the doll's arms and legs to hide the twists.

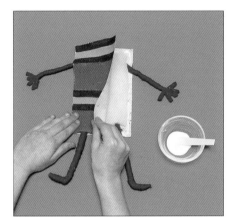

6 Assemble the pieces of the doll using the picture above as your guide, using glue to fix wadding between the pieces. Then glue the front piece of the doll's body in place as shown.

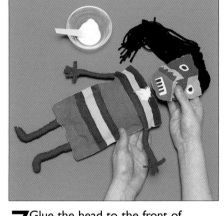

7 Glue the head to the front of the doll's body, making sure the hair does not become caught in the join. Leave the doll to dry completely before picking it up.

▲ Inca mask

This face mask is made of beaten gold and dates back to the 1100s or 1200s. It was made by a Chimú goldsmith and was laid in a royal grave.

Dolls such as these were placed in the graves of the Chancay people of the central Peruvian coast. The Chancay believed that grave dolls such as these would serve as helpers in the life to come.

Theatre and Entertainment

▲ Poets' corner

Poets such as Tao Yuanmin were highly respected in ancient China. Poetry dates back over 3,000 years in China. It was sung rather than spoken.

Throughout history, people from every country and culture have enjoyed listening to music, reading stories and poetry and watching dance, drama and shows. Artistic styles vary in different parts of the world, but representing important events and rituals in human society has always been a big part of our lives.

Many arts aim to entertain their audience by bringing an event or story vividly to life. The arts are also an excellent way of introducing people to new ideas. They are sometimes used to influence their audience's thoughts and beliefs.

◄ Festive times

Festivals were an important part of Inca society. This one is Situa, which was held in August to ward off illness. Music and dance played a large role during these occasions. People would play musical instruments such as drums, whistles and rattles all day.

An actor's disguise ▶

The ancient Greeks enjoyed music and art and went to the theatre regularly. The actors wore special masks during a performance. The top mask was used in tragedies, the one at the bottom in comedies.

◀ Arena of death

The Colosseum in Rome opened in AD80. Emperors staged huge games in its arena to win the favour of the Roman people. The Colosseum could hold as many as 50,000 people. Spectators jostled to watch specially trained gladiators fight each other to the death or face wild animals such as lions and tigers.

Plains drum

rattle

Time for music ▶

Native American instruments were made from everyday materials. Drums were the most important. There were various types of flat or deep drums, mostly made from rawhide (untreated buffalo skin) stretched over a base of carved wood. Reed flutes were sometimes played by Sioux men when they were courting their future wives.

wooden flute

drum and beater

◀ Medieval music

In the Middle Ages in Europe, rich nobles often employed their own full-time minstrels (musicians) to entertain them. Other musicians travelled from town to town, giving small public concerts.

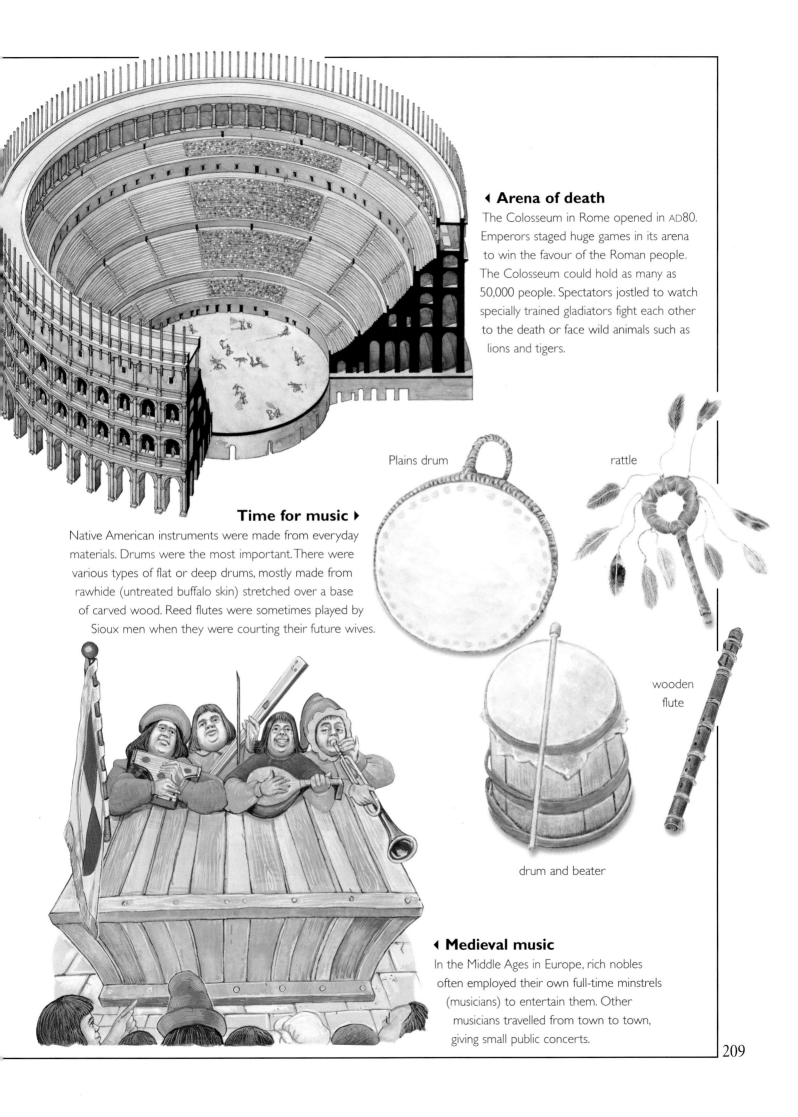

Greek Medusa's costume

In ancient Greek mythology, the Gorgons were three sisters called Stheno, Euryale and Medusa. They were the daughters of two sea monsters and had writhing, living snakes instead of hair, tusks like boars, gold wings and hands of bronze. Two of the Gorgons were immortal but the youngest sister, Medusa, was killed by the Greek hero Perseus. He cut off her head and gave it as a present to his guardian goddess Athene. She wore it ever after like a monstrous brooch on the front of her cloak.

YOU WILL NEED

2 x 2m green fabric, soft-leaded pencil, ruler, scissors, PVA glue and glue brush, sheet of thick card, pair of compasses, dark green acrylic paint, paintbrush, water pot, pair of green tights, 40 pipe cleaners, red card, needle and thread.

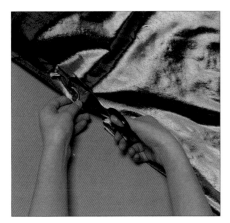

1 Fold the green fabric square in half. Along the centre of the fold, mark a narrow crescent shape 20cm long using a soft-leaded pencil. Cut out the crescent of fabric.

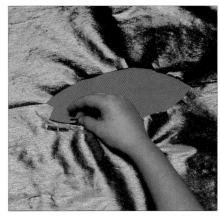

2 Make small cuts along the centre of the hole to create a series of flaps. Fold each flap over and glue it down as shown above. This gives the neck hole a neat, even edge.

3 Fold over and glue down any frayed edges of fabric to complete your gown. Leave it to one side to dry completely while you make the rest of the Medusa's costume.

4 Use the compasses and ruler to measure and draw a circle with a radius of 7cm (diameter 14cm) on to the sheet of thick card as shown. Carefully cut out the card circle.

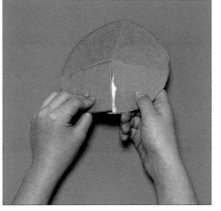

5 Cut into the centre of the circle. Bend the card slightly, overlapping the two edges, and glue them into position as shown above. Leave to dry, then paint the card dark green.

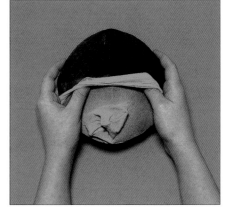

6 Cut the foot and an extra 20cm of the leg from a pair of green tights. Stretch the foot over the card circle so that it lies over the centre of the card as shown above.

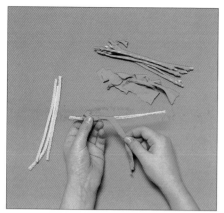

7 Cut the remainder of the tights fabric into small strips and wrap them around 40 pipe cleaners as shown above. Dab a spot of glue on each end to secure the strips in place.

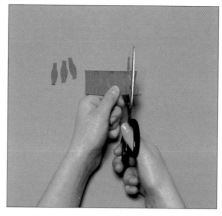

8 Draw small snake head shapes on the red card. Make 40 heads about 2.5cm long and 1cm wide at the ends. Cut them out. (You could fold the card over and cut out two at a time.)

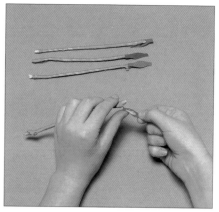

9 Glue the snake heads on to the ends of the pipe cleaners. Leave the snakes to one side until the glue is completely dry. You are now ready to fit the snakes to the head piece.

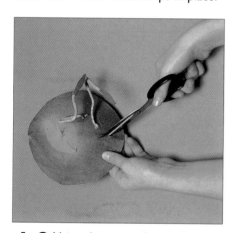

10 Using the pointed end of a pair of scissors, carefully pierce 20 small holes through the head piece you made earlier. Take care to space the holes out evenly.

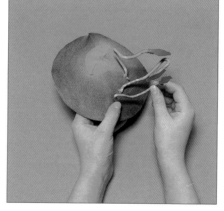

11 Poke a pipe cleaner through each hole. Bend the ends on the inside of the head piece to hold them in position. Form the pipe cleaners into twisted snake shapes.

12 Curve the unused pipe cleaners into twisty snake shapes. Use a needle and thread to sew them over the excess tights fabric that hangs around the card headpiece as shown.

To complete the gown, tie a green cord around your waist. If you have any extra fabric, make a scarf for your neck. Paint your face green to add to the scary effect. The only way to see a Gorgon without being turned to stone was to look at their reflection on a shiny surface. Clever Perseus, who defeated Medusa, used his shield.

211

Greek bird mask

The first Greek dramas were performed at temples in honour of the gods and goddesses. The stories they told were a mixture of history and myth. They featured the adventures of famous Greeks as well as the exploits of gods, goddesses and other legendary heroes. The all-male cast was backed up by a chorus of masked singers and dancers, who provided a commentary on the action.

Drama became so popular in Greece that large open-air theatres were built in major cities and at sacred places such as Delphi. Prizes were awarded to the best dramatists. Over 30 plays by Aeschylus, Sophocles and Euripides have survived, although they wrote many more than this. Some are still performed in theatres today. The works of another 150 known writers have been lost.

▲ Playing many parts
Actors in Greece used masks to represent different characters. The same actor could play different roles in one drama by changing his mask.

◄ Beware of the Minotaur
One popular Greek legend told of the Minotaur. This monster, half-bull and half-man, lived in a maze called the labyrinth. The hero Theseus took a sword and a ball of string into the maze. He unwound the string as he walked. After killing the Minotaur, he followed the string back to the entrance so he didn't lose the way.

YOU WILL NEED

Balloon, petroleum jelly, papier mâché (newspaper soaked in one part water to two parts PVA glue), black pen, scissors, acrylic paints, paintbrush, water pot, two pieces of ochre card (20 x 10cm), glue stick, pencil, pair of compasses, ruler, two pieces of red card (20 x 20cm), cord.

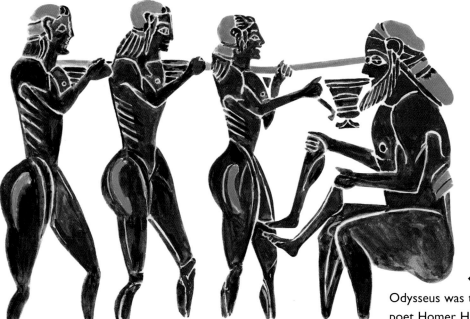

◄ Straight in the eye
Odysseus was the hero of *The Odyssey*, a story by the poet Homer. Here, with the help of his friends, he gouges out the eye of the Cyclops, a vicious one-eyed giant.

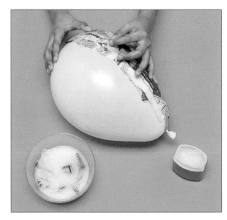

1 Blow up a balloon to slightly larger than your head. Cover half of the balloon in petroleum jelly, and add layers of papier mâché to cover this. When it is dry, pop the balloon.

2 Ask a friend to mark the position of your eyes and the top of your ears on the mask. Cut out small holes at these points. Paint the mask using turquoise acrylic paint.

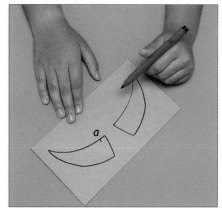

3 Draw and cut out four identical beak shapes, two on each sheet of ochre card. Mark a point 1cm along on the bottom of each pair (the edge marked *a* on the picture above).

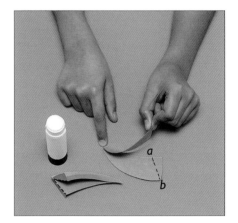

4 Draw a line from *a* to top edge *b* on identical beak shapes. Fold back the line. Glue the two shapes along the top edge as shown above. Repeat for the other pair of beak shapes.

5 Put the point of the compasses on the corner of the red card. Draw two arcs, one with a 10cm radius and one with a 20cm radius. Cut along each line you have drawn.

6 Cut a wavy feather shape into the top of the red card. Draw an arc 1.5cm from the bottom. Cut out 14 tabs as shown above. Repeat steps 5 and 6 for the other piece of red card.

7 Glue the two pieces of red card together at the top. Glue the tabs down to the top of the mask as shown. Glue the beak pieces to the mask. Then draw on a pair of eyes.

To wear your mask, thread a piece of cord through the holes on each side of the head. Tie the two ends together at the back. This mask is modelled on an original worn by the chorus in Aristophanes' comedy *The Birds*.

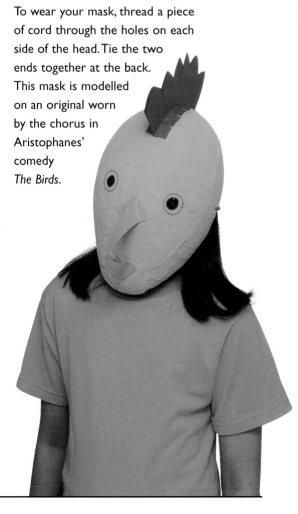

Chinese mask

The earliest Chinese poetry was sung rather than spoken. *Shijing* (the 'Book of Songs') dates back over 3,000 years and includes the words to hymns and folk songs. Music was an important part of Chinese life, and models of musicians were often put in tombs to provide entertainment in the afterlife.

Musicians were frequently accompanied by acrobats, jugglers and magicians. Such acts were as popular in the markets and streets of the town as in the courtyards of nobles. Storytelling and puppet shows were equally well loved. Plays and opera became popular in the 1200s, with tales of murder, intrigue, heroism and love acted out to music. Most of the female roles would be played by men. Elaborate make-up and fancy costumes made it clear to the audience whether the actor was playing a hero or a villain, a princess or a demon.

▲ **New Year dragon**
Dressing up is also a popular part of Chinese religion, with everybody joining in events such as Chinese New Year. Dragons symbolize happiness and good luck and represent the generous spirit of New Year.

YOU WILL NEED

Tape measure, self-hardening clay, cutting board, modelling tool, petroleum jelly, newspaper, PVA glue and glue brush, water, bowl for mixing glue and water, thick card, pencil, ruler, scissors, masking tape, two large white beads, acrylic paints, paintbrush, water pot, wood glue, needle, black wool, string.

▲ **Energetic opera**
Some ancient Chinese plays are still performed today. Modern theatre companies try to recreate how plays would have looked to their original audience.

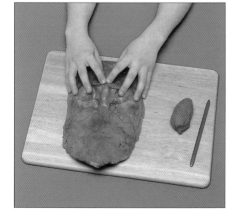

Measure the dimensions of your face using a ruler or tape measure. Mould a piece of clay to fit the size of your face. Carve out eye sockets and attach a clay nose. Leave to dry.

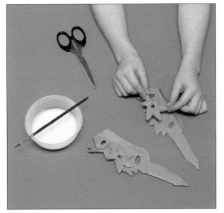

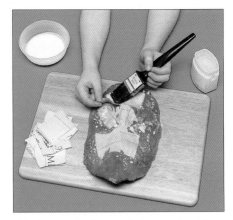

2 Smear the front of the mask with petroleum jelly. Apply six layers of papier mâché, made by soaking strips of newspaper in two parts PVA glue to one part water. Leave the mask to dry.

3 When it is dry, remove the mask from the clay mould. Cut a 2.5cm-wide strip of card long enough to fit around your face. Bend it into a circle. Tape it to the back of the mask.

4 Cut two pointed ear shapes as shown. Fold the card at the straight edges to make flaps. Cut out and glue on decorative pieces of card. Glue the ear flaps to the sides of the mask.

5 Glue two large white beads on to the front of the mask for the eyes. Cut out more small pieces of card. Glue these on for eyebrows. Glue on another piece of card for the lips.

6 Paint the entire mask in a dark blue-grey. Leave it to dry. Paint on more details using brighter colours. When the mask is dry, varnish it with wood glue.

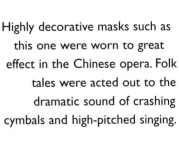

7 Use a needle to thread lengths of black wool through for the beard. Tape the wool at the back. Then thread string through the sides of the mask behind the ears to tie it on.

Highly decorative masks such as this one were worn to great effect in the Chinese opera. Folk tales were acted out to the dramatic sound of crashing cymbals and high-pitched singing.

Japanese Noh mask

Going to the theatre and listening to music were popular pastimes in ancient Japan. There were several kinds of Japanese drama, all of which developed from religious dances at temples and shrines, or from slow, stately dances performed at the emperor's court.

Noh is the oldest form of Japanese drama. It developed in the 1300s from rituals and dances that had been performed for centuries before. Noh plays were serious and dignified. The actors performed on a bare stage, with only a backdrop. They chanted or sang their words, and the performance was accompanied by percussion and a flute. Noh performances were traditionally held in the open air, often at a shrine. Kabuki plays were first seen around 1600 and were a complete contrast to the tragic Noh style. In 1629, the shoguns (military governors) banned women performers and so male actors took their places. Kabuki plays became very popular in the new, fast-growing towns.

▲ **Wooden expression**
This Noh mask represents a warrior. Noh drama did not try to be lifelike. The actors moved very slowly with stylized gestures to show their feelings.

YOU WILL NEED

Tape measure, balloon, petroleum jelly, mixing bowl, newspaper, PVA glue, water, pin, scissors, felt-tipped pen, self-hardening clay, bradawl, acrylic paints, paintbrush, water pot, piece of cord.

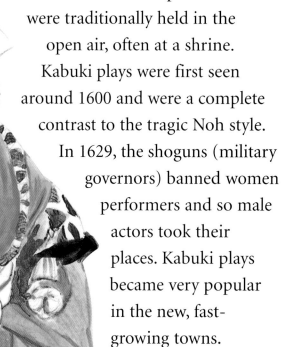

◀ **Plays made fun**
Kabuki plays were very different to the more serious Noh style theatre. They were fast-moving, loud, flashy and very dramatic. Audiences admired the skills of the Kabuki actors as much as the cleverness or thoughtfulness of the plots of these plays.

Ask a friend to measure around your head, above the ears, with a tape measure. Blow up a balloon to the same size. This will act as the mould for the papier mâché mask.

2 Smear the balloon with a layer of petroleum jelly. Then rip up strips of old newspaper and soak them in a bowl containing a mixture of two parts PVA glue to one parts water.

3 Cover the front and sides of the balloon with the papier mâché. You will need to add three or four layers of papier mâché. When the mask is dry, pop the balloon.

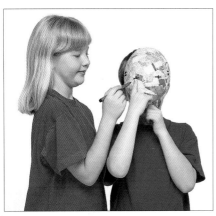

4 Trim the papier mâché to tidy up the edges of your mask. Then ask a friend to mark where your eyes and mouth are when you hold the mask to your face.

5 Cut out holes for the eyes and mouth using scissors. Then put a piece of clay either side of the face at eye level. Use a bradawl to pierce two holes on each side of the face.

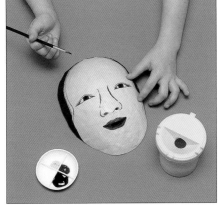

6 Paint the face of a calm young lady from Noh theatre on to your mask. You can use the picture above as your guide. In Japan, this mask would have been worn by a man.

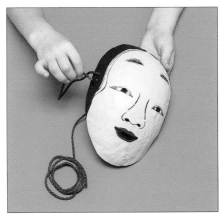

7 Fit a length of cord through the holes at each side of the mask. Tie one end of the cord. Once you have adjusted the mask to fit your head, firmly tie the other end of the cord.

Put on your mask and feel like an actor in an ancient Noh play. Noh drama was always about important and serious topics. Favourite subjects included death and the afterlife, and the plays were often tragic.

Celtic harp

The Celts enjoyed music, poems and songs as entertainment and for more serious purposes, too. Music was played to accompany Celtic warriors into battle and help them feel brave. Poems praised the achievements of a great chieftain or the adventures of bold raiders, and recorded the history of a tribe. Dead chieftains and heroes, and possibly even ordinary people, were mourned with sad laments.

On special occasions, and in the homes of high-ranking Celts, poems and songs were performed by people called bards. Roman writers described the many years of training to become a bard. Bards learned how to compose using all the different styles of poetry and memorized hundreds of legends and songs. They also learned how to play an instrument, and to read and write. Becoming a bard was the first step towards being a druid (priest).

◄ **Music from a god**
This statue shows a Celtic god playing a lyre. Music played an important part in many Celtic ceremonies. The Celts believed that, like religious knowledge, music was too holy to be written down. Sadly, this means that many Celtic poems and songs have been lost forever.

▲ **Making music**
Instruments such as this stringed lute have been played by humans as far back as 3500BC – long before the age of the Celtic civilization.

YOU WILL NEED
Sheet of thin card (49 x 39cm), pencil, ruler, scissors, thick card (49 x 39cm), felt-tipped pen, PVA glue and glue brush, acrylic paint, paintbrush, water pot, bradawl, coloured string, 16 brass split pins.

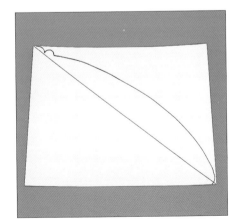

I Draw a diagonal line, from corner to corner, on the rectangle of thin card. Then draw a gently curving line, with a shape at one end, using the picture above as your guide.

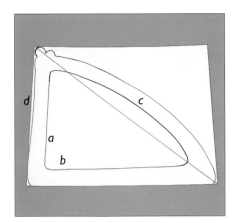

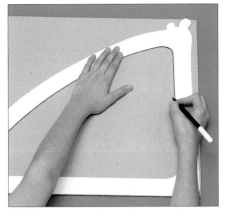

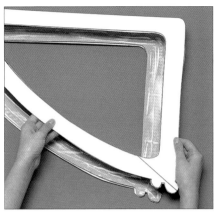

2 Using the picture above as your guide, draw two lines – *a* and *b* – 4.5cm in from the edge of the card. Join them with a curved line *c*. Finally, add a curved line *d* parallel with *a*.

3 Cut out the harp shape you have drawn and place it on the rectangle of thick card. Draw around it, inside and out, with a felt-tipped pen. Cut out the harp shape from the thick card.

4 Glue one side of the thin card harp shape to one side of the thick card harp shape. Apply two coats of dark brown paint, leaving the harp shape to dry between each coat.

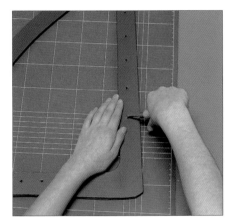

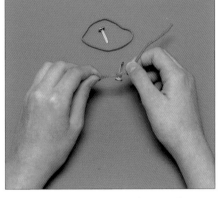

5 Use a bradawl to pierce a series of seven holes approximately 5cm apart along the two straight sides of the frame of your harp. These will be the holes for the strings.

6 Cut a 40cm length of string. Then cut six more pieces of string, each one 5cm shorter than the last. Tie a brass split pin to both ends of all the pieces of string.

Most Celtic poetry was not spoken, but sung or chanted to the music of the harp or lyre. Bards used the music to create the right atmosphere to accompany their words, and to add extra dramatic affects, such as shivery sounds during a scary ghost tale.

7 Push the split pins into the holes you made earlier so that the strings lie diagonally across the harp. Adjust each string so that it is stretched tightly across the frame.

Inca hand drum

Music and dance were very important to the Incas. Instruments, such as rattles, flutes, large drums, hand drums and panpipes, were made from wood, reeds, pottery and bone. At festivals, such as the Inti Raymi (Sun Festival), musicians would play all day without a break. Large bands walked in procession, each panpipe player picking out a different part of the tune. The Spanish influenced these festivals after the conquest, and they became known by the Spanish term, *fiesta*. However, many of the fiestas celebrated had their dances or costumes rooted in an Inca past.

▲ **Traditional music**
A modern street band plays in Cuzco, the ancient capital of the Inca Empire. Ancient tunes and rhythms live on in the modern music of the Andes.

▲ **Home of the Incas**
The Inca Empire in the Peruvian Andes was a world full of music and dance, especially during festivals.

Map labels: Quito, Spanish conquistador, Andes Mountains, Tumbes, Moche stirrup-spout pot, Chan Chan, Cajamarca, Moche, sun god mask, Chavin de Huantar, panpipes, alpaca, Machu Picchu, Nazca hummingbird figure, Paracas, Nazca, Cuzco, Lake Titicaca, reed boat, Tiwanaku

YOU WILL NEED

Pencil, ruler, thick card (100 x 20cm), scissors, masking tape, cream calico fabric, PVA glue and glue brush, acrylic paints, paintbrush, water pot, wadding, 30cm length of thick dowelling, coloured wool.

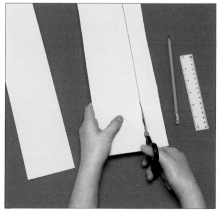

Use a pencil and ruler to mark two rectangles on the thick card, each one measuring 85 x 9cm. Cut the rectangles out carefully. They will form the sides of your Inca hand drum.

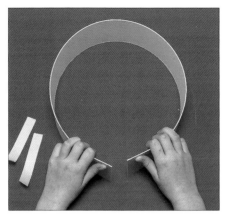

2 Bend one rectangle into a circle as shown above. Use strips of masking tape to join the two ends of the card ring together. It may be easier to ask a friend to help you do this.

3 Lay the ring on top of the cream calico fabric. Draw around the card ring on to the fabric, leaving a gap of about 2cm as shown above. Remove the ring and cut out the fabric circle.

4 Paint glue around the edge of the fabric circle. Turn the fabric over. Carefully stretch the fabric over the card ring. Keep the fabric taut and smooth the edges as you stick.

5 Draw a geometric Inca-style pattern on the second strip of card. Use bright colours to decorate the card as shown above. Lay the card flat and leave it to dry.

6 When the painted strip is dry, wrap it around the drum as shown. Use masking tape to fix one end of the ring to the drum. Then glue the rest of the ring around the drum. Leave to dry.

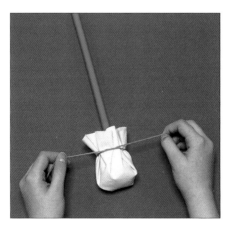

7 Cut out a 20cm-diameter circle of calico fabric. Make a drumstick by wrapping a piece of wadding and the calico circle around one end of the dowelling. Tie it with wool.

Women played hand drums like this one at festivals during Inca times. Some festivals were held in villages and fields. Others took place at religious sites or in the big Inca cities.

Playing the fool

Noble families often employed jesters full-time, so that they could be cheered up whenever they wanted. It was rather like having their own private comedy act. Jesters dressed in silly costumes with bells and played the fool. However, they were often skilled jugglers and acrobats, too. They sang songs and told funny stories and jokes, which were often very rude. They often made fun of their audience, and were great at passing on top-secret gossip that no one else would dare mention.

▲ Roll up for the fair
In the Middle Ages, jesters were often found entertaining merchants and traders at the local markets and fairs.

Juggling

YOU WILL NEED

Juggling: juggling balls.

Jester's rattle: pencil, yellow card (24 x 19cm), polystyrene ball, scissors, PVA glue and glue brush, 40cm length of dowelling (1cm in diameter), acrylic paints, paintbrush, water pot, seven bells, two 45cm lengths each of red and yellow ribbon.

1 Take a juggling ball in each hand. Throw both of the balls up into the air together in straight lines and catch them when they fall. This is the easy part of juggling!

2 Throw both juggling balls up together so that they cross in front of you. The trick is to make sure that they do not bump into each other. Catch each ball in the opposite hand.

3 Now try throwing both balls up together in straight lines again. This time, however, cross your hands over to catch the balls as they fall. You may have to practise this one a lot!

4 Throw the juggling ball in your right hand diagonally across your body. Just as it is about to drop, throw the other ball diagonally towards your right hand. Keep practising!

5 Catch the first ball in your left hand but keep your eye on the other ball still in the air. Catch this one in your right hand. Remember – practise makes perfect!

Jester's rattle

1 Use a pencil to draw a hat shape on to the piece of yellow card. Use the picture above to help you. Draw around the ball to make sure the curve at the bottom is the same diameter.

2 Cut out the hat shape. Put a strip of glue around the curve at the bottom of the hat. Press the ball into the glued section and hold it in place until it is firmly stuck down.

3 Use the pointed ends of a pair of scissors to make a hole in the bottom of the ball. Ask an adult to help if necessary. Fill the hole with glue and insert the piece of dowelling.

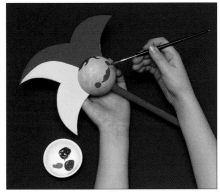

4 Paint the stick bright red. When it is dry, paint some eyes, a mouth, cheeks and hair on the ball to make a cheerful face. Then paint one half of the jester's hat red.

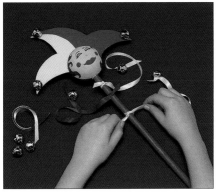

5 Glue three bells to the corners of the hat. Then tie four bells to the lengths of coloured ribbon. Tie the ribbons around the stick, using a simple knot to secure them.

Once you know how to juggle two balls, try to master the three-ball juggle. Professional jugglers who were not employed full-time travelled from castle to castle.

Important people often carried sticks in the Middle Ages, which they banged loudly on the floor to attract attention. The jester's small stick made fun of these.

Monster mask

Myths and legends involving beasts, ghouls and witches have captured the imaginations of people worldwide. Such scary stories have passed through the generations, at first by word of mouth, and then through books, plays, films and now via the Internet. The tale of Frankenstein's monster, created by the English writer Mary Shelley, is one such spine-chilling story. The monster was an ugly creature brought to life by a young scientist called Frankenstein. In this project, you can make a mask of Frankenstein's monster.

YOU WILL NEED

Balloon, newspaper strips, water, PVA glue and glue brush, pin, scissors, thick card (29 x 14cm, 22 x 12cm, 29 x 9.5cm and scraps), ruler, pencil, pair of compasses, brown gum tape, masking tape, two 3cm lengths of thin balsa dowelling, acrylic paints, paintbrushes, water pot, string.

1 Blow up the balloon. Soak strips of newspaper with half measures of glue and water to make papier mâché. Cover one side of the balloon with five layers of papier mâché. Leave it to dry.

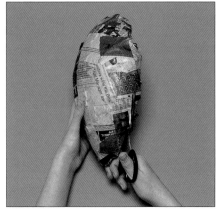

2 When the mask is completely dry, carefully burst the balloon using a pin. Take the papier mâché mask and trim off the excess to produce a rounded face shape.

3 Take the piece of card measuring 29 x 14cm. Use a ruler and pencil to draw a line 5cm in from one long edge. Then draw a pencil line across the middle as shown above.

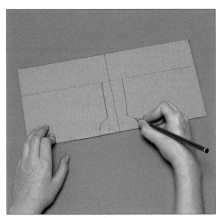

4 Draw the shape of the nose using the centre line in the middle as a guide. Make the nose 3cm wide on the bridge and 4cm at the nostril. Cut out the nose and the brow.

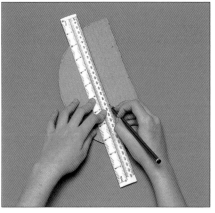

5 Set the compasses to 11cm. Draw a semicircle on to the 22 x 12cm piece of card. Cut it out. Draw a pencil line 5cm from the straight edge. Cut this 5cm piece off.

6 Line the edges of the semicircle with PVA glue. Stick it to the top edge of the nose piece as shown above. Hold the pieces together until the glue has dried.

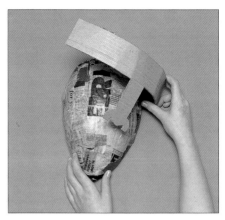

7 Cover the back of the head and nose piece with PVA glue. Stick this piece in position on top of the papier mâché face mask you made earlier. Leave the mask to one side to dry.

8 Draw a line in the centre of the 29 x 9.5cm piece of card. Draw a 10 x 4cm rectangle at the centre of the line touching the bottom edge. Cut the smaller rectangle out.

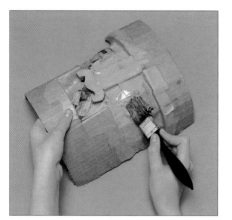

9 Cover the back of the card jaw piece with glue. Stick it over the lower part of the mask. Cover the gaps between the stuck-on face parts and the mask with brown gum tape.

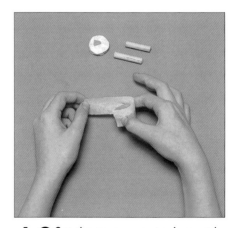

10 Set the compasses to 1cm and draw two circles on a scrap piece of card. Cut out the two circles and cover them with masking tape. Take the balsa dowelling.

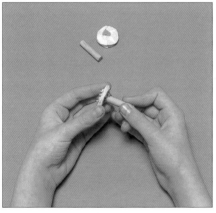

11 Make a hole in the centre of each card circle using your scissors. Push the balsa dowelling through the middle. Glue into position and paint the pieces black.

12 Paint the mask with a base colour, for example, grey or green. Wait for the base coat to dry before painting in the details of the face with other colours. Leave to dry.

13 Push the bolts through the sides of the mask. Glue them into position. Put the mask over your face and mark eyeholes. Take the mask off. Make eyeholes with the scissors.

To finish your Frankenstein mask, tie or tape string on to either side of the mask. If you can find old clothes, such as a shirt and dinner jacket, you could decorate them as well, perhaps with gruesome blood stains made with red paint.

Toys and Games

Game players

Archaeologists have found board games and toys among the remains of the great cities of the Indus Valley civilization. These people grew up nearly 5,000 years ago in the area occupied by present-day Pakistan.

People have always played with toys and games. Our early Stone Age ancestors played with small doll-like figures made of clay and whistles carved from bone. Toys dating from 5000BC have been found in China. Many games from the ancient world are still familiar to us today. Hopscotch and hide-and-seek were played in the ancient civilizations of Egypt, Greece and Rome. There were toys, too, such as rattles, yo-yos, dolls and spinning tops.

As well as being fun, games provided mental and physical challenges. Board games in particular showed children different ways of thinking and planning, and prepared them for the adult world.

◀ Martial arts

Kendo and several other martial arts that are popular today developed from the fighting skills of samurai warriors from ancient Japan. In kendo, combatants fight one another with long swords made of split bamboo. They score points by managing to touch their opponent's body, not by cutting or stabbing them.

Royal game ▸

A beautifully made board game was found in the Royal Graves of Ur, an ancient city of Mesopotamia. The board game was made of wood covered in bitumen (tar) and decorated with a mosaic of shell, bone, blue lapis lazuli (a kind of gemstone), red glass and pink limestone. The game may have been a bit like ludo, with two sets of counters and four-sided dice, but the rules have not been found.

◂ Ancient athletes

Sport was important to the ancient Greeks. In fact, it had religious significance. The first ever Olympic Games were held in 776BC in honour of the Greek god Zeus. Sports included throwing the discus and javelin, boxing, wrestling and the long jump. The games were only open to men – women were not even allowed to watch. They held their own games in honour of Hera, goddess of women.

Dangerous sports ▸

Wrestling was a favourite sport as long ago as 1000BC. Many kings in ancient India had the title *malla* (wrestler). They had to keep to strict diets and physical training programmes in camps known as *akharas*. Wrestling could be a highly dangerous activity. One inscription tells of a malla who was accidentally killed during a match.

Egyptian snake game

Board games such as mehen, or the snake game, were popular from the earliest days of ancient Egypt. In the tomb of the Pharaoh Tutankhamun, a beautiful gaming board made of ebony and ivory was discovered. It was designed for a board game called senet. Players threw sticks to decide how many squares to move at a time. Some of the squares had gains and some had forfeits. Senet was thought to symbolize the struggle against evil.

Another favourite pastime for the ancient Egyptians was sport. Armed with bows and arrows, sticks, spears and nets, they hunted wild animals for pleasure as well as for food. Wrestling was a popular spectator sport at all levels of society. Chariot racing, however, which was introduced around 1663BC, could only be afforded by the nobility.

▲ Tomb raider
A thief breaks into a pharaoh's tomb. Inside are the treasures that were important to him, including game boards and counters.

YOU WILL NEED

Self-hardening clay, rolling pin, cutting board, ruler, modelling tool, acrylic paint, paintbrush, water pot, cloth, varnish, 12 counters (six blue and grey and six gold and orange), two large counters, dice, pencil.

▲ Games in the afterlife
The walls of many Egyptian tombs were covered with everyday scenes. They were designed to show how life should carry on in the afterlife. In this tomb painting, an official of the Pharaoh Rameses II is playing the board game of senet with his wife.

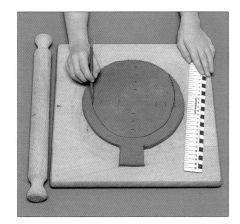

Roll out the clay on to a board and cut it into the shape shown above. Score on a snake shape and score lines across the body at intervals. Use the final project picture as a guide.

2 When the clay is completely dry, rub the board with diluted green paint to stain the lines. Wipe away the excess paint with a cloth. Leave the board to dry and then varnish it.

3 Each player takes six counters of the same colours, plus one large piece called a 'lion'. Place the counters so that the same colour faces up. Throw the dice. You need a '1' to start each counter.

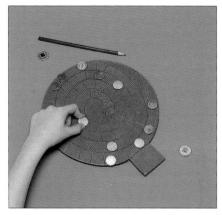

4 Your go ends if you throw another '1'. If it's another number, advance a counter that number of squares towards the centre of the board. Only move counters that have started on the board.

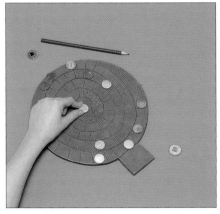

5 Throw exactly the right number to reach the centre. Then turn the counter over so that it can start the return journey. As soon as your first counter gets home, the lion piece begins.

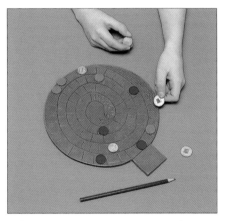

6 The lion counter moves to the centre of the board in the same way as the other counters. On its return journey, it can eat the opponent's counters if it lands on them.

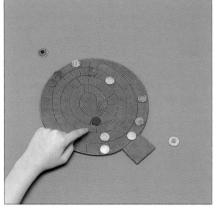

7 The winner is the person whose lion has eaten the largest number of counters. Work out the number of counters you got home safely, and see who has the most counters left.

▲ Two in one

This board game set, found in a pharaoh's pyramid, could be used to play senet and another game called tjau. It has a built-in drawer that contained all the loose pieces, such as counters, for the two games.

Mehen, the snake game, was popular in Egypt before 3000BC. The game was called snake because the stone board represented a coiled serpent with its head in the middle.

Egyptian lion toy

Wall paintings and goods found in Egyptian tombs have provided plenty of evidence that the ancient Egyptians enjoyed toys and games, such as spinning tops and rattles. Children had only a few years before serious education and work began. However, we know that they played with balls made from rags, linen and reeds. They also played with rattles and spinning tops made of glazed stone, and little wooden models of horses and crocodiles. Toy cats were especially popular, because cats were regarded as holy animals in ancient Egypt. A game called tip cat was also a favourite. In this game, players tried to hit a small, oblong piece of wood, called a cat, over a large ring in the ground.

Many ancient Egyptian artefacts have been preserved and are kept in museums throughout the world. In the *Staatliche Museen* (National Museum) in Berlin, Germany, there is a toy crocodile with a moving jaw, dating from more than 3,600 years ago. Equally remarkable are the hedgehog and lion on wheels dating from the same period, which were found in the Persian town of Susa.

▲ On guard
The Great Sphinx has the body of a lion and the head of a man. This massive stone statue guards the pyramids of Giza on the edge of modern Cairo. They were built for the Pharaoh Khufu, his son Khafre and the Pharaoh Menkaure.

▲ Paddle dolls
Egyptian children often played with a paddle doll. The hair of the doll on the left is made from dried mud. Both dolls date from c.1900BC.

YOU WILL NEED

Self-hardening clay, rolling pin, cutting board, modelling tool, piece of card, skewer, balsa wood, fine sandpaper, acrylic paints, paintbrush, water pot, masking tape, string.

1 Begin by rolling out the clay. Cut the clay into the shapes shown in the picture above. Mould the legs on to the body and the base. Leave the bottom jaw piece to one side.

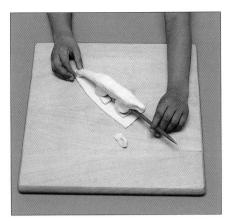

2 Use the modelling tool to make a hole between the upper body of the lion and the base section as shown above. The lower jaw of the lion will fit into this hole.

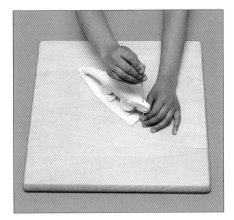

3 Insert the lower jaw into the hole you have made and prop it up with the piece of card. Then use the skewer to make a hole in the upper and lower jaws of the lion's head as shown above.

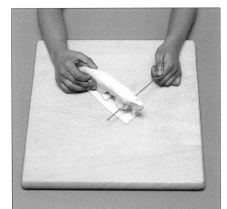

4 Now use the skewer to make a hole from left to right through the lion's upper body and lower jaw. When the figure is dry, you will thread the string through these holes.

5 Push a small piece of balsa wood into the mouth of the lion. This will form the lion's tooth. Leave the clay lion to dry. Sand down the surface of the figure with fine sandpaper.

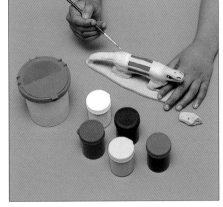
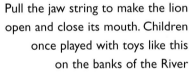

6 Paint the lion using bright colours as shown above. Use masking tape to ensure that the lines you paint are straight. Leave the lion in a warm place for the paint to dry.

Pull the jaw string to make the lion open and close its mouth. Children once played with toys like this on the banks of the River Nile. Originally, this toy would have been made of brightly painted wood, with a bronze tooth.

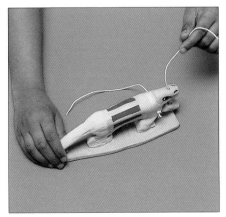

7 Thread the string through the holes in the upper body and tie it to secure. A second piece of string should then be threaded through the lower and upper jaws of the lion.

Greek knucklebones

The game of knucklebones played in ancient Greece is rather like the more modern game of jacks. It was not a game at all to begin with. The way the bones fell when they were thrown was interpreted to predict the future. The knuckles – little ankle bones of a sheep or cow – were called *astragalos* by the Greeks. Girls tended to play the game of knucklebones, while boys preferred to cast the bones like dice in a game of chance. Each of the four distinctively shaped sides of the bone was given a different numerical value.

One of the most popular board games in ancient Greece was a game of siege called *polis* (city). Another was the 'game of the five lines', in which the central, sacred, line had special significance. The exact rules are not known, but it is thought that it may have been rather like the later game of draughts. Board and picture games, and toys have been found in the tombs of children. Many archaeological finds have unearthed evidence of toys that are still played with today, such as hoops, rattles, dolls, spinning tops and balls.

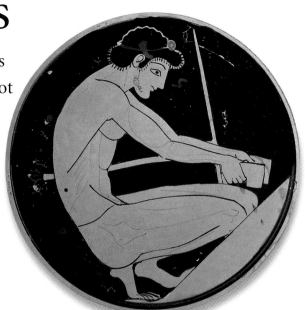

▲ **Fit for life**
A Greek athlete lifts weights, perhaps to get himself fit for battle, or for a sports competition. The Greeks were keen on sport for its own sake. Many cities had a public gymnasium, and games were a feature of religious festivals.

YOU WILL NEED
Self-hardening clay, rolling pin, cutting board, modelling tool, cream acrylic paint, paintbrush, water pot.

▲ **Knockout punch**
Boxing was one of the sports soon included in the Olympic Games after they began in 776BC. Other sports included weights, discus and javelin, running and wrestling.

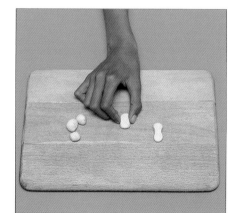

Divide the clay into five small pieces. Then roll each piece into the shape of a ball. Press each ball of clay into a figure-of-eight shape as shown in the picture above.

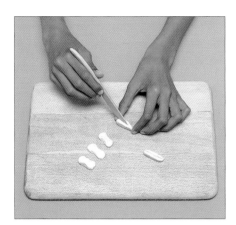

2 Use the modelling tool to carve out a ridge in the middle of each figure-of-eight. Then make small dents in the end of each piece with your finger. Leave the five shapes to dry.

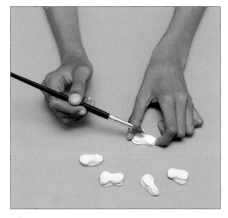

3 When they are dry, give the pieces two coats of paint. Use cream paint so that the pieces look like bone. When the paint is dry, you and a friend can play with them.

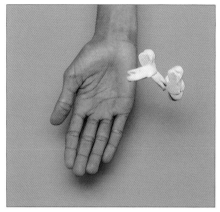

4 To play knucklebones, gather the five pieces in the palm of one of your hands. Throw all five pieces into the air at once as shown above. Then quickly flip your hand over.

5 Take turns to try to catch as many of the pieces as you can on the back of your hand. If you or your friend catch them all that person wins the game. If not, the game continues.

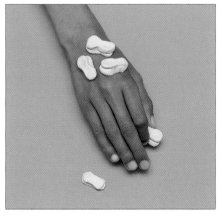

6 If you drop any of the pieces, try to pick them up with the others still on the back of your hand. Throw them with your free hand and try to catch them again.

Knucklebones were made from the ankle bones of animals such as sheep or cows. These small bones were used in different ways, depending on the type of game. The Greeks also used the knucklebones as dice.

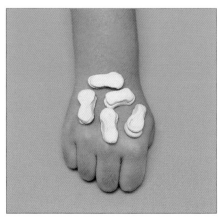

7 The winner is the first person to catch all the knucklebones on the back of their hand. It may take a few goes to get the hang of the game. But remember – practice makes perfect!

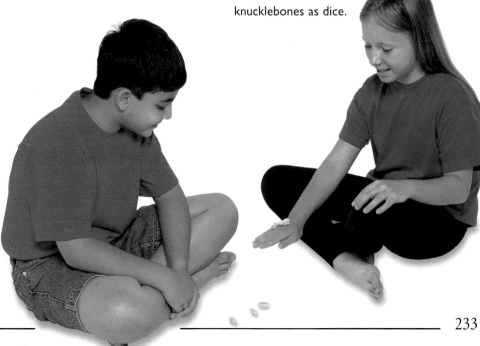

Roman dux game

The Roman game of dux was a little bit like the game of draughts. In terms of difficulty, it comes somewhere between the very simple games that Romans enjoyed playing, such as noughts and crosses, and more complicated games, such as chess. In some games, a die was thrown to decide how many squares they could move at a time.

Knucklebones was popular at public baths. The Romans learned how to play the game from the Greeks. Each player would throw the small anklebones of a sheep up into the air and try to catch them on the back of the hand. Knucklebones could also be played like dice, with each side of the bones having a different score.

Roman children played games such as hide-and-seek and hopscotch, and had dolls and toy animals of wood, clay or bronze. A child from a wealthy family might be given a child-sized chariot that could be pulled by a goat.

▲ Playing games

The mosaic dates from around the 1st century AD. It shows three Roman men playing a dice game. The Romans were such great gamblers that games of chance were officially banned. The one exception was during the winter festival of Saturnalia, when most rules were relaxed.

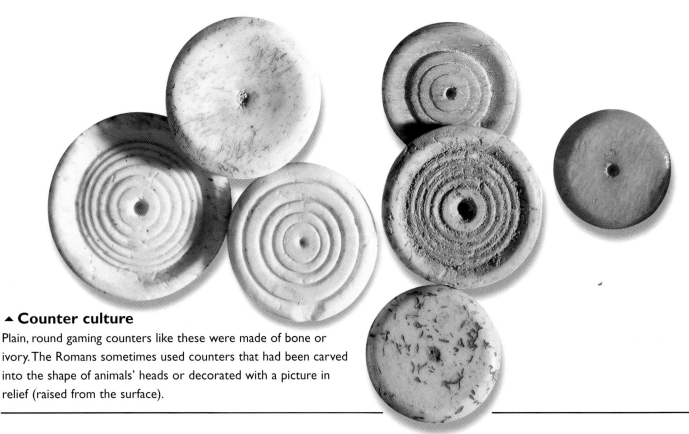

▲ Counter culture

Plain, round gaming counters like these were made of bone or ivory. The Romans sometimes used counters that had been carved into the shape of animals' heads or decorated with a picture in relief (raised from the surface).

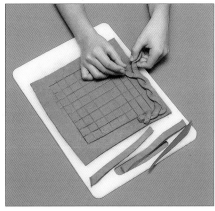

YOU WILL NEED

Self-hardening clay, rolling pin, cutting board, ruler, modelling tool, two different colours of glass mosaic tiles (16 of each), two glass beads (two colours; the same as your tiles).

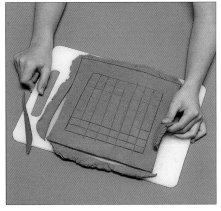

1 Roll out the clay, and trim it to about 25cm square. Use the ruler and modelling tool to mark out a grid eight squares across and eight squares down. Leave room for a border.

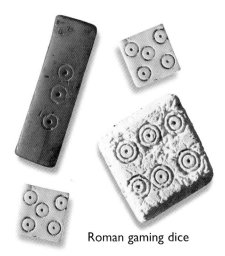

2 Decorate the border using the excess clay as shown. Leave the gaming board to dry. Each player then chooses a colour and has 16 tiles and a bead. The bead is the dux, or leader.

3 Players take turns to put their tiles on the squares, two at a time. The dux is put on last. Players now take turns to move a tile one square forward, backwards or sideways.

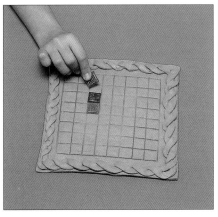

4 If you sandwich your opponent's tile between two of your own, his or her tile is captured and removed. You then get an extra go. The dux is captured in the same way as the tiles.

Roman gaming dice

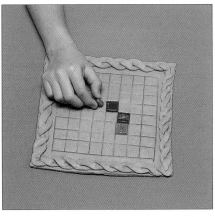

5 The dux can also jump over a tile on to an empty square as shown. If your opponent's tile is then trapped between your dux and one of your tiles, his or her tile is captured.

During the game, you must move a tile or a dux if it is possible to do so – even if it means being captured. The winner is the first player to capture all of the other player's tiles and dux.

Chinese kite

The earliest kite flying in China was recorded during the Han Dynasty (206BC–AD220). These early kites were made of silk and bamboo. They were flown high in the sky during battles to scare off the enemy. Gradually, kites were flown during festivals. In the Qing Dynasty (1644–1912), a festival called Tengkao (Mounting the Height) was introduced by the Manchu emperors. People flew kites from high ground in the belief that this would bring them good luck.

Ever since ancient times, the Chinese have loved to play games and watch displays of martial arts and acrobatics. The nobility also invited acrobats and dancers into their homes to amuse their guests. Performances often lasted for hours, especially during festivals and ceremonies. Sports, such as polo and football, were also enjoyed by the wealthy. One emperor, Xuanzong, enjoyed polo so much that he failed to keep up with his official engagements.

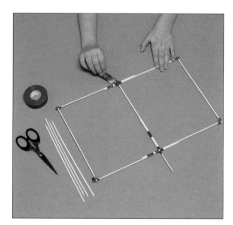

▲ Battleboard

The traditional game of xiang qi is similar to chess. One army battles against another, with round discs used as playing pieces. To tell the discs apart, each is marked with a name.

YOU WILL NEED

Thirteen barbecue sticks measuring 30cm long, ruler, PVA glue and glue brush, masking tape, scissors, white A1 paper, pencil, acrylic paints, paintbrush, water pot, 10m length of string, piece of wooden dowelling, small metal ring.

▲ Training for war

This figure shows an ancient Chinese polo player. Polo was originally played in India and Asia. It was invented as a training game to improve the riding skills of soldiers in cavalry units.

1 Make a 40 x 30cm rectangle by gluing and taping sticks together. Overlap the sticks for strength. Join two sticks together to make a central rod that sticks out on one side as shown.

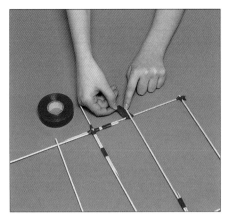

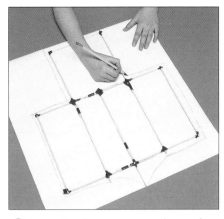

2 Use the last five sticks to make a rectangle measuring 40 x 15cm. Lay this rectangle on top of the first one at a right angle. Tape the two rectangles together as shown in steps 2 and 3..

3 Place the frame on to a sheet of white A1 paper. Draw a border around the outside of the frame, 2.5cm out from the edge. Add curves around the end of the centre rod.

4 Cut out the kite shape you have drawn. Using a pencil, draw on the details of the dragon design shown in the final picture on this page. Paint in the design and leave it to dry.

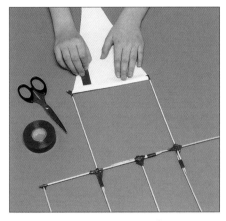

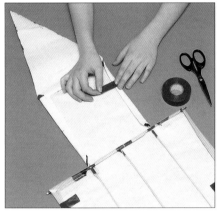

5 Cut a triangular piece of paper to make a tail for the end of your kite. Paint it and let it dry. Fold the tail over the rod at the bottom of the kite as shown. Tape the tail into position.

6 Carefully tape and glue your dragon design on to the frame of the kite. Fold the border over the frame and tape it on to the back of the kite as shown above.

7 Wrap the string round the dowelling and tie the end to a ring. Tie two pieces of string to the central rod of the frame. Make two holes in the kite, pass the strings through and tie to the ring.

Kites were invented in China around 3,000 years ago. They were often made into the shapes of animals or mythical creatures such as dragons. Today, Chinese children still play with home-made paper kites.

Japanese shell game

Perhaps one of the reasons why the Japanese invented the shell game was because shellfish have always been an important ingredient in Japanese food. Japan has a rich cultural history, and many pastimes have been handed down through the generations.

A game called menko, which has been played since the 1700s, involves throwing cards on the ground. Players try to flip their opponent's cards over by throwing their card on top of them. Karuta, another card game, has been popular since the 1600s. Karuta cards have pictures, words and poems written on them. In one version, known as iroha karuta, a player acts as the reader and keeps one set of karuta cards with sayings on them. The other players gather around a spread-out set of cards with the first letter or few words of the saying and a picture on them. When the reader starts reading a saying, the players try to find the matching karuta card. Whoever finds the card keeps it, and the player with the most cards at the end of the game wins.

▲ **Counters from the sea**
The Japanese often ate shellfish and kept the prettiest shells afterwards. They could then use them to play games such as this one.

YOU WILL NEED

Fresh clams, pan, water, bowl,

selection of acrylic paints,

paintbrush, water pot.

▲ **Playing to win**
Three court ladies play a card game, probably using karuta cards. These cards often included popular sayings from everyday Japanese life.

I Ask an adult to boil the clams. Leave them to one side to cool and then remove the insides. Wash the shells and leave them to dry. When they are dry, paint the shells gold.

2 When the gold paint is dry, carefully pull each pair of shells apart. Then paint an identical design on to each shell of the pair. Start by painting a round, white face.

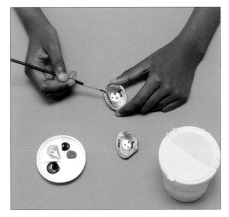

3 Add more features to the face, such as a mouth, hair and eyes. In the past, popular pictures, such as scenes from traditional stories, were painted on to the shell pairs.

4 Paint several pairs of clam shells with a variety of designs. Copy the ones here or make up your own. Make sure each pair of shells has an identical picture. Leave the painted shells to dry.

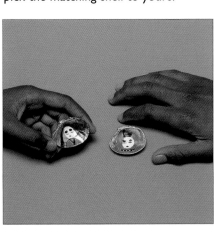

5 Now it is time to play the game. Turn all your shells face down and jumble them up. Turn over one shell and then challenge your opponent to pick the matching shell to yours.

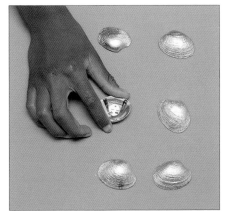

6 If the two shells do not match, turn them over and try again. If they do match, your opponent takes the shells. Take it in turns to challenge each other to find the matching pair.

The player with the most shells at the end of the game wins! Noble ladies at the imperial court enjoyed playing the shell game. This is a simplified version of the game they used to play.

Japanese streamer

There are thousands of local festivals in Japan each year. Most are based on ancient celebrations of the natural world, marking the yearly planting, growing and harvesting cycles. Each festival involves parades, dances, feasts and contests such as tug-of-war and kite flying.

Boys' Day, held on the fifth day of the fifth month each year, was originally a festival to prepare farm labourers for the hard work of transplanting rice seedlings. This festival was once known as the Sweet Flag Festival, named for the sweet flag plant that people hung outside their homes to keep evil spirits away. Gradually, the meaning of the festival changed to symbolize manliness and courage. Today, paper carp streamers hang from flagpoles above the houses of Japanese families on Boys' Day.

▲ **Swimming for boys**
Carp streamers such as these fly on Boys' Day. The carp swims against the current of a stream and therefore symbolizes strength and perseverance.

▲ **Festival fun**
A woodblock print shows celebrations during the New Year's festival. Kites filled the sky and traditional toys and games were enjoyed by everyone in Japan.

YOU WILL NEED

Pencil, two sheets of A1 paper, felt-tipped pen, scissors, acrylic paints, paintbrush, water pot, PVA glue and glue brush, picture or garden wire, masking tape, string, garden cane.

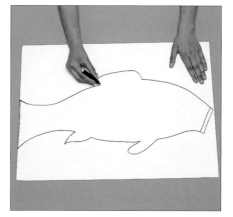

Take the pencil and one sheet of the A1 paper. Draw a large carp fish shape on to the paper like the one shown above. When you are happy with it, go over it in felt-tipped pen.

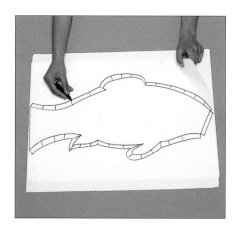

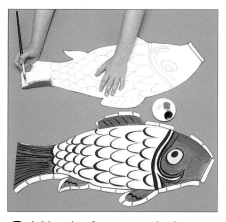

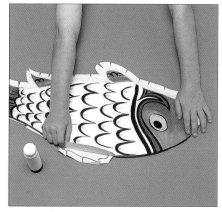

2 Put the second piece of paper over the first. Trace the outline of the fish shape on to the top sheet. Draw a narrow border around this fish shape and add tabs as shown above.

3 Add scales, fins, eyes and other details on both fish shapes as shown above. Cut the shapes out, remembering to snip into the tabs. Paint both fishes in bright colours.

4 Put the two fish shapes together with the painted sides facing outwards. Turn the tabs in and glue the edges of the fish shapes together. Do not glue the tail and mouth sections.

5 Use a small length of picture wire or garden wire to make a ring the size of the fish's mouth. Twist the ends together as shown above. Then bind them with masking tape.

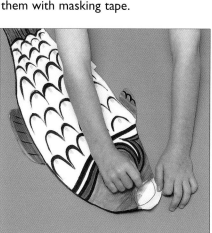

6 Place the ring inside the fish's mouth. Glue the open ends of the mouth over the ring. Tie one end of a length of string on to the mouth ring and the other end to a garden cane.

Families fly carp streamers on Boys' Day every year. One carp is flown for each son. The fish commemorate the ancient tale of a carp that once swam all the way to heaven to become a dragon. Most Japanese festivals are family occasions. The most important festival is the New Year. Many families go to a shrine to pray for good health and prosperity for the coming year.

Native American lacrosse

Between hunting expeditions and domestic tasks, Native Americans found time to relax and entertain themselves. Ball and stick games, such as lacrosse, were popular. There were also games of chance, gambling and tests of skill. Games of chance included guessing games, dice throwing and hand games where one person had to guess in which hand his opponent was hiding marked bones or wooden pieces. Archery, spear throwing and juggling were all fun to do and also helped to improve hunting skills.

Children loved to swim and take part in races. In the north, the girls and boys raced on toboggans. Active pastimes such as these helped to develop the skills a Native American needed to survive, such as strength, agility and stamina. Ritual foot races were also of ceremonial importance, helping the crops to grow, to bring rain and give renewed strength to the sun.

YOU WILL NEED

Thick card, ruler, pencil, scissors, masking tape, pair of compasses, barbecue stick, PVA glue and glue brush, bamboo stick (to reach your waist from ground level), string, brown paint, paintbrush, water pot, light ball.

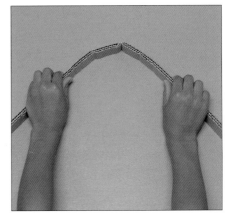

I Measure and then cut a strip of card 120 x 3cm. Fold it gently at the centre to make a curve. You could also cut two pieces of card measuring 60 x 3cm and tape them together.

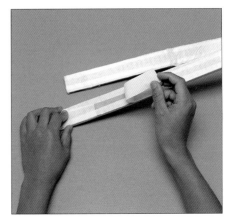

2 Completely cover the card strip with masking tape. Start from the edges and work your way around the strip, keeping the bent shape. Make sure you cover both sides of the card.

▲ **Twice the fun**

The ball game some Native Americans played used two sticks, although otherwise it was similar to lacrosse. The Cherokees called the game 'little brother of war'.

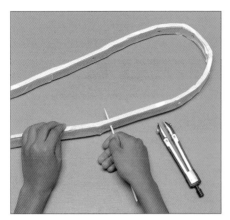

3 Use compasses to make two holes at the top of the bend, 10cm apart. Make two more holes 10cm from these and then two more 10cm further still. Enlarge with a barbecue stick.

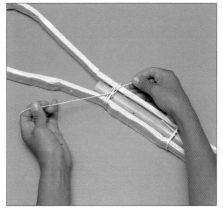

4 Glue the ends of the card strip to the top of the bamboo stick leaving a loop of card at the top as shown above. Tie a piece of string around the outside to keep it in place.

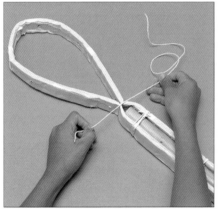

5 Pinch the card together where the loop meets the end of the stick. Tie it tightly with a piece of string, as shown above, and trim off the excess. Now paint the stick brown.

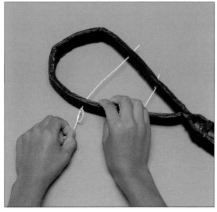

6 When the stick is dry, thread two pieces of string horizontally between the two sets of holes on the sides of the loop. Knot the pieces of string on the outside.

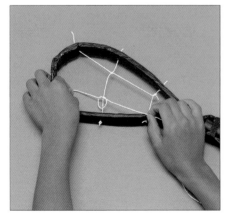

7 Now thread the vertical strings. Start at the holes at the top of the frame and tie the string around both horizontal strings. Tie the ends. Then try scooping up a ball with the stick.

The aim of the game of lacrosse is to get the leather ball between two posts to score a goal. It is a bit like hockey, but instead of hitting the ball, it is scooped up in the net of the stick.

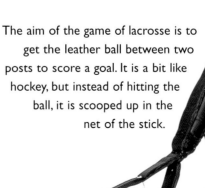

Mesoamerican patolli

Sports and games were enjoyed by Mesoamerican people after work and on festival days. Two favourite pastimes were tlachtli, a ball game, and patolli, a board game. Tlachtli was played in front of huge crowds of onlookers, while patolli was a quieter game enjoyed by two or more players.

Mesoamerican games were not just for fun. Both tlachtli and patolli had religious meanings. In the first, the court symbolized the world, and the rubber ball stood for the Sun as it made its daily journey across the sky. Players were meant to keep the ball moving to give energy to the Sun. Losing teams were sometimes sacrificed to the Sun god. In patolli, the movement of counters on the board represented the passing years.

▲ Playing the game

A group of Aztecs play patolli. This board game was played by moving dried beans or clay counters along a cross-shaped board with 52 squares. It could be very exciting, especially if players bet on the result.

YOU WILL NEED

Light fabric, ruler, black marker, acrylic paints, paintbrush, water pot, several sheets of differently coloured paper, scissors, PVA glue and glue brush, five dried broad beans or butter beans, self-hardening clay.

▲ Sacred circles

Volador is a ceremony performed on religious festival days. Four men, dressed as birds and attached to ropes, jump off a high pole. As they spin around, falling towards the ground, they circle the pole 13 times each. That makes 52 circuits – the length of the Mesoamerican holy calendar cycle.

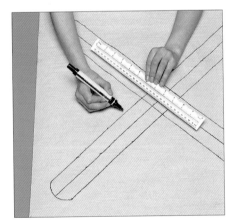

Measure a square of fabric about 50 x 50cm. Using a marker pen and ruler, draw six diagonal lines from corner to corner to make a cross shape as shown above.

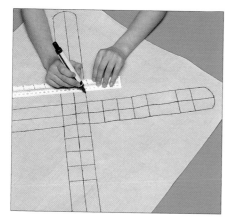

2 Draw six lines along each arm of the cross to give seven pairs of spaces. The third space in from the end of the cross should be a double space. Paint triangles in the double space.

3 Draw the heads of eight jaguars and then draw eight marigolds on sheets of coloured paper. Cut them out. Paint the face of the Sun God in the centre of the board.

4 Stick the jaguar heads and marigolds on to the board. Paint a blue circle at the end of one arm, and a crown at the opposite end. Repeat in green at the ends of the other arms.

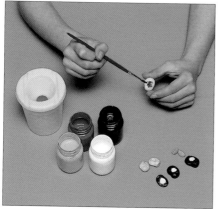

5 Paint the dried beans black with a white dot on one side. These will be used as dice. Finally, shape two small pieces of clay into counters. When they are dry, paint one green and one blue.

Most of the original rules for patolli have been lost. In this version, start each counter on the circle of the same colour. The aim is to move your counter to the crown of the same colour and back. Lose a turn if you land on a jaguar and get an extra turn if you land on a marigold.

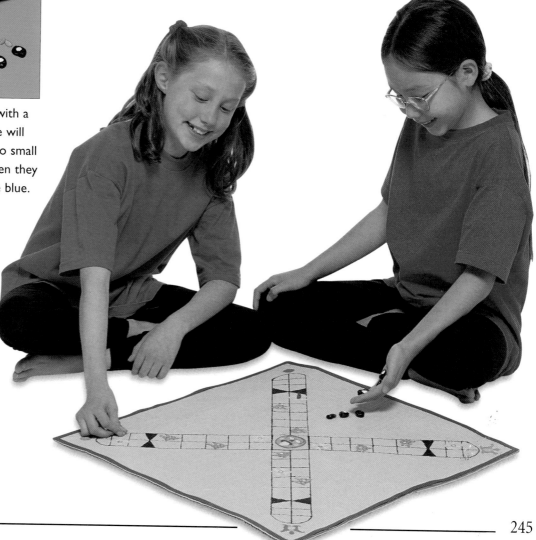

ARCTIC WORLD

ARCTIC WORLD

North
Sea

VIKING LANDS

North
America

CELTIC LAND

AZTEC & MAYA
EMPIRES

Gulf of
Mexico

Atlantic Ocean

Caribbean
Sea

Central
America
(Mesoamerica)

Pacific Ocean

INCA
EMPIRE

Andes Mountains

South
America

Cape Horn

ARCTIC WORLD

ARCTIC WORLD

VIKING
LANDS

Baltic
Sea

Europe

ROME

Black
Sea

ANCIENT
GREECE

Caspian
Sea

Mediterranean Sea

Asia

Sea of Japan

JAPAN

ANCIENT EGYPT

MESOPOTAMIA

CHINA

Persian
Gulf

ANCIENT
INDIA

Red Sea

Arabian
Sea

Bay of
Bengal

South
China
Sea

Africa

Indian Ocean

Australia

Cape of Good Hope

Glossary

A

acupuncture A part of traditional Chinese medicine that involves the insertion of fine needles into the body to relieve pain or to cure illness.

afterlife Life after death, as believed in by people of many world religions.

alabaster A type of white stone used to make ornaments.

alloy A mixture of metals smelted together to create a new material. Alloys have different properties from their constituent metals.

alpaca A llama-like animal native to South America, which is valued for its fine, silky wool.

amphitheatre An oval, open-air stadium surrounded by seats and used for public entertainment, such as for gladiator fights.

amphora A large, narrow-necked Greek or Roman jar with a handle on either side. Amphorae were used to store liquids such as wine or oil.

ancestor A member of the same family who died long ago.

Anno Domini (AD) A system used to calculate dates after the supposed year of Jesus Christ's birth. Anno Domini dates in this book are prefixed AD up to the year 1000, for example, AD521. After 1000 no prefixes are used.

anvil A heavy iron block on which objects can be hammered into shape.

aqueduct A channel for carrying water over long distances.

archaeologist Someone who studies ancient ruins and artefacts to learn about the past.

archaeology The scientific study of the past, which involves looking at the remains of ancient civilizations.

Arctic A vast, frozen area surrounding the North Pole.

aristocracy A ruling class of wealthy, privileged people, or government by such people.

armour A suit or covering worn by people or horses to protect them against injury during battle.

artefact An object that has been preserved from the past.

Assyrian An inhabitant of the Assyrian Empire. From 1530–612BC, Assyria occupied east of the Mediterranean Sea to Iran, and from the Persian Gulf to the mountains of eastern Turkey.

astrolabe A device invented by the Arabs, which consisted of a flat disc with a rod that could be pointed to the stars. Astrolabes helped sailors to navigate when travelling on water.

astrology The belief that stars, planets and other heavenly bodies shape the lives of people on Earth.

astronomy The scientific study of stars, planets and other heavenly bodies. In ancient times, astronomy was the same as astrology.

auxiliaries Foreign troops that help and support another nation that is engaged in war.

Aztec Mesoamerican people who lived in northern and central Mexico. The Aztecs were at their most powerful between 1350 and 1520.

B

barter An exchange of goods that does not involve money.

Before Christ (BC) A system used to calculate dates before the supposed year of Jesus Christ's birth. Dates are calculated in reverse. For example, 2000BC is longer ago than 200BC.

brahmin A Hindu who belongs to the highest of four social classes.

Bronze Age A period in human history, between 3000 and 1000BC, when tools and weapons were made from bronze.

Buddhism World religion founded in ancient India by the Buddha in the 6th century BC.

burin A chisel-like tool made from flint.

C

cartouche An oval border used in Egyptian hieroglyphs to show that the name it contains is royal or a god.

caste One of four social classes that divide the followers of Hinduism.

catapult A large wooden structure used to fire stones and iron bolts at the enemy during medieval sieges.

cavalry Soldiers on horseback.

Celt A member of one of the ancient peoples that inhabited most parts of Europe from around 750BC to AD1000.

century A unit of the Roman army, numbering up to 100 foot soldiers.

ceramics The art and technique of making pottery.

chainmail Flexible armour for the body, consisting of small rings of metal, linked to form a fine mesh.

chaps Over-trousers worn by cowboys to protect their legs.

chariot A lightweight, horse-drawn cart. Chariots were used in warfare and for sport.

chinampa An Aztec garden built on the fertile, reclaimed land on the lake shore. Layers of twigs and branches were laid beneath the surface of the water and weighted down with stones.

chiton Long tunics worn by both men and women in ancient Greece. Chitons were draped loosely over the body and held in place with brooches or pins.

circa (c.) A symbol used to mean 'approximately,' when the exact date of an event is not known e.g. c.1000BC.

citizen A Roman term used to describe a free person with the right to vote.

city-state A city, and the area surrounding it, which is controlled by one leader or government.

civil servant Official who carries out administrative duties for a government.

civilization A society that makes advances in arts, sciences, law, technology and government.

clan A group of people related to each other by ancestry or by marriage.

codex An ancient manuscript bound and folded into a book.

colonies Communities or groups of people who settle in another land but keep links with their own country.

conscription A mandatory term of service to the State whereby people have to work as labourers or soldiers.

coracle A small boat made of leather tightly stretched over a wooden frame.

crossbow A mechanical bow that fires small arrows called bolts.

crusades Eight holy wars from 1096 onwards, which were fought by Christians to recover the Holy Land (modern Israel) from the Muslims.

cubit An ancient unit of measurement equal to the length of a forearm.

cuirass Armour that protects the upper part of the body.

cultivate To prepare and use land or soil for growing crops.

cuneiform A type of writing that uses wedge-shaped figures, carved with a special tool. Cuneiform was developed by the Sumerians and also used by the Babylonians and Assyrians.

currency Form of exchange for goods such as money.

D

daimyo A nobleman or warlord from ancient Japan.

democracy A form of government in which every citizen has the right to vote and hold public office.

dictator A ruler with complete and unrestricted power.

dowel A thin cylindrical length of wood. Dowelling is available from hardware stores.

dugout canoe A canoe made by hollowing out a tree trunk.

dynasty A successive period of rule by generations of the same family.

E

edict An order issued by a ruler or by government.

electrum A mixture of gold and silver used for making coins.

emperor The ruler of an empire.

empire A group of lands ruled or governed by a single nation.

engrave To carve letters or designs on stone, wood or metal.

excavation A place where archaeologists dig up the ground to learn about past civilizations.

F

fiesta A religious festival with dancing and singing, especially common in Spain and South America.

firing The process of baking clay or glass paste in a kiln to harden it and make it waterproof.

fresco A picture painted on a wall while the plaster is still damp.

G

galley A warship powered by oars.

garrison A fort or similar place that is guarded by a group of soldiers. The word garrison can also refer to the group of soldiers themselves.

geisha A Japanese woman who entertains men with song and dances.

gem A precious or semi-precious stone or crystal, such as diamond or ruby. Gems often decorate jewellery or other ornaments.

gilding The process of applying a thin layer of gold to metal or pottery.

gladiator A professional fighter, slave or criminal in ancient Rome, who fought to the death in arenas for public entertainment.

glyph A picture symbol used in writing.

government The way in which a country or state is ruled.

greaves Armour worn to protect the shins.

groma An instrument used by Roman surveyors to measure right angles and to make sure roads were straight.

guilds Groups of skilled workers or merchants who checked quality standards, trained young people and looked after old and sick members.

H

haft The handle of an axe.

harpoon A spear-like weapon with a detachable head fastened to a rope.

hieroglyph A picture symbol used in ancient Egypt to represent an idea, word or sound.

hilt The handle of a sword.

Hinduism A world religion characterized by the worship of several gods and a belief in reincarnation.

hominid Humans and their most recent ancestors.

Homo sapiens The Latin species name for modern humans. The words *Homo* and *sapiens* together mean 'wise man'.

hoplites Greek fighting force made up of middle-class men. Their armour and weaponry was of the highest standard.

hunter-gatherer People who hunt wild animals for their meat and gather plants for food as a way of life.

I

ice age Several periods in Earth's history when the average temperature of the atmosphere decreased and large parts of the Earth's surface were covered with snow and ice. The most significant ice age occurred between 30,000 and 12,000BC.

igloo A dome-shaped Inuit shelter built from blocks of snow and ice.

ikebana The ancient Japanese art of flower arranging. The word ikebana means 'living flowers'.

immigrant A person who travels from his or her native country to live in another land.

Inca A member of an indigenous South American civilization living in Peru before the Spanish conquest.

indigenous Native or originating from a certain place.

inlay To set or embed pieces of wood or metal in another material so that the surfaces are flat.

inro A small, decorated box that is worn hanging from the sash of a Japanese kimono.

inscribed Lettering, pictures or patterns carved into a hard material such as stone or wood.

Inuit The native people of the Arctic and regions of Greenland, Alaska and Canada.

Iron Age The period when iron became the main metal used for producing tools and weapons. The Iron Age began around 1200BC.

iron ore Rock that contains iron in a raw, natural form.

irrigation Using channels dug into the earth to bring water to dry land so that crops can grow.

Islam A world religion founded in the 7th century AD by the prophet Mohammed.

K

kanji The picture symbols based on Chinese characters that were used for writing Japanese before about AD800.

kayak A one-person Inuit canoe powered by a double-bladed paddle. The wooden or bone frame is covered with sealskin.

kendo A Japanese martial art that involves fighting with bamboo swords.

kiln An oven or furnace used for firing bricks or pottery.

kimono A loose wide-sleeved robe, worn by both men and women in Japan.

knucklebones A favourite game of the Greeks and Romans. Knucklebones involved flipping small animal bones from one side of the hand to another without dropping them.

L

legion The main unit of the Roman army made up only of Roman citizens.

legislation Making laws.

loom A frame used for weaving cloth.

lyre A harp-like, stringed musical instrument common in ancient Greece.

M

magistrate A government officer of justice, similar to a local judge.

Maya An ancient civilization native to Mesoamerica.

medieval A term describing people, events and objects from a period in history known as the Middle Ages.

megalith A large stone, either standing on its own or used as part of a tomb, stone circle or other monument.

Mesoamerica A geographical area made up of the land between Mexico and Panama in Central America.

Mesopotamia An ancient name for the fertile region between the Tigris and Euphrates rivers in the Middle East. This area is now occupied by Iraq.

Middle Ages Period in history that lasted from around AD800 to 1400.

migration The movement of people to other regions, either permanently or at specific times of the year.

missionary A member of a religious organization who carries out charitable work and religious teaching.

monarchy A form of government in which the head of state is a king, queen or other non-elected sovereign.

mummy A human or animal corpse preserved in preparation for burial.

N

Native Americans The indigenous peoples of the Americas.

neolithic The new Stone Age. The period when people began to farm but were still using stone tools.

netsuke Small Japanese toggles that are carved from ivory and used to secure items from the sash of a kimono.

New Kingdom The period in ancient Egypt between 1550 and 1070BC.

nomads A group of people who roam from place to place in search of food or better land, or to follow herds.

O

Old Kingdom The period in ancient Egypt between 2686 and 2181BC.

oligarchy Government by a group of rich and powerful people.

oppidum A Latin word meaning town.

P

papier mâché Pulped paper mixed with glue, moulded into shape while wet and left to dry.

papyrus A tall reed that grows in the River Nile once used to make paper.

patolli A popular Aztec board game.

pharaoh A ruler of ancient Egypt.

plate armour Protective clothing made of overlapping plates of solid metal.

plumbline An instrument consisting of a weighted cord held up to see if a wall or other construction is vertical.

porcelain The finest quality of pottery. Porcelain is made with a fine clay called kaolin and baked at a high temperature.

prehistoric The period in history before written records were made.

priest An official who performs religious rituals, such as prayers, on behalf of worshippers.

pyramid A huge, stone, four-sided tomb built to house the mummy of an Egyptian pharaoh.

Q

quipu Knotted, coloured cords tied together and used by the Incas to record information.

R

ramparts The defensive parapets on the top of castle walls.

regent Someone who rules a country on behalf of another person.

relic Part of the body of a saint or martyr, or some object connected with them, preserved as an object of respect and honour.

relief A sculpture carved from a flat surface such as a wall.

republic A country that is ruled by an assembly of representatives elected by citizens rather than by a monarch or an emperor.

ritual A procedure or series of actions often performed for a religious purpose.

S

Saami The ancient people of Lapland in Scandinavia.

sacrifice The killing of a living thing, or the offering of a possession, in honour of the gods.

sadhu A nomadic Hindu.

samurai Members of the Japanese warrior class. Samurai were highly trained and followed a strict code of honourable behaviour.

sari A traditional garment worn by Indian women. A sari consists of a long piece of fabric wound round the waist and draped over one shoulder and sometimes the head.

scabbard The container for the blade of a sword. It is usually fixed to a belt.

scribe A professional writer, clerk or civil servant.

Senate The law-making assembly of ancient Rome.

shield boss A metal plate that is fixed to the centre of a shield to protect the hand of the person holding it.

shinden A single-storey Japanese house.

Shinto An ancient Japanese faith, known as the way of the gods and based on honouring holy spirits.

shogun A Japanese army commander. Shoguns ruled Japan from 1185–1868.

shrine A place of worship or a container for holy relics such as bones.

siege A long-lasting attack to capture a fortified place or city by surrounding it and cutting off all supplies.

Silk Road The ancient, overland trading route between China and Europe, used mainly by merchants travelling on camels.

smelt To extract a metal from its ore by heating it in a furnace.

society All the classes of people living in a particular community or country.

soldered Something that is joined together with pieces of melted metal.

spindle A rod used to twist fibres into yarn for weaving.

staple food The major part of the diet. For example, rice was the staple food of people from ancient India.

Stone Age The first period in human history in which people made their tools and weapons out of stone.

subject A person who is ruled by a monarch or government.

surcoat A long, loose tunic worn over body armour.

T

tachi The long sword that was carried by Japanese samurai.

tax Goods, money or services paid to the government or ruling state.

template A piece of card cut in a particular design and used as a pattern when cutting out material. You can use a photocopier to enlarge the templates in this book. Alternatively, copy the templates on to a piece of paper, using a ruler to make sure the size follows the measurements given in the book.

temple A building used for worship or other spiritual rituals.

tesserae Coloured tiles made of stone, pottery or glass and pressed into soft cement to form mosaics.

textile Cloth produced by weaving threads, such as silk or cotton, together.

tipi A conical tent made up of skins stretched over a framework of wooden poles. Tipis are still used by some Native American tribes.

toga A loose outer garment worn by the upper classes in ancient Rome. A toga consisted of a large piece of cloth draped round the body.

tomb A vault in which the bodies of dead people are placed.

torii The traditional gateway to a Shinto shrine.

trading post General store where people from a wide area traded or swapped goods.

treadwheel A wooden wheel turned by the feet of people or animals and used to power mills or other machinery.

tribe A group of people who shared a common language and way of life.

tribute Goods given by one person or nation to another as a form of taxation.

trident A three-pronged spear.

trireme A warship used by the ancient Greeks. Triremes were powered by men rowing in three ranks.

tundra A treeless area where the soil is permanently frozen under the surface.

U

umiak A rowing boat used by peoples native to the Arctic. Umiaks are made from whalebone, covered with walrus hide and waterproofed with seal oil.

underworld A mysterious place to which the spirits of the dead were believed to travel after death and burial.

V

Viking One of the Scandinavian peoples who lived by sea raiding in the early Middle Ages.

villa A Roman country house, usually part of an agricultural estate.

volador A religious Aztec ritual in which four men spun round and round a tall pole.

Z

Zen A branch of the Buddhist faith that was popular among Japanese samurai warriors.

ziggurat A pyramid-shaped temple built by the ancient Babylonians with a broad, square base and stepped sides.

Index

Acknowledgements

This edition is published by Southwater

Southwater is an imprint of Anness Publishing Ltd
Hermes House, 88–89 Blackfriars Road, London SE1 8HA
tel. 020 7401 2077; fax 020 7633 9499 www.southwaterbooks.com; info@anness.com

© Anness Publishing Limited 2001, 2004

UK agent: The Manning Partnership Ltd; tel. 01225 478444; fax 01225 478440;
sales@manning-partnership.co.uk
UK distributor: Grantham Book Services Ltd; tel. 01476 541080; fax 01476 541061;
orders@gbs.tbs-ltd.co.uk
North American agent/distributor: National Book Network; tel. 301 459 3366; fax 301 429 5746;
www.nbnbooks.com
Australian agent/distributor: Pan Macmillan Australia; tel. 1300 135 113; fax 1300 135 103;
customer.service@macmillan.com.au
New Zealand agent/distributor: David Bateman Ltd; tel. (09) 415 7664; fax (09) 415 8892

A CIP catalogue record for this book is available from the British Library.

Publisher Joanna Lorenz
Managing Editor, Children's Books Gilly Cameron Cooper
Consultants Rachel Halstead and Struan Reid
General Editor Leon Gray
Contributing Editors Gilly Cameron Cooper, Rebecca Clunes, Louisa Somerville
Editorial Readers Diane Ashmore, Penelope Goodare, Jonathan Marshall, Richard McGinlay, Joy Wotton
Assistant Editor Sarah Uttridge
Designer Sandra Marques/Axis Design Editions Ltd
Jacket Design Axis Design Editions Ltd
Photographers Paul Bricknell and John Freeman
Illustrators Rob Ashby, Julian Baker, Andy Beckett, Mark Beesley, Mark Bergin, Richard Berridge,
Peter Bull Art Studio, Vanessa Card, Stuart Carter, Rob Chapman, James Field, Wayne Ford, Chris Forsey,
Mike Foster, Terry Gabbey, Roger Gorringe, Jeremy Gower, Peter Gregory, Stephen Gyapay, Ron Hayward,
Gary Hincks, Sally Holmes, Richard Hook, Rob Jakeway, John James, Kuo Chen Kang, Aziz Khan,
Stuart Lafford, Ch'en Ling, Steve Lings, Kevin Maddison, Janos Marffy, Shane Marsh, Rob McCaig,
Chris Odgers, Alex Pang, Helen Parsley, Terry Riley, Andrew Robinson, Chris Rothero, Eric Rowe,
Martin Sanders, Peter Sarson, Mike Saunders, Rob Sheffield, Guy Smith, Don Simpson, Donato Spedaliere,
Nick Spender, Clive Spong, Stuart Squires, Roger Stewart, Sue Stitt, Ken Stott, Steve Sweet, Mike Taylor,
Alisa Tingley, Catherine Ward, Shane Watson, Ross Watton, Alison Winfield, John Whetton,
Mike White, Stuart Wilkinson, John Woodcock
Stylists Jane Coney, Konika Shakar, Thomasina Smith, Melanie Williams

10 9 8 7 6 5 4 3 2 1

The publishers would like to thank Scallywags and all the children modelling in this book.

Picture credits

Bryan and Cherry Alexander: 77bl, 82bl; Ancient Art & Architecture Collection Ltd/R.Sheridan: 230tr,
234tr; The Art Archive: 88tr, 102t/Oriental Art Museum Genoa/Dagli Orti, 136tr/Dagli Orti, 204cl,
218bl/Conseil Général Saint Brieuc/Dagli Orti, 228bl/Eileen Tweedy, 229bl/British Museum/Jacqueline
Hyde, 232tr/Museo Provinciale Sigismondo Castromediano Lecce/Dagli Orti, 234b & 235cr/Musée Alésia
Alise Sainte Reine France/Dagli Orti, 238bl/Private Collection/Dagli Orti, 242bl/Chateau de
Blerancourt/Dagli Orti; The Bridgeman Art Library: 30cl/Christe's Images, 236bl/Oriental
Museum/Durham University, 240bl/Victoria & Albert Museum; Christies Images: 102b; Corbis: 182cl/Dave
G. Houser, 214bl/Dean Conger, 216tr/Werner Forman, 232bl/Dave G. Houser; The Hutchison Library:
87t/Robert Francis, 88b/Liba Taylor, 220tr/H. R. Dönig, 240tr/Jon Burbank, 244bl, 244tr; Japan Information
and Cultural Centre: 23t, 30b; South American Pictures/Diego Rivera: 87b.

Every effort has been made to trace the copyright holders of all images that appear in this book. Anness
Publishing Ltd apologizes for any unintentional omissions and, if notified, would be happy to add an
acknowledgement in future editions.